Praise for *Reclaiming the Commons*

"If you ever wondered what a Saint would look like in our modern era, search no further. Vandana Shiva has emerged as one of the globe's most effective advocate for family farmers, the poor, safe, nutritious food, dignified communities, humane working conditions, democracy, and biodiversity. Her profound spiritual dimension forms the platform for her ideals, and gives her the resilience to withstand daily slanders, vilification, and censure from the global power centers. She risks her life, safety, and freedom in a fierce struggle against the Chemical Cartel: tyrannical governments and the homicidal corporations conspiring in tandem to privatize the commons, commoditize the planet, subjugate its people, and to censor dissent.

In her new book, *Reclaiming the Commons*, Vandana argues that "the commons", the shared assets of community–air, water, wildlife–form a social safety net for the poor, and provide the essential foundation stone for dignified, democratized, communities. Vandana brilliantly and pragmatically lays out the philosophical and logistical underpinnings of her battle to preserve the commons as public asset, and to protect them from privatization by the wealthy, authoritarian elite."

— Robert F. Kennedy Jr.
Environmental Lawyer, Activist

"A powerful, deeply moving call to rethink the very way we understand life, including our own. We will protect and, ultimately–save–life on this planet only as we experience ourselves in relation to all–only as we move from the manufactured fear of scarcity to fall in love with the majesty our connectedness. *Reclaiming the Commons* is about reclaiming ourselves. I love this book."

— Frances Moore Lappé, author of *Diet for a Small Planet*
Co-founder of Small Planet Institute, Cambridge, MA

"As she has, nonstop for 30 years, Vandana Shiva has done it again. *Reclaiming the Commons* is a vital political aid to a magnificent local resistance movement in India. At a crucial moment in history, as a handful of corporations are aggressively seeking ultimate control over worldwide agricultural resources and products, Shiva steps forward and leads the movement to block their incursions, both globally, and notably in her native India, where corporatists' powers seek full take-over.

Shiva brilliantly articulates what is at stake in the battle between "two paradigms", that of an age-old system based on local community rights, and the outrageous over-reach of global corporations seeking invasion and control of local systems, notably food and agriculture. This is a profound and disturbing book by one of the most powerful global voices on these matters. It is a vital and illuminating work; timely and profound."

— Jerry Mander, author of *Paradigm Wars*
Founder and President, International Forum on Globalization

RECLAIMING THE COMMONS

RECLAIMING THE COMMONS

Biodiversity, Indigenous Knowledge, and the Rights of Mother Earth

VANDANA SHIVA

Foreword by Ronnie Cummins

with the Navdanya Team

Anugrah Bhatt • Prerna Anilkumar • Neha Raj Singh

SANTA FE & LONDON

Published by Synergetic Press 1 Bluebird Court, Santa Fe, NM 87508 & 24 Old Gloucester St. London, WC1N 3AL England

Library of Congress Cataloging-in-Publication Data

Names: Shiva, Vandana, author.
Title: Reclaiming the commons : biodiversity, indigenous knowledge, and the rights of Mother Earth / Vandana Shiva ; foreword by Ronnie Cummins with the Navdanya Team, Anugrah Bhatt, Prerna Anilkumar, Neha Raj Singh.
Other titles: Enclosure and recovery of the commons
Description: [New edition]. | Santa Fe : Synergetic Press, [2020] | New edition of: The enclosure and recovery of the commons : biodiversity, indigenous knowledge, and intellectual property rights / Vandana Shiva ... [et al.]. New Delhi : Research Foundation for Science, Technology, and Ecology, c1997. | Includes bibliographical references and index.
Identifiers: LCCN 2020019730 (print) | LCCN 2020019731 (ebook) | ISBN 9780907791782 (paperback) | ISBN 9780907791799 (ebook)
Subjects: LCSH: Ethnobotany--India. | Ethnoscience--India. | Biodiversity--India. | Ethnobotany. | Ethnoscience. | Biodiversity.
Classification: LCC GN635.I4 E53 2020 (print) | LCC GN635.I4 (ebook) | DDC 304.2--dc23
LC record available at https://lccn.loc.gov/2020019730
LC ebook record available at https://lccn.loc.gov/2020019731

Cover and book design by Ann Lowe
Managing Editor: Amanda Müller
Printed by Versa Press, USA on 55# Tradebook Cream
Typeface: Adobe Caslon Pro and Caslon Antique

RECLAIMING THE COMMONS

TABLE OF CONTENTS

DEDICATION

To the indigenous and traditional communities who are dependent upon biodiversity and are jointly experts in the crucial biodiversity knowledge that we need for the future of humanity and all species. Who live in the commons through commoning; who have freely shared their innovation and creativity with others; who have engaged in a struggle to protect this culture of caring, sharing, and who resist the enclosure of the biodiversity and Intellectual commons, and to our small farmers who have been seed savers, breeders, and conservers of millennia, keeping alive the Seeds of Life, the Seeds of Hope, and the Seeds of Freedom.

ACKNOWLEDGMENTS

To Chakravarty Raghavan, editor of SUNS, earlier head of PTI, who woke me up to GATT in 1987; To Shri SP Shukla who as GATT Ambassador defended India's sovereignty, and continued to lead the People's campaign on WTO after retirement; To the late Shri Keayala who created the National working on Patent Laws and worked tirelessly with the Government and Parliament to ensure TRIPS implementation put India and her civilization values first; To the late Shri Chaturan Mishra, then Agriculture Minister, who invited me to be part of the Expert group on Plant Variety Protection and Farmers' Rights Act as a *sui generis* alternative UPOV; To Shri Suresh Prabhu who as Environment Minister, and Shri BP Singh, Secretary of Environment, invited me as an expert to draft The Biodiversity Act of India; To the late Justice Krishna Iyer who guided us at every step on earth jurisprudence and the commons; To the all-party parliamentary group who ensured that Article 3, including 3(j), clearly defined what are not inventions; and to all colleagues who have continued to defend India's sovereignty with creativity, consistency, and clarity.

This book is a product of a collective and cumulative effort.

It was first published in 1997 as *The Enclosure and Recovery of the Commons* and was used widely in the national and international debates on biodiversity and Intellectual Property Rights (IPRs). The new edition is being published in 2020. Much has happened in twenty years, many laws we were working towards to protect our biodiversity and were proposing in 1997 are now in place.

The Navdanya team has also changed over the last two decades. However, our dedication to resist the enclosures of the commons and creatively recover the commons has remained unchanged. To build and strengthen the struggle of our people to live peacefully and sustainably, with true abundance that comes from biodiversity.

One man robbing another of food,
Can this custom last?
One man watching another suffer,
Can such life survive?
Survive before our eyes,
Survive here in our midst?
Lovely gardens, spacious fields,
Innumerable enrich this land,
Fruits and tubers, and grains in plenty,
Immeasurably it yields,
Forever and ever it yields!
(Long live Bharat Commonwealth)

– Subramania Bharati

FOREWORD BY RONNIE CUMMINS

It is no exaggeration to place Vandana Shiva as one of the most important visionaries, authors, public speakers, and activists of our era. Once 'profit at any cost' agriculture and globalization is finally defeated, once we turn around the climate crisis and the crisis of democracy, and join hands together across borders and continents to celebrate; we need Vandana Shiva, the traditional farmers, rural villagers of India, and the indigenous world to sit at the head of the table.

I have worked with, and been inspired by, Vandana for almost three decades starting with a solidarity picket line and press event that I helped organize on October 2, 1993 (Gandhi's birthday) in Boca Raton, Florida. Together, we protested the W.R. Grace Company's attempt to patent India's neem tree with a simultaneous protest against Cargill, Monsanto, and 'Patents on Life' in front of the Minneapolis Grain Exchange.

In October of 1994, the network that I helped coordinate, The Pure Food Campaign, joined forces with Navdanya, Vandana's India-based organization, and activists in over two dozen nations to launch the Global Days of Action Against Genetically Engineered Foods. This was the beginning of a global grassroots movement *against* GMOs and *for* organic and regenerative agriculture that has persevered until this day, nurturing not only resistance, but a healthy and organic alternative to what Vandana aptly calls 'the Poison Cartel'. At the close of the twentieth century, Vandana and our growing global movement helped organize the teach-ins and protests at the 'Battle of Seattle', successfully blocking Monsanto and the Gene Giants from extending their monopoly patents and control over seeds and agriculture across the entire world. More recently, in 2015, Vandana and I, along with a network of food and climate activists, met in Costa Rica and formed Regeneration International, dedicated to reversing global warming through regenerative food, farming, and land-use. Vandana and I currently serve together on RI's international steering committee.

The so-called 'Green Revolution' of industrialized, energy and chemical-intensive agriculture, GMO foods, and seed patents have not only degraded our health, our biodiversity, our environment, and driven hundreds of millions of small farmers and rural villagers into poverty, forced migration, and desperation–they now threaten our very existence. As world scientists and our own everyday experience points out, we are facing nothing less than a climate catastrophe and a Sixth Great Extinction of biodiversity that will unravel the fragile life-support systems of our planet. Along with the continued burning fossil fuels, our current degenerative food, farming, and land-use practices are pumping billions of tons of climate-destabilizing greenhouse gases into the atmosphere and our oceans every year.

Fortunately, people all over the world are turning against the fossil fuel corporations, Bayer-Monsanto, and all the other multinational corporations and indentured politicians that threaten our well-being and the future of humankind and turning back to nature and taking back control over their health, diets, and political destinies. As we move forward out of these dark times, let's remember and celebrate the history of our struggles for seed and food sovereignty, the preservation of indigenous knowledge, and our precious biodiversity. *Reclaiming the Commons* is a strong reminder of this history and of how the forces of life and biodiversity, inspired by Mother Earth and indigenous tradition, have managed to hold back the forces of corporate greed and monopoly control, not only in India, but at many of the front lines of grassroots struggle throughout the world. Long live Mother Earth and inspired visionaries such as Vandana Shiva!

INTRODUCTION

My Thirty-Year Journey on Biodiversity, Biopiracy and Intellectual Property

In 1987 I was invited to a meeting in Bogeve, France and the United Nations in Geneva on Laws of life and emerging Biotechnologies.[1] Agrichemical corporations were present at this meeting. There, it was stated, that at the turn of the century (2000) there would be only five corporations controlling food and health, and those who would 'win the race' would have the largest number of mergers, acquisitions, and patents on seeds. Additionally, it was said that new biotechnologies based on recombinant DNA–which allowed moving genes across species boundaries to make GMOs–were going to be the basis of these patents on seeds.

Today, with the merger of Bayer with Monsanto, Dow with Dupont, and Syngenta with ChemChina, there are precisely three megacorporations controlling global food and health through seeds, agrichemicals, pharmaceuticals, as well as large scale biopiracy from nature and indigenous communities.

It was this very meeting in Bogeve that started me on the journey to protect biodiversity and seeds with local communities, working both with our government and parliament to evolve laws to protect biodiversity, people's traditional knowledge, as well as protecting national sovereignty in our laws.

As a scientist I have worked for more than thirty-five years on conservation and the sustainable utilization of seeds and biodiversity, on defending Farmers' Rights, and on IPRs related to seeds.

This book marks the long legal journey to protect our biodiversity and indigenous knowledge from the unscientific, unethical frameworks that corporations try to impose on us in order to own life on Earth and collect rents from farmers as seed royalties. I felt then, and feel even now, that the claim that Monsanto 'invented' the seed and has a 'right' to collect royalties from our farmers, and farmers all over the world, is both epistemologically and ethically wrong. Seeds are not 'machines' 'invented' by corporations. Indian laws and international laws were fortunately shaped, not by Monsanto's bullying and false claims, but by the scientific fact that the biodiversity and living organisms are self-organized, highly complex, and constantly make and renew themselves. Indigenous communities, including traditional farmers, co-create and co-evolve biodiversity with nature. This book is about the common creativity of the earth, her biodiversity, and people's knowledge. It is also about the scientific, legal, political and cultural struggle to defend the sovereignty of biodiversity, indigenous cultures, and national systems.

Since the beginning of this journey, I have worked with our government on the negotiations on the Convention on Biodiversity (which was signed in Rio at the Earth Summit in 1992). I have worked on TRIPS/GATT/WTO, as well as serving as an expert involved in drafting India's Plant Variety Protection, Farmers' Rights Acts, and the National Biodiversity Act. I have also worked closely with the National Working group on Patent Law and the all-party group in Parliament on the Amendment of the Patent Act to implement TRIPS which resulted in Article 3(j) that excludes plants, animals, and seeds from patentability.

In addition to the work I've done to help protect our national sovereignty and public interests; I have also served as an expert in monitoring the epidemic of biopiracy of indigenous biodiversity and knowledge, challenging and winning cases against the biopiracy of neem and wheat in the European Patent Office. Our research on biopiracy monitoring and the resulting victories are also summarized in this book.

Further, I have intervened in the High Court Karnataka case on Monsanto's challenge to the Seed Price Control Order of the Government, as well as the Delhi High Court case related to 3(j), whose decision Monsanto has repeatedly challenged in the Supreme Court.

Monsanto has further attempted to challenge the Competition Commission of India's (CCI) investigation into its *prima facie* monopoly on Bt cotton, with the false claim that it has a patent on Bt cotton. It is in cases such as this, and other such false claims in the context of the Bayer-Monsanto merger, for which I have been a representative to the CCI.[2]

Monsanto's refutation of article 3(j) of India's Patent Act through the commercial case no. 132/2016 was dismissed by the High Courts. Monsanto subsequently appealed to the Supreme Court to overturn the High Court ruling but failed on May 7, 2018.

Reclaiming the Commons first written in 1997 as part of the public debate taking place across the country in the context of the implementation of the Convention on Biodiversity (CBD) and the Trade Related Aspects of Intellectual Property Rights (TRIPS) Agreement of the WTO. Its objective was to protect our sovereign rights and community rights to biodiversity in the Biodiversity Act and our Amended Patent Act.

The CBD is an international, legally binding agreement, which recognizes the sovereign rights of countries to their biological resources. It also acknowledges ecological innovation within indigenous communities. The CBD gave us an opportunity to change the regime of biopiracy at the global level and replace it with a sustainable and just system in which biodiversity, diverse knowledge systems, and the rights of communities—whose survival depends on this biodiversity and knowledge—are simultaneously protected.

Two decades ago, in the heyday of globalization, there was an attempt by global corporations and some countries representing corporate interest, to privatize and enclose our biological and intellectual commons. The expansion of 'Intellectual Property Rights' into the domain of life forms and biodiversity, and the globalization of this regime through the TRIPS Agreements of GATT/WTO, were direct attempts at the enclosure the biological and intellectual commons. We were successful in our laws to prevent these enclosures and protect our rights in our national laws, adopting the sovereign path and avoiding recolonization of our biodiversity and living wealth.

The 'enclosure of biodiversity and biodiversity related knowledge through patents and intellectual property rights' is the final step in the series of enclosures of the commons that began with the rise of colonialism. Therefore, biodiversity and biodiversity related knowledge needs to be adequately protected in light of the continued attempt at making 'private property' out of long-held traditional knowledge and life forms.

Juridical innovation was required to recognize and protect biodiversity and the cultural integrity of indigenous communities from piracy and privatization, allowing them to continue to use their resources freely, as they have done since time immemorial.

The global context is driven by two forces–the commitment of the international community to protect the conditions of life on earth through the Convention on Biodiversity on the one hand, and the pressure from global corporations for limitless markets, profits, and privatization of the earth's resources on the other.

Thus, the new context since the 1990s required that:

- Under CBD, India implemented laws to conserve biodiversity and ensure its sustainable and equitable utilization
- Under the Leipzig Global Plan of Action, India evolved and implemented laws to conserve plant genetic resources for agriculture
- India implements the TRIPS Agreement, taking into account the full range of options available

The legal changes are being made in the context of the existing reality of:

- A rich biodiversity wealth in spite of massive erosion
- A rich and ancient heritage of indigenous knowledge for the utilization of biodiversity
- An epidemic of biopiracy which includes the piracy of our biological resources and indigenous knowledge

The three most significant legal changes that have been made in Indian law to protect our biodiversity and indigenous knowledge are:

- Implementation of the Biodiversity Act 2002
- Introduction of the Plant Variety and Farmers' Rights Act 2002
- Amendments to the Indian Patents Act 1970 which was made in 2005

Within this context of existing realities and emergent challenges, over the last two decades India chose the sovereign route to implement national laws. Sovereignty over biological resources and indigenous knowledge has been recognized by the CBD, specifically in Articles 3 and 15. This recognition has changed the open access regime that was prevalent under colonial systems in which Third World genetic resources were treated as the 'common heritage of mankind' available to use freely, while plant varieties and products developed from this rich biodiversity were treated as intellectual property of northern corporations.

The Colonial Option

Treats indigenous knowledge and Third World biodiversity as open access systems and 'common heritage of mankind'. But the products developed from this knowledge and biodiversity require intellectual property protection.

Adopts western style IPR systems blindly and makes the protection of private property in life forms the only objective of the legal systems, thus promoting the monopoly of TNCs over knowledge and biodiversity.

The Sovereign Option

Recognizes the sovereign rights over the biological and intellectual heritage. Therefore, evolves a jurisprudence and legal framework appropriate to the protection of our biological and cultural diversity and the protection of biological and intellectual commons; and creates the balance of public and private interest as the main objective of our legal system.

The recovery of the commons is different from the open access system of 'common heritage of mankind'. Commons are based on community control and community management and are not open access systems. In fact, community control over common resources is the only real mechanism for ensuring sovereign control over natural resources.

Again, India chose the sovereign issue to frame her laws to implement CBD and the TRIPS Agreement. However, the forces that wanted to use both CBD and TRIPS to colonize our biological and intellectual heritage by having unregulated access to our rich biodiversity, taking patents on biodiversity, living resources and seeds, are still trying to undermine the legal framework we have evolved. Both the colonial option as well as the sovereign option recognize the value of biodiversity and the value of indigenous knowledge systems. However, they differ in the fact that in the colonial option, India's biological and intellectual heritage will not serve the economic interests of India's people as it is based on corporate values. In the sovereign option, the biodiversity and knowledge that has evolved in India will continue to meet the economic needs of India's people, and continue to evolve on the basis of the value on which it has been sustained over centuries.

The sovereign option and colonial option emerge from two different paradigms and worldviews, leading to two conflicting ownership systems: an age-old system based on community rights, still the dominant one in rural and indigenous communities, combined with national sovereignty, and the ownership system of corporate defined IPRs based on individual private property and enclosures of the commons. The sovereign option in the context of traditional knowledge and biodiversity requires the reinvention of sovereignty to be centered on people since local communities are the conservers of both the resources and knowledge.

The reinvention of sovereignty has to be based on the reinvention of the state so that the state becomes a partner of the people and is thus not reduced to a corporate state. Sovereignty cannot only reside in the centralized state structures, nor does it disappear when the protective functions of the state, with respect to its people, start to wither away. The partnership for national sovereignty needs empowered communities which assign and set the duties and obligations on which the state structures itself. On the other hand, TNCs and international agencies promote not only the separation of community interests from state interest, but also the fragmentation and divisiveness of communities.

The sovereign option adopted by India for its legal systems for biodiversity, conservation, and protection of traditional knowledge, recognize the sovereign rights of the country as well as the rights of communities, and not merely the rights of corporations. In the IPRs context, we have evolved articles that recognize real inventions and do not reward biopiracy and patents of living resources which are not inventions.

As we look back over the last thirty years, we feel grateful that we have been of service to the earth, our country, our farmers, and our tribals. We feel satisfied that the laws we were struggling to put in place when we first wrote *The Enclosure and Recovery of the Commons* are now the law of the land. I was personally part of the expert groups that drafted our Biodiversity Act, our Plant Variety Protection and Farmers' Rights Act, and our Tribals, and Forests Dwellers Rights Act.

Today, there is a renewed attempt by the privateers to own life on earth by eroding the sovereign laws of India. The arguments they use are the same tired arguments of two decades ago–of presenting biopiracy as 'invention', with the assumption of colonial superiority. We are therefore bringing out a new edition, highlighting the uniqueness of India's biodiversity related laws to protect our unique natural heritage, our civilization, revisiting the timeless debates about the commons and their enclosures, sovereignty vs colonialism, and sustainability vs non-sustainability.

As the 'miracle' of globalization and of new GMO technologies fades, the limits of the greed driven global market and the mechanistic paradigm of the dominant stream of Western corporate science are recognized, the potential of biodiversity, biodiversity-based knowledge systems, and of biodiversity-based economies to the common good become signposts for the future.

Reclaiming the Commons is about the thirty-year journey on the recovery of the biological and intellectual commons. Commons for communities are not the same as the open access unregulated systems industry has been trying to create. The commons as managed by communities and defended through laws of national sovereignty are vital to protect the common good, to protect the web of life, hence protecting life itself. They are vital in protecting our humanity, and to help us remember we are part of one earth family. Especially for the two-thirds of India who live outside the livelihood provided by the state, and the market, in what is referred to as the biodiversity-based economy. The biodiversity-based economy of India represents the poorest communities in marginalized regions, their access to biodiversity and use of their indigenous knowledge and skills is their primary means of livelihood security.

Additionally, this book touches on the evolution of Navdanya's efforts in protecting our biological and intellectual commons over the last three decades, our contribution to the legal framework for the protection of biodiversity; as well as the foundation of our civilization, our culture, our economies, and our knowledge systems.

The main contributions we have made are:

- Conservation of biodiversity and creation of community seed banks to defend seed as a commons
- Strengthening of Farmers' Rights in the area of agricultural biodiversity
- Strengthening Rights of traditional medical practitioners in the area of medical plants
- Strengthening Rights of craft communities using biodiversity
- Providing alternatives to the western industrial corporate model of IPRs as experts in drafting the Biodiversity Act, the Plant Variety Protection Act, and working with Parliamentarians on amendments to the Patent Act, specially the introduction of Art 3(j)

- Monitoring cases of biopiracy, legally challenging and winning the cases of biopiracy of our neem, basmati, and wheat

The IPR system as it has evolved in western industrial societies is, in effect, a denial of the collective innovation our people that has been developed over thousands of years. The expansion of such narrowly defined IPRs to biodiversity and knowledge of its utilization results in enclosures of the biological and intellectual commons which have supported local communities and indigenous cultures over millennia. Biopiracy becomes the inevitable outcome of such a regime.

The piracy of the indigenous innovation through patents on nature and the diversion of their biological resources to global markets without regulation through laws like our Biodiversity Act have prevented the undermining of the livelihood of two-thirds of India: women, tribals, peasants, pastoralists, and fisher folk. It also threatens the biodiversity base which they have protected because their survival depends on it.

The defense of the rights of traditional communities to their biodiversity and traditional knowledge is based on recognition by the state that communities have their own rights, knowledge, and values, needing protection by the state. This recognition by the formal legal systems does not give the state the right to intrude in local biodiversity utilization patterns based on community rights, but it creates an obligation on the state to prevent external actors from "pirating local resources and indigenous knowledge, and from imposing property rights regimes that counter community rights, and cultural values." This is precisely what our national Biodiversity Act has ensured.

This rectification is necessary because in the absence of strong community rights protection, the state is merely an instrument of the protection of foreign investment and a promoter of the predation of biodiversity and indigenous knowledge.

The implementation of the Panchayati Raj Act in scheduled areas (the provision of the Panchayats {extension to the scheduled areas} Act 1996), has already set precedent for the recognition of communities as their own competent authority for decision making on resource use, cultural values, traditions, and community rights to common resources as the building blocks of a decentralized democracy.

Global corporations are still trying to establish an unfair regime in which biological and intellectual resources flow freely from poor countries to rich countries, without regulation, and from the poorest communities to the richest corporations. Biological resources come back in patented form resulting in a double loss for poor countries and their communities; the first through the theft of their intellectual and biological wealth, and second through royalty payments for what has been derived from their collective, cumulative innovation and biodiversity.

Two decades ago, they tried to prevent regulation for the fair, equitable, sustainable, and just use of biodiversity. Today the laws for equity and sustainability are in place both nationally and internationally. The attempt now is to dilute and subvert them. Our work today, as thirty years ago when we started Navdanya, is to protect our biodiversity, our sovereignty, our commons.

We are at a new watershed. In the 1990s we were defining a new partnership between the sovereignty of the country and the sovereignty of local communities. Today–with strong laws that exclude the false claim to invention of life forms, laws for Biodiversity Conservation, and regulation for access and benefit sharing–we can take the next quantum leap in the form of a new partnership between the creativity of nature and her diverse species, the innovation of traditional communities, and our sovereignty as a nation.

During the next thirty years of India's formal independence, it is appropriate to expand our policies to reflect our civilizational philosophy of *Vasudhaiva Kutumbkam,* that the Earth is one family, one community in diversity. Living as one family in a diverse, complex, fragile world requires the evolution of living democracies and living economies. Navdanya has catalyzed the living democracy, and living economy movement by creating community seed banks, community biodiversity registers, and local living biodiversity economies. India's true democratic spirit rests on deepening movements for decentralized democracy throughout the country by recognizing the knowledge, innovation, and biodiversity that have evolved through community rights and community responsibility. What is more, the recognition of community rights is a precondition for both the protection of biodiversity and the protection of people's rights. This recognition is also the only means for protecting our natural wealth in the form of our biological and intellectual heritage and our national sovereignty.

Species are disappearing at more than 10,000 times the normal rate. Scientists are now talking of the sixth mass extinction, including the imminent threat to the survival of our own species. Conserving biodiversity and cultures that conserve biodiversity is not an issue we can ignore or devalue. It has become imperative to our very survival.

We dedicate this book to the human potential and human will to cultivate the possibility of a better future.

– Dr. Vandana Shiva

WHERE THE MIND IS WITHOUT FEAR . . .

Where the mind is without fear and the head is held high;
Where knowledge is free;
Where the world has not been broken up into fragments by narrow domestic walls;
Where words come out from the depths of truth;
Where tireless striving stretches its arms towards perfection;
Where the clear stream of reason has not lost, it's way into the dreary desert sand of dead habit;
Where the mind is led forward by thee into ever-widening thought and action–
Into that heaven of freedom, my Father, let my country awake.

– Rabindranath Tagore

The Universe is the creation of the supreme power meant for the benefit of all creation. Each individual life form must, therefore, learn to enjoy its benefits by forming a part of the system in close relation with other species. Let not any one species encroach upon others' rights.

– Ishopanishad

ONE

The Duty to Protect Biodiversity

THE CONVENTION ON BIODIVERSITY AND THE BIODIVERSITY ACT

Protecting Our Rich Biological and Intellectual Heritage

INDIA IS A CIVILIZATION whose knowledge, economies, and democracy are based on diversity. India possesses a unique wealth of biological diversity—from the ecosystem level to the species and genetic levels—which have been preserved, protected, and evolved by our indigenous peoples and traditional cultures over thousands of years. It is estimated that over 75,000 species of fauna and 45,000 of flora are found in India. Of the estimated 45,000 plant species, about 15,000 species of algae, 1,600 lichens, 20,000 fungi, 2,700 bryophytes, and 600 pteridophytes. The 75,000 species of animals include 50,000 insects, 4,000 mollusks, 200 fish, 140 amphibians, 420 reptiles, 1,200 birds, 340 mammals, and other invertebrates. Thus, India is a home to about two lakh species of living organisms.

In addition, our farmers have bred diversity in grains, pulses, oilseeds, vegetables, and fruits; gifting the world 200,000 varieties of rice, 1,500 varieties of wheat, 1,500 varieties of mangoes, and 4,500 varieties of brinjal (eggplant).

It is the biodiversity of our spices, our cotton, and our indigo that was the source of India's wealth in pre-colonial times and was the reason for colonization. Today there is a new attempt to colonize our biodiversity–our seeds and medicinal plants through biopiracy and patenting.

Ancient, intricate systems of traditional indigenous knowledge for biodiversity utilization have been evolving steadily, reflecting the continuous, cumulative and collective innovation of the people. Traditionally, the knowledge has been freely available within and between communities in the commons.

Most of the people in our country derive their livelihood and meet their survival needs from the diversity of living resources; as forest dwellers, farmers, fisher folk, healers, and livestock owners. Indigenous knowledge systems existing in medicine, agriculture, and amongst fishers are the primary base for meeting the food and health needs of the majority of our people.

The immense resources of natural heritage have been protected, preserved and conserved over the years by India's indigenous peoples, who have had a reverence for their natural heritage. Conservation and utilization have always been delicately, sensitively, and equitably combined in the indigenous knowledge system and cultures of India.

There are two paradigms of biodiversity conservation. The first is held by communities whose survival and sustenance is linked to local biodiversity utilization and conservation. The second is held by global commercial interests whose profits are linked to the utilization of global biodiversity for the production of inputs into large scale homogeneous, uniformly centralized and global production systems. For local indigenous communities, conserving biodiversity means to conserve the integrity of ecosystems and their species, the right to these resources and knowledge, and their production systems based on biodiversity. For them, biodiversity has intrinsic value as well as high use value. Where commercial interests are concerned, biodiversity itself has no value; it is merely 'raw material' for the production of commodities, for the 'mining of genes' and for the maximization of profits.

Most people in India, even today, live in the first paradigm of biodiversity utilization. According to an ethnobotanical survey, there are 7,500 species used as medicinal plants by the indigenous medical traditions of India. These traditions are kept alive by 360,740 Ayurveda practitioners, 29,701 Unani experts, and 11,644 specialists of Siddha. In addition, millions of housewives, birth attendants and herbal healers carry on village-based traditions. In the 1990s, before the impact of globalization, 70 percent of health care needs in India were still based on traditional systems which are centered around the use of medicinal plants. Eighty percent of seeds used by farmers still came from farmers' seed supplies. Thus, India was still predominantly a biodiversity-based economy. Impacts of globalization have eroded the biodiversity and knowledge sovereignty of local communities, pushing them into deep poverty and unemployment.

The utilization of biodiversity in a people's economy is guided by a plurality of knowledge systems. The knowledge of the properties, characteristics, and uses of this biodiversity is held by local epistemological frameworks.

Nature's diversity and the diversity of knowledge systems is, however, undergoing a major process of destabilization with the expansion of patents and intellectual property rights as defined by corporations into the domain of biodiversity. While nationally we have taken steps to protect our biodiversity, biopiracy alongside the patenting of indigenous knowledge is growing rampantly.

As we enter the third millennium, we need to find ways to protect biological diversity, the intellectual heritage of India, and the world for future generations. On the one hand, emergent ecological concern for the conservation of biological diversity and the growing awareness of the western paradigm of reductionist mechanistic knowledge provides a new opportunity to value the indigenous knowledge of local communities. On the other hand, emergent forms of private property in knowledge and life forms threaten the continuity of biodiversity and related knowledge for the poorer two-thirds of India. This awareness also creates an opportunity to recover and reclaim the commons. The renewed incentive to conserve comes from commitments India has made in international conservation agreements such as the Convention on Biological Diversity (CBD).

The threats to our rich biological and intellectual heritage come from the expansion of western style "industrial intellectual property rights" regime to biodiversity.

The CBD recognizes that traditional knowledge, innovations, and practices are of vital importance to the conservation of biological diversity and that local, indigenous communities have a close reliance on biological resources. Their livelihood and lifestyles often depend on it and are shaped by it. As such, in accordance with Article 10(c), contracting parties are obliged to protect and encourage customary use of biological resources in line with traditional cultural practices to conserve and sustainably use these resources. Further, according to Article 18.4, the contracting parties are also obliged to develop and use indigenous and traditional technologies to conserve biological diversity and sustainably use its components.

The Convention on Biological Diversity

In 1992 the international community adopted the CBD at Rio de Janeiro at the Earth Summit, along with the United Nations Framework Convention on Climate Change. These two international environmental agreements are the fragile threads that hold our future.

The CBD was seen as a way to reclaim lost ground on the unchecked exploitation of genetic resources in developing countries. While no mandatory obligations arise out of this legal instrument it lists three important aims:

- Conserving biological diversity
- Sustainable use of resources
- Fair and equitable sharing of benefits that arise out of commercial use

Though it is still a form of Northern 'taking' with which a 'giving' to the South is attached, its aims of justice and fairness mandate the sharing of benefits with resource providers. The CBD has carved an institutional framework for benefit sharing arrangements which have sprouted across the world through which the resource users (corporations and scientists) compensate the resource providers and stewards (indigenous peoples, communities, etc.,) through the idiom of "benefits."

Article 8(j) reads: "Subject to its national legislation, respect, preserve and maintain knowledge, innovations and practices of indigenous and local communities embodying traditional lifestyles relevant for the conservation and sustainable use of biological diversity and promote their wider application with the approval and involvement of the holders of such knowledge, innovations and practices and encourage the equitable sharing of the benefits arising from the utilization of such knowledge, innovations and practices."

The CBD reaffirmed the recognition of "the intrinsic value of biological diversity and the ecological, genetic, social, economic, scientific, educational, cultural, recreational, and aesthetic values of biological diversity and its components."[1]

The objectives of the Convention are stated in Article 1.

Article 1 Objectives:

"The objectives of this Convention, to be pursued in accordance with its relevant provisions, are the conservation of biological diversity, the sustainable use of its components, and the fair, equitable sharing of the benefits arising out of the utilization of genetic resources by appropriate access to genetic resources, by appropriate transfer of relevant technologies, taking into account all rights over those resources and to technologies, and by appropriate funding."

The primary objective of the CBD is the conservation of biodiversity. While recognizing that conserving biodiversity is a common concern for humanity, the Convention clearly recognized the sovereign rights of states and closed the door for unregulated access, exploitation and ownership through patents by global corporations with commercial interests. It strengthened the sovereign option in the area of biodiversity and shut down the colonial choice of "free access" to our biodiversity, only to be sold back to us as patented commodities for health and agriculture.

Article 3 of the Convention states:

"States have, in accordance with the Charter of the United Nations and the principles of international law, the sovereign right to exploit their own resources pursuant to their own environmental policies, and the

responsibility to ensure that activities within their jurisdiction or control do not cause damage to the environment of other States or areas beyond the limits of national jurisdiction."

The regulation on access to biodiversity flows from this principle of sovereignty.

According to Article 15(1) on Access to Genetic Resources:
"Recognizing the sovereign rights of States over their natural resources, the authority to determine access to genetic resources rests with the national governments and is subject to national legislation."

The Convention also recognized that indigenous knowledge needs to be protected in order to conserve biodiversity. Article 8(j) on *in situ* conservation states:
"Subject to its national legislation, respect, preserve and maintain knowledge, innovations and practices of indigenous and local communities embodying traditional lifestyles relevant for the conservation and sustainable use of biological diversity, and promote their wider application with the approval and involvement of the holders of such knowledge, innovations and practices and encourage the equitable sharing of the benefits arising from the utilization of such knowledge, innovations and practices."

Finally, under Article 19(3) the CBD created an obligation for biosafety–i.e., prevention of large-scale loss of biological diversity–in the context of genetically modified organisms, or living modified organisms:
"The Parties shall consider the need for and modalities of a protocol setting out appropriate procedures, including, in particular, advance informed agreement, in the field of the safe transfer, handling and use of any living modified organism resulting from biotechnology that may have adverse effect on the conservation and sustainable use of biological diversity."

I was appointed to the expert group that created the framework for the protocol on Biosafety under Article 19.3 of the Convention. The Cartagena Protocol on Biosafety is the international law on the biosafety of GMOs.[2]

The Nagoya protocol on Access and Benefit Sharing is another protocol of the CBD. It is meant to advance the objective of the CBD which is to ensure "fair and equitable sharing of benefits arising from the utilization of genetic resources." This was becoming especially significant in the context of the growing rush to patent and commodify biodiversity, genetic resources, and indigenous resources. At the seventh meeting of the parties of the ad hoc, open-ended Working Group on Access and Benefit-sharing there was a mandate to elaborate and negotiate an international regime on access to genetic resources and benefit-sharing in order to effectively implement Articles 15 (Access to Genetic Resources) and 8(j) (Traditional Knowledge) of the Convention and its three objectives.

Article 15 of the CBD laid out the narrative on:

- Mutually agreed terms in *Article 15(4):* "Access, where granted, shall be on mutually agreed terms and subject to the provisions of this Article."
- Prior informed consent in *Article 15(5):* "Access to genetic resources shall be subject to prior informed consent of the Contracting Party providing such resources, unless otherwise determined by that Party."
- Benefit sharing in *Article 15(7):* "Each Contracting Party shall take legislative, administrative or policy measures, as appropriate . . . with the aim of sharing in a fair and equitable way the results of research and development and the benefits arising from the commercial and other utilization of genetic resources with the Contracting Party providing such resources."

The lineage of CBD was carried forward in the sixth Conference of Parties (COP) which led to the creation of the Bonn Guidelines on

Access to Genetic Resources and Fair and Equitable Sharing of Benefits Arising out of their Utilization in COP 10, resulting in the Nagoya Protocol on Access to Genetic Resources and Fair and Equitable Sharing of Benefits Arising out of their Utilization.

The Nagoya Protocol on Access to Genetic Resources and Fair and Equitable Sharing of Benefits Arising out of their Utilization

On October 29, 2010 the Nagoya Protocol was adopted in Nagoya, Japan with the aim to establish an international, legally binding framework for the transparent and effective implementation of Access and Benefit Sharing (ABS) concept at regional, national, and local levels.[3] It was a movement forward in cementing a new vocabulary of biocultural entitlements, calling for the creation of set duties and obligations on the parties engaging with indigenous communities for the use of genetic resources and knowledge.

The Protocol noted in its preamble that "the interrelationship between genetic resources and traditional knowledge, their inseparable nature for indigenous and local communities, the importance of the traditional knowledge for the conservation of biological diversity and the sustainable use of its components, and for the sustainable livelihoods of these communities."

The preamble also stated that it was mindful of "the right of indigenous and local communities to identify the rightful holders of their traditional knowledge associated with genetic resources, within their communities."

Article 6 dealt with aspects of access to genetic resources where its subsection (1) clearly stated that "in the exercise of sovereign rights over natural resources, and subject to domestic access and benefit-sharing legislation or regulatory requirements, access to genetic resources for their utilization shall be subject to the prior informed consent of the party providing such resources . . . or a party that has acquired the genetic resources in accordance with the Convention, unless otherwise determined by that Party."

Article 6(2) emphasized that "in accordance with domestic law, each party shall take measures, as appropriate, with the aim of ensuring that the prior informed consent or approval and involvement of indigenous and local communities is obtained for access to genetic resources where they have the *established right* to grant access to such resources."

Article 6(3)(g) established the idea of mutually agreed terms where it called to "establish clear rules and procedures for requiring and establishing mutually agreed terms."

Article 7 affirmed similar ideas for access to traditional knowledge associated with genetic resources.

Article 12(1) clarified that "in implementing their obligations under this protocol, parties shall in accordance with domestic law take into consideration indigenous and local communities' customary laws, community protocols and procedures, as applicable, with respect to traditional knowledge associated with genetic resources."

Furthermore, Article 12(4) emphasized that "parties, in their implementation of this Protocol, shall, as far as possible, not restrict the customary use and exchange of genetic resources and associated traditional knowledge within and amongst indigenous and local communities in accordance with the objectives of the Convention."

By ensuring that prior informed consent and mutually agreed terms are set forth before actually accessing the knowledge, Article 6 affirmed the idea of an established agency of the indigenous communities to control and govern the uses of the traditional knowledge while ensuring that their customary laws are respected.

Article 14 called for establishing an Access and Benefit-sharing clearinghouse as part of the clearinghouse mechanism under Article 18(3) of CBD which would serve as a means for sharing of information related to access and benefit-sharing. An internationally recognized certificate of compliance which is issued by the resource provider to act as an evidence of prior informed consent, and mutually agreed terms would have to be made available to this clearinghouse.

In the domain of benefit sharing, the Nagoya Protocol, thus, institutionalized various biocultural rights and entitlements of indigenous communities in accordance with the domestic laws of the parties. However, this Protocol restricts access only to global players, ignoring the access of local communities; it prioritized only utilization for research and commerce, ignoring the survival needs of local communities. This was legalized biopiracy, as it enabled the transfer of genetic wealth from local communities to global corporations, undermining the biodiversity economies and cultures that have conserved biodiversity and are necessary for its future.

However, despite this, the protocol successfully provided a legal framework for the fair, equitable sharing of benefits arising out of the utilization of genetic resources for research and commercialization purposes. At present, more than 100 countries have acceded to the Protocol, making it mandatory for them to set down an access and benefit regime in compliance with it. Furthermore, patent and IPR regimes are required to respect the obligations under the Nagoya Protocol for access and benefit sharing.

The protocol followed the Indian Biodiversity Act by eight years. Countries of the world were inspired by the forward thinking Indian legal framework.

The Indian Biodiversity Act 2002

As part of our international commitment, the Indian government enacted the Biological Diversity Act (BDA) in 2002.[4] This is one of the major instruments available to the government for the protection of indigenous knowledge systems. I was appointed a member of the expert group to draft the national law, both because of my experience on an international level at the CBD as well as my experience with creating Navdanya, the movement for the conservation of biodiversity, which preceded both the national and international law on biodiversity conservation.

The preamble of the act states that it is "an Act to provide for the conservation of biological diversity, sustainable use of its components, and fair and equitable sharing of the benefits arising out of the use of biological resources, knowledge, and for matters connected therewith or incidental thereto."

The Act defines biodiversity as follows:

"Biological diversity" refers to the variability among living organisms from all sources and the ecological complexes of which they are part, including diversity within species or between species and of ecosystems."

As a national implementation of the United Nations Convention on Biodiversity 1992 it reaffirms:

"The sovereign rights of the States over their biological resources and the duty to protect their rich biological diversity and associated traditional and contemporary knowledge system relating thereto."

It also ensures fair and equitable benefit sharing; given that both biodiversity and biodiversity knowledge is collectively held by local communities, who have been defined as "benefit claimers" in the act:

"'Benefit claimers' means the conservers of biological resources, their by-products, creators and holders of knowledge and information relating to the use of such biological resources, innovations and practices associated with such use and application."

The act defines "commercial utilization" in 2(f):

"'Commercial utilization' refers to the end uses of biological resources for commercial utilization such as drugs, industrial enzymes, food flavors, fragrances, cosmetics, emulsifiers, oleoresins, colors, extracts, and genes used for improving crops and livestock through genetic intervention, but does not include conventional breeding or traditional practices in use in any agriculture, horticulture, poultry, dairy farming, animal husbandry or beekeeping;"

The permission of State Biodiversity Boards is necessary for commercial utilization to ensure fair and equitable benefit sharing with the communities from whom the resources and traditional knowledge have been taken:

> *"No person, who is a citizen of India or a corporate body, association or organization which is registered in India, shall obtain any biological resource for commercial utilization, bio-survey and bio-utilization for commercial utilization except after giving prior intimation to the State Biodiversity Board concerned:*
>
> *Provided that the provisions of this section shall not apply to the local people and communities of the area, including growers and cultivators of biodiversity, and vaids and hakims,* who have been practicing indigenous medicine."*

This law established itself as a model law, later becoming the basis of the Nagoya Protocol on Access and Benefit Sharing; it regulates commercial actors, while respecting the freedoms of traditional communities who have conserved biodiversity and age-old knowledge.

The Biodiversity Act 6(1) also links biodiversity to intellectual property to prevent biopiracy:

> *"No person shall apply for any intellectual property right, by whatever name called, in or outside of India for any invention based on any research or information on a biological resource obtained from India without obtaining the previous approval of the National Biodiversity Authority before making such application.*
>
> *Provided that if a person applies for a patent, permission of the National Biodiversity Authority may be obtained after the acceptance of the patent but before the sealing of the patent by the patent authority concerned."*

The institutional mechanisms created by the Act are as follows: the arrangement of a National Biodiversity Authority (NBA), State Biodiversity Boards (SBBs), and Biodiversity Management Committees (BMCs) in local bodies. The NBA consists of a chairperson, ten *ex officio*

* Those who practice Ayurveda are known as Vaids
* In India, Hakims are those who practice Unani

central government representatives, and five non-official specialists/experts. Its main functions are to lay down procedures and guidelines to govern activities such as granting permission to foreign companies for obtaining any biological resource, and for transferring the results of any research, exemption of certain biological resources normally traded as commodities, etc. The NBA and SBBs are required to consult BMCs in decisions relating to the use of biological resources/related knowledge within their jurisdiction; and the BMCs are to promote the conservation, sustainable use, and documentation of biodiversity. Their main role is to prepare the People's Biodiversity Register (PBR) in consultation with local people, which includes comprehensive information on the availability of local biological resources, and the traditional knowledge associated with them.

Chapter II of the Act covers the Regulation of Access to Biodiversity. Section 3 deals with the certain persons (a non-citizen, a non-resident, a company not incorporated/registered in India) who should not undertake biodiversity related activities without approval of the National Biodiversity Authority. Section 4 pertains to the results of research which shall not be transferred to certain persons (a non-citizen, a non-resident, a company not incorporated or registered in India) without approval of the National Biodiversity Authority. Section 6 revolves around the application for intellectual property rights and says that:

> *"No person shall apply for any intellectual property right, by whatever name called, in or outside of India for any invention based on research or information on a biological resource obtained from India without obtaining the previous approval of the National Biodiversity Authority before making such application."*

Chapter V of the Act gives certain mechanisms for the equitable sharing of benefits. The NBA, under Section 19 and Section 20, demands equitable sharing of benefits which arise out of the use of accessed biological resources, their by-products, innovations, and practices associated with their use and applications and related knowledge. Furthermore, if any amount of money is ordered by way of benefit sharing, the NBA may direct the amount to be deposited in the National Biodiversity Fund.

The various arrangements for benefit sharing as elaborated under the Act are:

- Grant of joint ownership of intellectual property rights to the National Biodiversity Authority, or where benefit claimers are identified, to such benefit claimers
- Transfer of technology
- Location of production, research, and development units in such areas which will facilitate better living standards to the benefit claimers
- Association of Indian scientists, benefit claimers, and the local people with research and development in biological resources, bio survey and bio utilization
- Setting up of venture capital fund for aiding the cause of benefit claimers
- Payment of monetary compensation and non-monetary benefits to the benefit claimers as the National Biodiversity Authority may deem fit

The corporations who wanted free access to our biodiversity and knowledge to then make patents are very active through their lobby groups in trying to erode the Biodiversity Act. Thus, the Association of Biotechnology Led Enterprises (ABLE), a lobby group of the biotechnology industry has made "recommendations on Biodiversity Law provisions and its compliance." ABLE has also tried to challenge the Seed Price Control Order which the government passed to address the agrarian crisis and farmers' distress. I intervened in the case in the High Court of Bangalore, and ABLE's case on behalf of Monsanto and the biotechnology industry was dismissed while the Seed Price Control Order was upheld.

After having wreaked havoc with farmers' rights and in farmers' lives, as well as illegally collecting royalties from Indian farmers for Bt cotton, in spite of not having a patent under 3(j) of the Patent Act, the biotechnology industry is trying to subvert our sovereignty, our national legislation for the conservation of biodiversity, our people's rights, as well our Patent Act by claiming that:

"As the BDA is currently being interpreted, the effect on agricultural research is adverse at best and crippling at worst. If access to biological resources is blocked or the route is made so difficult to traverse, the development of new and improved varieties will be affected. This, in turn, affects the availability of the latest tools and products to Indian farmers."

The distorted logic of the industry is based on the false claim that their GMOs have helped farmers, and therefore they should have unconditional, unregulated access to India's biological and genetic wealth, and be able to take patents.

The claim is false because as Section 6 shows, Bt cotton has resulted in a severe crisis for Indian farmers. Secondly, Monsanto does not, and cannot have patents on seeds under Section 3(j) of India's Patent Law. Thirdly, it is now recognized that industry might introduce new varieties, but these are not "improved" in the context of health, nutrition, resource use efficiency, or climate resilience.

On totally false claims, industry is trying to dismantle laws that we have put in place in order to protect our biodiversity and our communities. It is deliberately trying to cover up its technological failures, sell these failed technologies as "miracles", burdening farmers with high cost seeds that fail to control pests, while also claiming a right to biopiracy.

If a particular industry recommends that no permission should be taken for accessing biological material from India for making a patent application in India or anywhere in the world according to section 6(1) of the Biodiversity Act it (ABLE and the biotechnology industry) represents the desire to have a right to biopiracy.

Not only are corporations trying to undermine the Biodiversity Act, they are also trying to undermine the Patent Act.

Section 10(4)(ii)(d) of the Patents Act [2005] requires that the Patent Applicant should disclose the source and geographical origin of the biological material in the description of the patent application. Industry is falsely presenting this requirement as independent of the Biodiversity Act by citing the transitional arrangement of 2002 as final law when it was merely a temporary mailbox arrangement. They then falsely mention that the Biodiversity Act was not in place at the time of the Patent Amendment 2002, therefore making the two unrelated.

Contrary to their misleading claim, the Patent Amendment Act of 2005 is the final Act, and it has fully taken the Biodiversity Act into account. Industry is trying to argue that patent applications in countries outside India cannot be subjected to Indian laws. This has been the basis of all biopiracy. And preventing biopiracy through regulation of access is one of the objectives of the Biodiversity Act. Again, the demand by industry to undo the access clauses in the act is a demand for a right to engage in biopiracy.

They want to unscientifically claim that organisms in wastewaters such as sewage waste and agricultural waste are not biological resources.

Additionally, they want to claim that if they say they are contributing to conservation and sustainable use of biodiversity, they should have no obligation to follow the rules of the Biodiversity Act.

My work on biodiversity conservation, shaping laws to protect biodiversity and our knowledge began when the chemical companies wanted to use GMOs to claim patents, imposing those patents on seeds and lifeforms through TRIPS. Luckily, we have been successful in implanting Biodiversity and Patent laws that protect the planet and people, not just corporate profits. Even after thirty years, the chemical industry, which is now the biotechnology industry, is still trying desperately to own life for limitless profits. Thirty years ago, they were trying to impose IPRs for their monopolies. We contested them then, preventing TRIPS from becoming an instrument of colonization. The contest between sovereignty and colonization, between biodiversity, corporate greed, and unaccountability continues. Our national laws related to Biodiversity and IPRs are shaped by the sovereignty of biodiversity, of farmers, and of local communities.

Defending the Biodiversity and Knowledge Commons: Navdanya's Community Biodiversity Register (CBR)

While we worked on laws to protect our biodiversity, we also built the movement to defend biodiversity and knowledge commons within communities.

A Community Biodiversity Register performs the function of documenting knowledge of communities at the local, regional, and national levels by the people themselves for the purpose of rejuvenating the ecological basis of agriculture and the economic status of farmers.

CBRs recognize both the differing needs of farmers and consumers as well as their contribution towards meeting these needs. Navdanya has helped form more than 5000 CBRs over the years. CBRs serve the needs of local agricultural communities and not the needs of non-local commercial interests who exploit biodiversity for raw material. Therefore, the documentation has to branch out of local community registers which are ecosystem specific, culture specific, and which are the primary level of utilization for community rejuvenation.

Documenting farmers' varieties of seed is a vital countervailing force to the predatory nature of the IPR regime because it refutes the terms "landraces" and "germplasm" (both of which contribute to the concept that farmers' varieties are not gifts of nature, and thus can be appropriated freely for corporate benefit) and invalidates corporate claims to originality and innovation by placing it, beyond doubt, with the farming community. CBRs, by making farmers varieties freely accessible to other farmers across the country, rejuvenate agricultural biodiversity, people's knowledge, and encourage sustainable agriculture.

Access to traditional varieties revitalizes the role of the farmer as a plant breeder and strengthens his resistance to seed monopolies. Seed exchanges between farmers inevitably shrink the market for corporate seeds. Such exchanges thus help farmers and farming communities to retain agricultural freedom and economic control over agriculture.

At Navdanya, we have been compiling such a community register. Navdanya's community biodiversity register acts as a document of indigenous resources and indigenous knowledge, as a platform for the assertion of Common Intellectual Rights, and as a seed catalogue for interested individuals and groups to get access to organic seed, the first link in the organic food chain.

Navdanya believes that conservation of agricultural biodiversity is impossible without the participation of the communities who have evolved and protected the plants and animals that form the basis of sustainable agriculture. In agriculture, *in situ* conservation strategies are impossible to separate from sustainable utilization and production methods.

Why has documentation of community knowledge become necessary?

Documentation of community knowledge is becoming imperative because of:

- Erosion of resources: non-sustainable production and consumption patterns in agriculture have led to the erosion of land, water and agricultural biodiversity in farmers' fields. For example, the 'miracle seeds' of the green revolution replaced indigenous varieties of rice, many of which are like amaranth–and in the process of being replaced by crops like rice and wheat–are also threatened by extinction.
- Erosion of knowledge: communities which are identified and innovated have traditionally had free exchange of knowledge of their resources within the community and outside it. When such resources are eroded and lack common use, common knowledge is eroded over time.

- Disappearance of sustainable utilization alternatives: when both the resource and knowledge about it disappear from the commons, the space for utilization of alternatives in a sustainable manner, or rather, the space for a return to sustainable agricultural production and consumption shrinks.
- Intellectual piracy: the removal of knowledge from the commons leaves it vulnerable to being claimed as the private intellectual property of someone else. This is particularly true when the common knowledge has no recorded originator or innovator but has traditionally been treated as community knowledge. The IPR regimes ensure that the pirates of such knowledge become the new owners of the knowledge and share it only for profits.
- Biopiracy: intimately linked with intellectual piracy is biopiracy. The removal of resources from the commons leaves it vulnerable to piracy both directly by the IPR regimes and by collections made by organizations (nationally and internationally, government or private).
- IPRs and monopolies: together, intellectual piracy and biopiracy mean that the resource is now in the monopoly control of corporations. In agriculture, this reduces all innovation to innovation by the corporations for profits, with agricultural production and consumption becoming conditional on corporate interests.

TWO

TRIPS, Biodiversity, and Section 3(j) of India's Patent Act

How India defended the sovereignty of Biodiversity, Farmers and the country in the GATT/WTO.

IN 1995 THE WTO CAME INTO FORCE and one of the agreements that emerged from the WTO was the Trade Related Property Rights Agreement (TRIPS).[1] The objectives of the TRIPS Agreement are stated in Article 7:

"The protection and enforcement of intellectual property rights should contribute to the promotion of technological innovation and to the transfer and dissemination of technology, to the mutual advantage of producers and users of technological knowledge and in a manner conducive to social and economic welfare, and to a balance of rights and obligations."

The principles on which TRIPS is based clearly allows countries to frame laws to promote the public interest:

"Members may, in formulating or amending their laws and regulations, adopt measures necessary to protect public health and nutrition, and to promote the public interest in sectors of vital importance to their socio-economic and technological development, provided that such measures are consistent with the provisions of this Agreement."

Monsanto has admitted, on record, that it tried to write the TRIPS Agreement for its own benefit. James Enyart of Monsanto is on record at a conference illustrating just how deeply the TRIPS Agreement was supposed to be aligned with corporate interest and against the interests of farmers, nations, and their citizens:

"Industry has identified a major problem for international trade. It crafted a solution, reduced it to a concrete proposal and sold it to our own and other governments... The industries and traders of world commerce have played simultaneously the role of patients, the diagnosticians, and the prescribing physicians."

Through our work with our negotiators, our government, and our parliamentarians, we ensured that TRIPS did not become a Monsanto law, and our Patent Amendment to implement TRIPS protected the integrity of biodiversity, lifeforms, and *ordre public.* Our negotiators at the GATT introduced exclusions for plants and animals and a *sui generis* option in the TRIPS Agreement in Article 27.3(b). We were successful in excluding life forms from patentability in TRIPS, in India's Patent Act, as well as implementing the unique Plant Variety Protection and Farmers' Rights Act.

TRIPS article 27.3(b) on Patents on life, including seeds, gives parties the sovereign right to exclude from patentability plants and animals. It also gives the option to parties to protect plant varieties, i.e., seeds of plants either through patents or a *sui generis* system.

Article 27.3(b) of the TRIPS Agreement states: "Parties may exclude from patentability plants and animals other than micro-organisms, and essentially biological processes for the production of plants or animals other than non-biological and microbiological processes. However, parties shall provide for the protection of plant varieties either by patents or by an effective *sui generis* system or by any combination thereof."

With the Uruguay Round of GATT, corporations had tried to colonize the biodiversity and peoples of the planet by expanding their industrial patents and IPR regimes geographically. Western style IPR regimes were then attempted to be universalized through the TRIPS Agreement.

Patents, trademarks, and copyrights have always been subject to national jurisdiction. They are definitely not part of international trade.

The international platform for intellectual property was constituted by the World Intellectual Property Organization (WIPO). However, the WIPO did not have the "teeth" that were intended to be brought into the Uruguay Round of GATT through the dispute settlement system of GATT (which earlier had just been an agreement and not an institution). These rounds then resulted in the formation of the World Trade Organization (WTO), which came into force on January 1, 1995 after the Marrakesh meeting in 1994.

Rich, industrialized countries with an eye on commercial interests, especially the US, got together in the 1980s and imposed their idea of IPRs on the world's countries and people. Because Intellectual Property was not part of trade, they added 'trade related', making it 'Trade Related Intellectual Property Rights' (TRIPS) and dragging patents into the Uruguay Round of GATT. Thus, the US introduced intellectual property issues into the GATT Ministerial in Punta Del Este 1986.

The TRIPS Agreement of GATT was not a product of careful negotiation. The US decided to forcefully impose it on the world alongside its corporations. It has been imposed by transnational corporations on the earth and us, the citizens of the world, by manipulating the governments of industrialized countries.

The framework for the TRIPS Agreement was conceived and shaped by the industry group in the Intellectual Property Committee (IPC) which consisted of the Intellectual Property Committee (USA), Keidanren (Japan), and UNICE (Europe). The IPC was a coalition of thirteen major US corporations dedicated to the finalization of TRIPS in GATT. The members of the IPC were Bristol Meyers, Dupont, General Electric, General Motors, Hewlett Packard, IBM, Johnson and Johnson, Merck, Monsanto, Pfizer, Rockwell, and Warner. Keidanren was the Japanese Federation of Economic Organizations. UNICE was the Union of Industrial and Employees Confederation of Europe and was recognized as an official spokesman for European Business and Industry.

After the Punta del Este, the then US Trade Representative (USTR), Clayton Yeutter made a suggestion to members of the IPC about what to do next, as Edmund Pratt, Chairman of Pfizer stated:

"Having been successful in getting 'TRIPS' on the GATT agenda, the government asked the US private sector to provide specific proposals for an agreement, and to form an international private sector consensus to achieve it.

In conjunction with more than a dozen companies from all relevant sectors of US business, Pfizer and IBM co-founded the Intellectual Property Committee or IPC. The US Trade Representative was impressed and suggested that we increase our effectiveness internationally by joining forces with UNICE, the principal pan-European business group, and its counterpart in Japan, Keidanren."[2]

Thus, the US government and corporate representatives sat side-by-side in the negotiations on the CBD as well as the GATT.

A text which had a major influence on the IPR negotiations in the GATT was released in Washington in June 1988, entitled 'Basic Framework of GATT Provisions on Intellectual Property: Statement of Views of the European, Japanese, and United States Business Communities.'

The Basic Framework, written by corporations, required that a "patent shall be granted for . . . products and processes without discrimination to the subject matter," i.e., that plants, animals and seeds can be patented.

These groups worked closely to introduce intellectual property protection into the GATT. James Enyart of Monsanto, commenting on the IPC strategy stated:

"Besides selling our concepts at home, we went to Geneva where we presented (our) document to the staff of the GATT secretarial. We also took the opportunity to present it to the Geneva based representatives of a large number of countries. What I have described to you is absolutely unprecedented in GATT. Industry has identified a major problem in international trade. It crafted a solution, reduced it to a concrete proposal and sold it to our own and other governments. Industries and traders of the world played simultaneously the patients, the diagnosticians and the prescribing physicians."

It is this usurpation of the rights of diverse social groups by commercial interests that would have ultimately led to the displacement of ethical, ecological, and social concern from the substance of the TRIPS Agreement if countries like India, Argentina, and Brazil had not intervened.

TRIPS, as imposed by corporations, was changed through democratic negotiations between the larger public and their governments in the Third World, and the contribution of Third World negotiators at the WTO to uphold the integrity of life forms and people's rights to seeds and medicines. The imposition of values and interests of northern TNCs on the diverse societies and cultures of the world was unsuccessful.

At the conceptual level, Trade Related Intellectual Property Rights (TRIPS) were intended to be restrictive, being shaped and defined by global corporations and hence weighted in their favor, and pitted against biodiversity, the rights of species, citizens in general, and particularly Third World peasants and forest-dwellers. Traditional knowledge is the result of centuries of cumulative, collective innovation. Denial of the rights of communities who have evolved traditional knowledge related to biodiversity over centuries is an epistemic and human rights violation. People everywhere are innovative and creative. In fact, the poorest people have to be the most innovative, since they have to create their means of survival while it is threatened on a daily basis. So too, women have been important innovators and protectors of seeds and genetic resources.

Limited concepts of innovation and knowledge, along with limited categories of intellectual property rights, as construed by corporations and rich countries in the trade negotiations, operate on a number of levels.

The first limited view is the shift from common to private rights. The preamble of the TRIPS Agreement states that intellectual property rights are recognized only as private rights. This excludes all kinds of knowledge, ideas, and innovations that take place in the 'intellectual commons,' in the communities, in the villages among farmers, in forests among tribals, and even in universities among public scientists. TRIPS, therefore, was originally meant to be a mechanism to privatize the intellectual commons and de-intellectualize society, so that in effect, collective wisdom becomes a corporate monopoly.

The second limitation is that intellectual property rights are recognized only when knowledge and innovation generate profits, not when they meet social needs and ecological needs, including improving food quality, taste, nutrition, and climate resilience. According to Article 27.1.9, to be recognized as an IPR, innovation must be capable of industrial application. Only profits and capital accumulation are recognized as viable uses of creativity. Under corporate control social creativity as well as social and common good are discounted.

Lastly, the most significant limitation of IPRs is achieved by way of the prefix 'trade-related.' The majority of innovation by women, peasants, and tribals is for domestic, local, and public use rather than international trade. The TNC's innovation often based on biopiracy is for the sole purpose of increasing their share in global markets and international trade; and the TRIPS in GATT in its corporate form would only have enforced the TNC's rights to monopolize all production, distribution, and profits from biodiversity at the cost of all citizens and small producers worldwide.

Article 27 on patentable matter, which is a reflection of the basic framework for TRIPS prepared by the corporations, is a clear indication that in the Uruguay Round an attempt was made to remove all prior boundary conditions on patent regimes. Article 27(1) states that:

> *"Patents shall be available for any inventions, whether products or processes, in all fields of technology, provided that they are new, involve an inventive step, and are capable of industrial application."*

This was an attempt to nullify the exclusions built into national patent laws for the protection of the public and national interest. For example, in the Patent Act of India 1970, methods of agriculture and horticulture were excluded and not considered patentable whereas the TRIPS text would have included these as patentable if we had not introduced exclusions in Article 27.3 which excluded seeds, plants, animals, and their parts from patentability.

Exclusions of Article 27.3(b) of TRIPS and Section 3(j) of India's Patent Act

TRIPS article 27.3(b) on Patents on Life, including seeds, gives parties the sovereign right to exclude plants and animals from patentability. It also gives the option to parties to protect plant varieties, i.e. seeds of plants either through patents or a *sui generis* system.

India's laws are consistent with the TRIPS Agreement of the WTO, whilst simultaneously protecting biodiversity, public interest, and national interest. This flexibility is provided in Article 27 of the TRIPS Agreement:

> *"Members may also exclude from patentability: diagnostic, therapeutic, and surgical methods for the treatment of humans or animals.*
>
> *Plants and animals other than micro-organisms, and essentially biological processes for the production of plants or animals other than non-biological and microbiological processes. However, Members shall provide for the protection of plant varieties either by patents or by an effective sui generis system or by any combination thereof. The provisions of this subparagraph shall be reviewed four years after the date of entry into force of the WTO Agreement."*

Section 3(h) of the Indian Patent Act excludes from patentability a method of agriculture or horticulture.

In regard to patenting life in this context, Monsanto was not able to be the "patient, diagnostician, and physician" all in one because an alliance of sovereignty worked together. Initially, I had got involved in the TRIPS/GATT issue because of the Chakravarty Raghavan wakeup call at the "Laws of Life" meeting in UN Geneva, March 1987 where he alerted us that neither the WIPO nor UNCTAD were international platforms for IPR issues being enforced by corporations. GATT was their preferred platform. Our alertness and engagement changed the evolution of patent laws in the context of plants, animals, and seeds.

As a result, we were able to introduce exclusions in the above Patents on Life clause. This was the article used by the Indian Patent Office to examine the Monsanto patent application for Bt cotton, subsequently rejecting most of its claims in two examinations. Further, this same article was used by the Indian Patent Office to reject a Monsanto patent on climate resilient seeds.

Under the Indian Patent Act, only process patents can be granted to food, medicines, drugs, and chemical products but under the WTO, the Third World had to grant product patents in this area also. A mailbox arrangement was implemented in a 2002 amendment of India's Patent Act.

In 2002, India very clearly defined what is not an invention and this included evergreening of medicines.

When India amended her patent acts, safeguards to defend national and public interests consistent with TRIPS were introduced. Section 3 defined what is considered to be unpatentable subject matter.

Section 3(d) excludes as inventions "the mere discovery of any new property or new use for a known substance."

This was the article under which Novartis's patent claim to a known cancer drug was rejected. Upon rejection, Novartis tried to challenge this article in the Supreme Court but lost.

Section 3(h) of the Indian Patent Act excludes from patentability a method of agriculture or horticulture.

IPRs in the area of seeds and plants are governed by the Plant Variety Protection and Farmers' Rights Act, because they are excluded under 3(j) and 3(h) in the Patent Act.

I was a member of the expert group that drafted the law, helping to ensure the clause on Farmers' Rights.

Section 3(j) is also an important aspect of the *ordre public* exemptions allowed in TRIPS Article 27.2 which states:

"Members may exclude from patentability inventions, the prevention within their territory of the commercial exploitation of which is necessary to protect ordre public or morality, including to protect human, animal or plant life or health or to avoid serious prejudice to the environment, provided that such exclusion is not made merely because the exploitation is prohibited by their law."

We are all members of the earth family, single strands in the interconnected web of life. We are not outside nature, nor masters and owners of biodiversity. We are not inventors of life, but rather participants in it. Yet corporations who claim legal personhood, are now asserting the role of creator. They have declared the seed to be their "invention," hence their patented property. A patent is an exclusive right granted for an "invention," which allows the patent holder to exclude everyone else from making, selling, distributing and using the patented product. Patents on seed imply that the farmers' right to save and share seed is now in effect defined as "theft" and "intellectual property crime."

This was the discussion in the 1987 Bogeve meeting on the new biotechnologies that led me to saving biodiversity, seeds, and defending farmer's rights in practice and in law.

The door to patents on seed and patents on life was opened by genetic engineering. By adding one new gene to the cell of a plant, corporations claimed they had invented and created the seed, the plant, and all future seeds which, in turn, become their property. In other words, GMO meant 'God Move Over'.

In defining the seed as their creation and invention, corporations like Monsanto tried to shape the Global Intellectual Property and Patent Laws on the unscientific grounds that by adding one gene, they create a seed and plant, and all its future generations so that they could prevent farmers from seed saving and sharing. This is how the Trade Related Intellectual Property Rights (TRIPS) Agreement of the World Trade Organization was introduced into a trade agreement.

Over these 30 years in international and national fora and in international and national courts, I have witnessed Monsanto continuing to defend patents on GMOs while shifting their arguments since they have been losing the false ground on which they claim patents on seeds and life forms. First, they said they had invented a life form. However, as we showed that the seed is a complex, self-organized living system, and not an invention nor manufactured; in addition, as section 3(j) was clear that life forms are not inventions, Monsanto changed its arguments. They are now saying they have invented a chemical product.

Monsanto and Bayer Monsanto are still trying to be the "patient, diagnosticians, and prescribing physicians" when it comes to seeds and rights to seed. They are now also trying to be the "hospital."

While we in India have kept scientific accuracy, national sovereignty, the *ordre public,* ethics, and equity at the center of our Biodiversity and IPR laws, the US has no such laws, and decisions are made under corporate influence, without the guidance of science and law.

Section 3(j) of the Indian Patent Act excludes from patentability plants and animals in whole or in any part thereof, seeds, varieties, species, and essentially biological processes for production or propagation of plants and animals.

This was the article used by the Indian Patent Office to reject a Monsanto patent on climate resilient seeds, rejecting most claims on Bt cotton. The decision was upheld by the High Court of Delhi.[3]

While the Indian patent office rejected Monsanto patents on the basis of 3(j), the US Supreme Court ruled on behalf of Monsanto against a farmer, Vermon Hugh Bowman, who had not bought seeds from Monsanto but purchased soybeans from an Indiana grain cultivator. The US Supreme court ruling created intellectual property in future generations of a grain or seed. This was, and still is, biologically and intellectually incorrect because all that Monsanto had done was add a gene for resistance to its proprietary herbicide Roundup. Adding a gene of Roundup resistance does not amount to "inventing" or "creating" a soya bean seed and its future generations.

This is why 3(j) in India's Patent Law excludes essential biological processes from being counted as an invention. Our patent laws are more scientifically, ecologically, and epistemologically sophisticated than the US, which has no biodiversity law and only ad hoc court decisions to shape its IPR laws.

India's patent laws are sovereign laws. Our laws are different from US decisions because we are a sovereign country. Being different from US norms and orders (which are clearly Monsanto influenced) is not to be TRIPS inconsistent. In fact, for the protection of biodiversity, food security, farmers' rights, and real innovation, US law needs to learn from Indian law and the decisions on patents our courts have upheld.

India and other countries were successful in preventing the imposition of patents on life during the GATT negotiations on TRIPS. Article 27.3(b) of TRIPS has a *sui generis* option for protection of plant varieties. Thus, countries do not *have to* allow patents on seeds, nor do they *have to* adopt UPOV.

The thrust of Western IPR regimes in the area of biodiversity is diametrically opposed to indigenous knowledge systems. Knowledge is considered to be individual creativity, based on Western scientific thought, systems of knowledge creation, and gathering. Due to this, the resource base and indigenous knowledge that is pirated is merely viewed as 'raw material.' In this paradigm, IPRs represent the property rights to products of mind and thereby narrowly define knowledge and creativity while ignoring the creativity of nature and non-western knowledge systems.

The two categories of IPRs that have a direct impact on the erosion of the prior rights of communities are patents and plant breeders' rights. Plant breeders' rights negate the contribution of Third World farmers as breeders, and hence undermine farmers' rights. Patents allow the usurpation of indigenous knowledge as "Western invention" through minor tinkering and trivial translation.

The Union for the Protection of New Varieties of Plant Convention (UPOV) represents a Western devised (therefore internationally 'acceptable') form of plant variety protection, other than patenting. This form of intellectual property rights protection, referred to as the Plant Breeders' Right (PBR), was promoted as the most favorable form for adoption under the sui generis option for developing nations by the developed nations. Furthermore, under the 1991 revision of the UPOV Convention, the new clauses severely restricted farmers' rights by removing all rights for them to save seed for sowing the following year. They also removed researchers' rights to save the seed of new protected varieties. This meant that protective varieties could still be used as an initial source of variation for the creation of new varieties, but such new varieties could not be marketed or sold without the permission of the holder of plant breeders' rights.

There now exist very little differences in the restrictions set by plant breeders' rights and those set by patents for farmers. The UPOV is a monopoly system that embodies the philosophy of the industrialized north who want to protect the interests of corporate biotechnology and powerful seed companies' systems. I worked as an expert in the group created by the agriculture ministry to implement the *sui generis* option in TRIPS. We did not adopt UPOV and instead implemented the Plant Variety Protection and Farmers Rights Act. The UPOV would have encouraged the free flow of agricultural biodiversity based on centuries of breeding off the fields of Indian farmers, while forcing them to pay royalties to the seed industry for the varieties derived from farmers' varieties.

India was successful in introducing a *sui generis* option for plant variety protection. IPRs in the area of seeds and plants are now governed by the Plant Variety Protection and Farmers Rights Act because they are excluded under 3(j) and 3(h) of the Patent Act.

In 2015 because of the high costs of Bt cotton seed, and the rising agrarian distress, the government introduced a Seed Price Control Order. [4]

When India amended her patent acts, safeguards consistent with TRIPS were introduced. Article 3 defines what is not patentable subject matter.[5]

Article 3(d) excludes as inventions "the mere discovery of any new property or new use for a known substance."

This was not only the article under which Novartis's patent claim to a known cancer drug was rejected, but also the article that Novartis tried to challenge in the Supreme Court and lost.

Section 3(j) of India's Patent Law does not allow patents on seeds. Section 3(j) excludes from patentability "plants and animals in whole or in any part thereof other than microorganisms but including seeds, varieties, species, and essentially biological processes for production or propagation of plants and animals."

This was the article used by the Indian Patent office to examine Monsanto's patent application for Bt cotton, rejecting most of the claims in two examinations. In addition, this was the article upheld by the High Court of Delhi. Monsanto has appealed the High Court Decision on article 3(j).

India has been unique in framing her sovereign laws to protect the rights of biodiversity and all species, the rights of farmers, tribals, and fisher folk whose livelihoods depend on the biodiversity economy. Furthermore, India continues to keep alive the challenge to biopiracy at the International level in WTO, having successfully created the exclusion for patenting life forms in TRIPS during the mandatory review in 1999 for article 27.3(b) India made the following submissions:

> *"Clearly, there is a case for re-examining the need to grant patents on lifeforms anywhere in the world. Until such systems are in place, it may be advisable to: (a) exclude patents on all lifeforms;"*

The African Group too stated:

> *"The African Group maintains its reservations about patenting any life forms as explained on previous occasions by the Group and several other delegations. In this regard, the Group proposes that Article 27.3(b) be revised to prohibit patents on plants, animals, microorganisms,*

> *essentially biological processes for the production of plants or animals, and non-biological and microbiological processes for the production of plants or animals. For plant varieties to be protected under the TRIPS Agreement, the protection must clearly, and not just implicitly or by way of exception, strike a good balance with the interests of the community as a whole and protect farmers' rights and traditional knowledge, and ensure the preservation of biological diversity."*

This mandatory review has been subverted by governments within the WTO: this long overdue review must be taken up to reverse patents on life and patents on seed as well as biopiracy; as well as completed both in the context of false claims to invention as in the Monsanto Bt cotton case, and in the epidemic of biopiracy.

Since biopiracy is theft, not invention, no patents should be granted for appropriation of traditional knowledge and associated biological resources. Further, full disclosure of source or origin of genetic resource by patent applicants, submission of evidence of prior informed consent of local communities, and evidence of fair and equitable sharing of benefits under the relevant national regimes needs to be made mandatory in the TRIPS Agreement.

In 2001 the Doha Ministerial Declaration had tasked the TRIPS Council of the WTO to examine the relationship between the TRIPS Agreement and the Convention on Biological Diversity, and the protection of traditional knowledge and folklore. This is important for countries like India in addressing biopiracy.

The WIPO has also taken up the issue of Intellectual Property and Traditional Knowledge.[6]

In June 2018, India joined Brazil, South Africa, and China for WTO talks on checking the theft of traditional knowledge including Ayurveda, Yoga, and Naturopathy.[7] Because of India's persistence the WTO took up the issue of IPRs and biodiversity during the talks.

Section 3(j) of the Indian Patent Act and Monsanto's Bt cotton case: A story of violation of Indian patent laws, pseudo-science, and illegal royalty collection from farmers

On May 7, 2018, in an appeal in the Supreme Court to overturn a High Court decision that upheld the exclusion of patents on seeds in India's Patent Law: Monsanto stated that Indian companies had been using "their patent for eighteen years," filing a case against Indian seed companies on the basis of "infringement," claiming that it had a patent on Bt cotton. The case was dismissed by the High Court of Delhi in its Final Judgment dated November 4, 2018.[8] Monsanto did not, and does not have a patent on Bt cotton, contrary to its claims in the courts.

Monsanto filed their patent application on January 5, 2001 to the Indian Patent Office (IPO) entitled "Methods for Transforming Plants to Express Bacillus Thuringiensis Delta-Endotoxins." As the title indicates and as also repeatedly stated in their complete specification, the invention claimed pertains to "transgenic plants having insecticidal capabilities." The specification states that "the present invention encompasses any transgenic plant or plant cell prepared by the use of a DNA construct disclosed herein." Further, it adds that "the present invention also encompasses a seed produced by the transformed plant, a progeny from such seed, and a seed produced by the progeny of the original transgenic plant, produced in accordance with the above process." In a nutshell, the claims (fifty-nine in total) submitted along with the application, even more explicitly seek to assert monopoly over a plant, its tissues, cells, and methods of production of transgenic plants.

While the Indian Patent Office, through two examinations, had rejected most claims made by Monsanto, US Patent IN214436 was granted in favor of Monsanto Technology LLP., (Appellant no. 1 herein) on February 12, 2008 for a period of 20 years with effect from November 4, 1999 (i.e., due to expire on November 3, 2019).

On March 30, 2006, the First Examination Report (FER) issued by the Patent Examiner raised a series of objections on patentability and patent eligibility of the invention. In particular, the FER noted that "Claims 1–40, 48–56, 57, 58 are [not] allowable under Section 3(j)."

On August 7, 2006, the patentee (i.e., Monsanto) vastly amended their claims and specifications.

On October 16, 2006, the Patent Examiner issued a Second Examination Report (SER) and once again sought to reject the amended claims 4, 26-28 and 32-36 under Section 3(j).

On November 30, 2006, in reply, Monsanto stated that "the claims have been suitably amended to overcome the objections raised by the Examiner. The applicant has deleted claims 4, 26 to 28 and 32 to 36 as objected under section 3(j) of the Indian Patents Act." Along with the response, the Patentee submitted their amended Claims–i.e., 27 in total. Of relevance, claims 25 to 27 pertained to "a nucleic acid sequence" which was the subject matter of current dispute.*

The High Court ruled that claims 25–27 were 'unpatentable' and excluded from patent protection by virtue of Section 3(j) of the Patents Act, 1970 (hereinafter the act). On grounds that article 3(j) of India's patent law does not allow patents on seeds, plants, or their parts.

Having started trying to claim Bt cotton, its progeny and future generations as their invention, Monsanto has now shifted its ground and says that the subject patent (viz., Claims 25–27) covers a 'Nucleic Acid Construct' or 'Artificial Gene' ('Bt. Gene') which is purely a chemical product; therefore, cannot form 'part' of a seed or plant excluded under Section 3(j).

In Monsanto's fifty-eight claims, most related to plants and claims 1–40, 48–56, 57, and 58 were rejected as not allowable under 3(j) on March 30, 2006 by the Patent Office. Claims 41, 43, and 59 were rejected under 3(b) and other grounds. Only claims 45, 46, 47 were not objected to. These were the subset of claims on nucleic acid sequence.

The patent office had therefore clearly implemented 3(j) on a scientific basis. As the HC order recognized, "ultimately what was granted

* A chart containing the details of claims submitted by the Appellant and the objections raised by the Examiner is annexed at the end of the chapter.)

was not a patent over the product, or even a method, but the identification of the place in the genetic sequence of the DNA where the cryAB2 protein is in the plant cell."[9]

Our laws recognize that adding a gene to a seed is not an "invention" of the seed. Seeds are not machines, they are self-organized living systems that evolve, reproduce, multiply and renew. They can be manipulated, but not "invented." Changing the tiles of a bathroom floor in a house is neither the making of the house, nor the basis of its ownership, and with ownership, the right to collect rents, royalties, or trait fees.

India's Patent Law is clear; life forms are not inventions and hence not patentable. The government has reiterated again and again that Monsanto does not have a patent in India.[10]

Monsanto had falsely defined seed to be their 'invention' and paved such scientifically unjustified claims as their route to monopoly over seed. With the HC judgment, they have shifted their language, but not their intent for monopoly. They now refer to genes and DNA as 'chemical products' and are trying to say their patent is for the product, not a process.

The shifting sands of Monsanto's illegal patent claim to Bt cotton

Having lost the argument on patents on seeds and plants in the High Court, Monsanto changed its tactics in the Supreme Court.

Having failed to get a patent on plants in its patent application, and having failed to mislead the HC with scientific and legally fraudulent arguments, Monsanto is now (2018) trying to mislead the Supreme Court, both by reducing transgenic material it has manipulated to a 'chemical', and then trying to claim they have a product patent. Monsanto cites the mailbox arrangement made in the 2002 Amendment of the Patent Act to accept applications in the 'mailbox' of Section 2(q) and Section 5 of the Patents Act 1970 which did not allow product patents on chemicals and only process patents. This was the basis of India's strong generic drugs industry. This clause for applications for a mailbox was a temporary interim arrangement which was replaced by the final amendment of 2005 which repealed Section 5 altogether, and inserted Article 3, including 3(j).

The 2005 Amendment is what applies to the subject matter.

Monsanto's arguments on a patent are thus in violation of the law, which is the 2005 Amendment, not the 2002 interim mailbox arrangement. While product patents could be applied for in 2002, the grant was to be based on the 2005 Amendment.

Monsanto is presenting its attempt of corrupt India's Patent Laws. It has failed to mention that its original application was for patents on plants, and that is still its intent. Now by referring to the genes as a chemical, as a product and as their 'intellectual property' they want total freedom to collect rents and royalties. They even go to the extreme of claiming intellectual property "through genetic contamination" as in the famous Percy Schmeiser case referred to in the High Court judgment. That case also falsifies Monsanto's rendering of genetic modification as 'chemical production' in a 'subcellular' container which is not part of the plant, and that the "presence of the artificial gene is reversible, and the gene can be removed /deleted."

In paragraph 15 of Monsanto's appeal it called for a scientific committee to assist the court. This was a tremendous insult to India's Patent Controller, to the learned High Court Judges and also the learned Supreme Court judges. It was a desperate attempt to continue its patent fraud on the nation and her farmers and should have been dismissed with costs and payment for damages.

In the Supreme Court, on May 7, 2018, Monsanto stated:

"We have invented a chemical that transforms plants into super plants. The seed is merely a container."

Further, in their appeal they said, "seed is merely a carrier of their chemical, artificial gene/nucleic acid construct and the presence of the construct in seed is a reversible process." They say that through cross pollination and backcrossing the artificial gene/nucleic acid construct can be removed/deleted.

These are false claims.

Once a gene is put in a GMO it is an irreversible part of the GMO and cannot be removed. Once it is released in the environment, the transgene does not stay 'contained' in the plant. It moves into the soil, it spreads genetic contamination through pollination and wind, as happened in the case of Percy Schmeiser.

A "nucleic acid sequence" in biology is simply a chain of nucleotides arranged in a particular sequence, encoding information. There are only four known nucleotides which are well known (A, T, C, and G). Nowhere in claim 25 do they address it as a chemical. Labeling it as a chemical is an afterthought and an attempt to escape the purview of Section 3(j). A nucleic acid sequence is, in fact, a biological molecule or 'biomolecule.'

No gene can be removed/deleted without consequence (often lethal) for the organisms. They can be replaced by an allele of the same gene which leads to a different expression of the same characteristics (for example, replacing the gene for susceptibility to a disease with a resistant allele). This is what breeders usually do with naturally occurring genes in plant breeding. Therefore, the 'removal/deletion' of a gene is scientifically absurd because it potentiates fatal consequences for the organism whose range depends on how large the portion of DNA which was removed/deleted was.

Once the Bt gene or any transgene is introduced, it becomes part of the plant, spreading and contaminating, without being able to be removed or recalled. The transgene outside the transgenic plant has no function and no value in itself as a 'chemical product' to be traded in the market as other chemical products are. It was created with the intent of introducing the GMO Bt cotton.

In the best of cases, the transformation through backcrossing usually leaves several fragments of the transgenes scattered around the crop genome which collectively are a lot harder to breed out or even identify. If they are very small fragments, e.g. less than about 10-15 base pairs, they usually cannot be detected reliably. So, it is not possible to ensure that they would be removed by backcrossing.

Monsanto is unscientifically trying to argue that a gene is merely a chemical; a plant is a machine into which the chemical can be mechanically introduced and removed at will. They are trying to make a fallacious argument that Bt cotton is not a plant and Bt genes modified by them is not a part of a plant or plant variety. Genes are part of living organisms. Subcellular organelles are parts of living organisms.

Monsanto is also trying to say their patent is for a 'product', not a 'process' to try and escape from the restrictions of Article 3(j) while indirectly continuing their attempt to establish monopoly over seed, now through claiming Bt as a product. A product patent on Bt would become a patent on the seeds containing the Bt. However, the patent title itself clarifies that patent number 214436 is for "methods for transforming plants to express *Bacillus thuringiensis* delta-endotoxins." It is therefore false for Monsanto to argue that the patent is a product patent and not a process patent. Once the transgenic gene made with Bt toxins is extracted from the organism (*Bacillus thuringiensis*), with genes for antibiotic resistance markers and genes that act as viral promoters, and then introduced into cotton it becomes Bt cotton: a plant variety which is not patentable under 3(j).

Besides falsely claiming patents on Bt cotton seeds first as patents on plants, then as patents on genes that are modified in a lab, and now as patents on chemicals, Monsanto is distorting science at the most basic level and wanting to corrupt our national laws which are based on the highest scientific understanding of the biology of living organisms, genes and GMOs.

By referring to Bt genes as a 'technology' and now a chemical product added to plants, Monsanto is hiding from the courts that a 'gene', even when described in its chemical form as a nucleic acid sequence, becomes part of the plant and its future generations through the essential biological process of plant reproduction and future breeding.

Unlike other technologies, where the technology of production and the technology of the product are separable, genetically modified seed, like Bt cotton and the Bt gene, once introduced into the seed through genetic engineering in the lab, becomes part of the seed which produces and reproduces itself as a biological organism, not a machine. The Bt gene–which Monsanto misleadingly calls 'technology' and 'technology trait'–inevitably becomes part of the Bt cotton seed and cannot be separated from it.

Bt is a gene (from a soil bacterium *Bacillus thuringiensis)*, not a technology, not a mere chemical, but part of a life form. Genetic engineering is the technology through which a gene of bacteria has been added to a plant, in this case cotton, another life form. Indian law has evolved with deep scientific understanding of how plants and GMOs work.

On the same scientific basis, the 'technology fees' charged for the 'technology trait' of Bt are intrinsic to the price of seed, with the farmers paying for it with their very lives. The technology fees and seed price are inseparable. That is why the Seed Price Order was introduced under the Essential Commodities Act of India. Monsanto then challenged this Act, but I intervened in the HC of Karnataka, and the case was dismissed.

3(j) of the Indian Patent Act is based on the best of science, not the fraudulent claims Monsanto has been using that the seed is a 'mere container' or 'carrier' into which they put a gene; a gene which can be removed through conventional breeding without the interference of genetic engineering–as seeds are complex self-organized living organisms, not containers.[11]

A gene, whether artificial or natural, is a fundamental component of, essentially, "biological processes for the propagation of plants and animals:" again, the seed is not 'merely a carrier.' It is the essence of the future plants for whose development, not only the genes but several other cellular constituents are of fundamental importance. In fact, the seed itself is a living organism which is capable of remaining alive at the lowest water content of many other organisms. The idea that seeds/ plants are simply inert vessels that carry these genes is contrary to all we know about genetics. They have many interactions with other genes, expressed as pleiotropy and epistasis.

Genetic science has shown that the mechanistic paradigm on which Monsanto's claims are based is false. The genome is a fluid, self-organizing living system in which every part, including the introduced gene, interacts with every other part, including the environment. The gene is not a 'master molecule' as the false science of genetic determinism projects.

Monsanto has not made a chemical in the lab, but merely mixed existing genes found in natural organisms into a transgene referred to as Bt (cry2Ab) and introduced the transgene into the cells of the cotton plant through a 'gene gun' or, particle gun.

The Bt gene was taken from the naturally occurring Bt organism in the soil, Bacillus thuringiensis. This is not an 'invention' of a chemical in the lab as Monsanto claims, but an extraction from a naturally occurring organism. The name Bt is derived from the naturally occurring soil organism.

In the case of Bt Brinjal, a case was started against Monsanto for biopiracy of the Bt.[12]

Besides the Bt from the soil, Monsanto has used other naturally occurring microorganisms to extract genes for antibiotic resistance markers and viral promoters, including *Arabidopsis thaliana* and the cauliflower mosaic virus. These are not chemicals 'invented' in the lab but known organisms with known functions which are public knowledge, even available on Wikipedia. [13]

This is not the 'manufacture' of a 'chemical' but the manipulation of existing genes in naturally occurring microorganisms. Article 3(d) of the patent law combined with Section 3(j) forbids such patents in India.

Article 10 of the Patent Law along with Article 3 and 6 of the Biodiversity Act require that Monsanto disclose the source of the microorganisms. Monsanto's false claim to patents on Bt cotton is in violation of Section 10(4) of the Indian Patent Act which states that:

"Every complete specification shall:

(a) Fully and particularly describe the invention and its operation or use and the method by which it is to be performed;

(b) Disclose the best method of performing the invention which is known to the applicant and for which he is entitled to claim protection; and

(c) End with a claim or claims defining the scope of the invention for which protection is claimed;

(d) Be accompanied by an abstract to provide technical information on the invention:

Provided that–

(i) The Controller may amend the abstract for providing better information to third parties; and

(ii) If the applicant mentions a biological material in the specification which may not be described in such a way as to satisfy clauses (a) and (b), and if such material is not available to the public, the application shall be completed by depositing the material to an international depositary authority under the Budapest Treaty and by fulfilling the following conditions, viz.,:

(a) The deposit of the material shall be made not later than the date of filing the patent application in India and a reference thereof shall be made in the specification within the prescribed period;

(b) All the available characteristics of the material required for it to be correctly identified or indicated are included in the specification including the name, address of the depository institution and the date and number of the deposit of the material at the institution;

(c) Access to the material is available in the depository institution only after the date of the application of a patent in India or if a priority is claimed after the date of the priority;

(d) Disclose the source and geographical origin of the biological material in the specification, when used in an invention."

Therefore, in terms of Section 10(4)(d)(ii), if the patent application describes biological material, it is to be deposited in terms of the Budapest Treaty with an IDA before the application is made. This process is obligatory.

The Hon'ble Delhi High Court noted, "Monsanto nowhere states that in terms of Section 10(4), the biological material was deposited with an International Depositary Authority (IDA), as a precondition for its application under the Patents Act." Monsanto has allegedly failed to:

> *"(a) Disclose the source and, origin as well as accession details, of B. thuringiensis from which the Cry2A gene was isolated; (b) disclose source and origin as well as accession details of Agrobacterium tumefaciens from which nopaline synthase gene and octopine synthase gene were isolated and used; (c) disclose source and origin as well accession details of potato and tomato from which 3' end of the protease inhibitor I or II genes were isolated; disclose source and origin as well as accession details of a plant, particularly maize plant from which the PTPs have been isolated; disclose source and geographical origin as well as accession details of Arabidopsis thaliana from which PTPs have been isolated; disclose source and geographical origin along with, the accession/variety details of maize, cotton, and tobacco plants being used in the examples; disclose source, geographical origin as well as the accession/variety details from; which the FMV35S promoter has been isolated; (e) disclose details of petunia heat shock protein (HSP70), maize heat shock protein (HSP70) is absent; and disclose the source, geographical origin and accession details of . . . (ineligible) phosphotransferase gene (NPTII)."*

While noting that Claim 25–27 are not with respect to microorganisms the Honorable High Court observed that even if for the sake of argument, the subject matter of Claims 25–27 were considered as *microorganisms* the said Claims would still fail as necessary conditions of Section 10(4)(d)(ii) were not fulfilled and on that ground also the patent was liable to be set aside.

It is submitted that Section 10(4)(d)(ii) applies to all *biological materials* and not just *microorganisms*. Notwithstanding, the creative relabeling of nucleic acid sequence described in Claim 25 variously as chemical product/chemical compound/artificial gene, etc. 'Nucleic acids' are genetic material and whether outside the cell or inside the cell they are *biological material* and are subjected to fulfill conditions of 10(4)(d)(ii).

The national laws of many countries, including India, require that *biological material* and not just *microorganisms* be deposited; therefore, in practice, various IDAs provide the facilities to deposit the said *biological material.* It is pertinent to note that the official website of the Budapest Treaty lists the various kinds of 'microorganisms' that can be deposited at various IDAs. Many of these IDAs in practice accept the deposit of nucleic acids, genetic material, genes, nucleic acid preparations, and so forth. It is thus amply clear that biological materials that include nucleic acid sequences are required to be submitted to IDAs.

Biological material access is also governed by the Biodiversity Act and by the Nagoya Protocol on Access and Benefit Sharing as mentioned in the prior chapter. That is why the biotechnology industry is trying to undermine the obligations under both the Patent Act and the Biodiversity Act. They are still under the delusion that they take biological resources without regulation, and then impose patents which have not been granted.

The summary on the official website of the Budapest Treaty also states the following:

> *"The main feature of the Treaty is that a contracting State which allows or requires the deposit of microorganisms for the purposes of patent procedure must recognize, for such purposes, the deposit of a microorganism with any 'international depositary authority,' irrespective of whether such authority is on or outside the territory of the said State. Disclosure of the invention is a requirement for the grant of patents. Normally, an invention is disclosed by means of a written description. Where an invention involves a microorganism or the use of a microorganism, disclosure is not possible in writing but can only be affected by the deposit, with a specialized institution, of a sample of the microorganism. In practice, the term "microorganism" is interpreted in a broad sense, covering biological material the deposit of which is necessary for the purposes of disclosure."*

The Long History of Illegal Royalty Collections on False Claim of Patents on Bt Cotton

While Monsanto does not have a patent on Bt cotton in India, it goes outside the law to collect royalties as 'technology fees'. The majority of the 300,000 farmers' suicides in India since 1995, when WTO came into force, are concentrated in the cotton belt. Today, 95 percent of cotton in India is controlled by Monsanto.

While stating in the Supreme Court that it is not claiming patents on seed, every case Monsanto has filed against India's laws, rules, and institutions is based on the false claim that it has patents on Bt cotton. This legal history is part of the case in the SC.

Monsanto has fraudulently claimed it has patents on Bt cotton seeds, challenging the Seed Price Control Order of 2015 in its licensing agreements with the Indian Seed Industry, and its legal challenge to the Competition Commission of India (CCI) when the CCI started an investigation on Monsanto's *prime facie* monopoly on Bt cotton. It used its rejected patent claims as a means to trap the Indian seed industry to collect illegal royalties which in turn are royalties collected from farmers.

Monsanto has made its false claim to patents on Bt cotton central to the investigation of its monopoly on Bt cotton by challenging the CCI Order on February 10, 2016 in reference case no. 02/2015 on the false grounds that it has a patent on Bt cotton seed. [14]

Monsanto–which is being acquired by Bayer–has been systematically distorting the science of the seed and misrepresenting India's patent law, making false IPR claims in establishing their monopoly. False claims to patents on seed are central to Monsanto's seed monopoly.

Even in the case of the CCI order of February 10, 2016 in reference to case no. 02/2015 and 107/2015 on monopoly over Bt cotton seed, Monsanto used its nonexistent patents on Bt cotton seed to challenge the order of the CCI in the High Court. The first page of the Writ Petition submitted on February 27, 2016 states that the CCI cannot investigate a *prima facie* case of monopoly because of Monsanto's "right to license the Intellectual Property Rights which vest in its favor, i.e., right in the US Patent IN214436 in respect of genetically modified hybrid cotton seeds and in the trademarks 'Bollgard' & 'BOLLGARD II' and to prevent unauthorized use thereof."

In 2019, the CCI concluded in its findings that Mahyco Monsanto Biotech Ltd (MMBL) has abused its dominant position in the market for Bt cotton technology by charging unfair licensing fees and entering into pricing agreements directly aimed at overcharging farmers who use Bt cotton seeds.

It is through a backdoor that Monsanto in the Supreme Court appeal is trying to claim that the technology is for a chemical, and the patent is for a product to introduce patents on seed and patents on life.

The collection of illegal royalties from farmers is based on the unfair, untruthful agreements Monsanto signed with Indian companies on the false claim to patents on seed.

Knowing that Monsanto could not have a patent on seeds, including genetically engineered Bt cotton seeds, Monsanto misled Indian seed companies that it had a patent and locked them into unfair licensing arrangements which led to Monsanto controlling 95 percent of the Bt cotton seed market.

Monsanto falsely claims patent rights to seed in the sublicensing agreements with Indian seed companies.

Paragraph 1.24 of the agreement signed with Rasi Seeds on February 1, 2015 clearly states: "'Monsanto Patent Rights' shall mean all patents relevant to hybrid cotton planting seed containing the Monsanto technology and any patent application or issued patent in the US or any other country or jurisdiction, as well as any extension or other government actions which extend any of the subject matter of such patent application or patent, and any substitutions, confirmations, registrations, or revalidations of any of the foregoing, in each case, that are owned or controlled by Monsanto or its affiliates."

The licensing agreements which have established Monsanto's monopoly on Bt cotton in India are based on the illegal claim that patents in the US apply in India. Patent Laws are sovereign laws, and India has its own Patent Act. US law and US Patents do not become applicable in India. That is why companies have to apply for patents in the Indian Patent Office, and the Indian Patent Office grants patents according to Indian Patent Law. Since Indian Patent Law, through article 3(j), excludes patents on seeds and plants, Monsanto cannot have a patent on Bt cotton seeds.

It is through this false claim to patents that Monsanto locked Indian farmers through the Indian seed industry into dependence on Bt cotton and collected illegal royalties from Indian farmers, trapping them in debt and in many cases these debt-trapped farmers committed suicide.

Monsanto is *not* licensing to Indian seed companies the use of tools of genetic engineering (used for introducing genes from non-related organisms into a plant). These tools are only two: a gene gun, or an agro-bacterium. What Monsanto *is* transferring to Indian companies is not the technology for creating transgenic plants, but the Bt cotton seed–which includes the genes within the seed–to multiply, hybridize, and sell under their monopoly. That is why the HC has rightly recognized that the law which should govern the contracts and licensing arrangements between Monsanto and Indian seed companies is the Plant Variety Protection and Farmers Rights Act. The mystification through the use of the term 'technology trait' and 'technology fees' is hiding the fact that the cases including the present application for a combination is about seed, and the price of seed. And the price of seed has become a life and death issue for Indian farmers.

Monsanto continues to behave as if it can write laws for establishing its monopoly on the vital sector of seed in India. This is what the Bt cotton case is about, its license agreements state that Monsanto's patent rights which will govern the contract include rights granted in the USA. Thus through writing contracts on false grounds, both in terms of its non-existent patents on Bt cotton seed in India and the false claims that Bt cotton will control pests it is subverting India's laws, including Intellectual Property Rights related to seed and plants, biosafety laws, the Essential Commodities Act, and the Competition Act.

When it introduced Bt-I, it had no patent. The trait value collected was therefore illegal. It did get a patent for Bollgard II, but not for the seed, only the transgenic transformation in the lab.

As recorded in the proceedings of the competition commission: *"Monsanto Holding Private Limited (MHPL) is a 100 percent subsidiary of Monsanto Inc. USA (MIU) in India and it is engaged in marketing of Bt cotton hybrid seeds (trade name–Paras) and other field crop seeds. MAHYCO is also an Indian company, engaged in research and development, production, processing and marketing of hybrid seeds and open pollinated seeds in India. MHPL holds 26 percent stake in MAHYCO. Monsanto Mahyco Biotech Ltd (MMBL) is a 50:50 joint venture formed between MHPL and MAHYCO, engaged in the sublicensing of the Bt cotton technology of MIU in India.*

In 1998, MIU licensed its Bt cotton technology to MMBL for further sublicensing to seed manufacturers in India, to incorporate this technology in the existing cotton seeds/hybrids produced by Indian seed manufacturing companies. As per the facts made available, first sublicensing took place in 1999 and it was subsequently renewed as per the terms of various agreements between MMBL and Indian seed companies. The resultant modified seeds were claimed to possess insect resistant traits termed as Bt cotton seeds. In India, substances and products which contain genetically engineered organisms can be produced, sold, imported or used only with the approval of the Genetic Engineering Appraisal Committee (GEAC). It is stated that BG-I was approved for commercialization by GEAC in 2002 whereas, BG-II was approved for commercialization in 2006."

In spite of not having a patent, Monsanto started to collect royalties on its illegally introduced Bt cotton. It collected an upfront, one-time non-refundable fee of 50 lakh rupees from each licensee as well as a recurring fee. Since it did not have a patent, it cooked up a category called "Technology Trait" to collect a 'trait fee', just another name for royalty. In the end, this royalty is extracted from poor farmers.

India's peasants are too small and too many to do contracts for a nonexistent IPR. Monsanto locked in Indian seed companies to collect royalties on their behalf–very much like the British arbitrarily appointed Zamindars to collect taxes and revenues from peasants in colonial times, ruining a rich and prosperous land, leaving us in poverty and destitution.

Such agreements are illegal because when Monsanto locked Indian companies into these agreements to extract royalties and trait fees, it had no approval for commercial planting. Further, it did not and cannot have patents on seed under Indian Patent Law. US Patents do not apply in India. The agreements are fraudulent and Indian farmers, Indian seed companies, and India have been cheated by extracting 'royalties' on the basis of a nonexistent right.

In 1999 Monsanto did not have commercial approval for Bt cotton. By signing agreements for licensing before approval, Monsanto was engaging in illegal action.

Secondly, Monsanto changes its technology trait value every season, showing again that the issue is seed price. As the Competition Commission of India records:

"Many Indian seed companies entered into sublicense agreements with the MMBL for procuring its Bt cotton technology in consideration of an upfront one-time non–refundable fee of 50 lakh rupees and recurring fee called 'trait value.' The 'trait value' is the estimated value for the trait of insect resistance conferred by the Bt gene technology. It forms a significant portion of the Bt cotton seed prices. It is stated that the trait value is determined by MMBL on the basis of Maximum Retail Price (MRP) of 450 g seed packet (hereinafter 'per packet'), in advance for each crop season. It is also stated that out of this trait value, some amount is disbursed as royalty to MIU and the royalty paid to Monsanto US by the MMBL is a small portion (between 15-20 percent) of the trait

> *value it collects. The HC has now said this trait value be treated as benefit sharing in the case under the PPVFR Act, since Bt cotton lies outside the scope of patentability under 3(j) of the Patent Act . . ."*

Once an upfront fee has been paid for seeds with a Bt toxin trait, the technology fee is an unfair, greedy means of increasing seed prices to increase profits in a monopoly market. The MRTP had also made this observation forcing Monsanto to concoct 'trait fees'.

The reality is that the Monsanto Company is still behaving as the "patient, physician, and diagnostician" and moreover as a criminal who is simultaneously his own lawyer and judge. It has tried to create its own laws, defining its own rules outside the law of the land. Now, Monsanto rules are coming in direct conflict with India's sovereign laws that we have put in place over the last decade, and the courts are now upholding the Government to act in accordance with its duty–to protect the public and the national interest.

No commercial interest can act outside of the law. Even commercial contracts have to be within the boundary conditions of justice and fundamental rights of people set by a country's constitution. The right to profit is not absolute. Rather, it is limited by the human rights of citizens as defined in their constitution. The issue of the price of seed as an essential commodity which farmers can afford, and which is reliable has to be settled in the context of farmers' fundamental rights with the duty of government to protect the life and livelihood of farmers. It cannot be decided arbitrarily by a company with the sole objective of maximizing its own profits at the cost of farmers' lives.

Bt cotton, a failed technology for pest control

Monsanto's lawyers claimed in the Supreme Court that they have added a chemical that makes the cotton a 'super plant' that resists pests. The primary justification for the genetic engineering of Bt into crops is that this will reduce the use of insecticides. One of the Monsanto brochures had a picture of a few worms and stated, "You will see these in your cotton and that's OK Don't spray." However, in Texas, Monsanto faced a lawsuit filed by twenty-five farmers over Bt cotton planted on 18,000 acres which suffered cotton bollworm damage and on which farmers had to use pesticides in spite of corporate propaganda that genetic engineering meant an end to the pesticide era.

The sublicensing agreements also declare in 1.17 (Rasi):

"'Insect Tolerance' or 'Insect tolerant' shall mean reduced damage from boll worms (as well as from certain other insects of Lepidoptera which may be sublicensed to fruiting parts of cotton plants which have been genetically modified by recombinant DNA technology including but not limited to Bt genes."

Thus, not only were Indian farmers harmed as consumers because Monsanto created a monopoly in Bt cotton seeds, they were also faced with crop failure and damage because the Bt did not work in controlling pests. Monsanto was well aware that GMO Bt technologies were not sustainable as pest control technologies before it introduced Bt cotton to India.[15]

The Bt cotton is not a 'super plant', but a plant that produces toxic genes in every cell of the plant and is failing to control the bollworm counter to the claim of Monsanto.[16]

Monsanto, now known as Bayer, must be held liable for the costs borne by farmers because Monsanto has collected technology fees as royalties, and because it has pushed its Bt cotton on farmers with the false claim that Bt cotton controls pests and farmers will not need to use pesticides.

According to the Central Cotton Research Institute, the average gross income from cotton cultivation was Rs 73,200 per hectare (/ha) during 2010-2015 while net income was Rs 9,259/ ha. Net income showed a negative trend during 2010-15 (fig. 1) while the gross income remained stagnant. Net income decreased from Rs 24,682 /ha during 2010-201111 to Rs 15,604 /ha during 2013-2014, and it was negative (Rs 6,318/ha) during 2014-2015.[17]

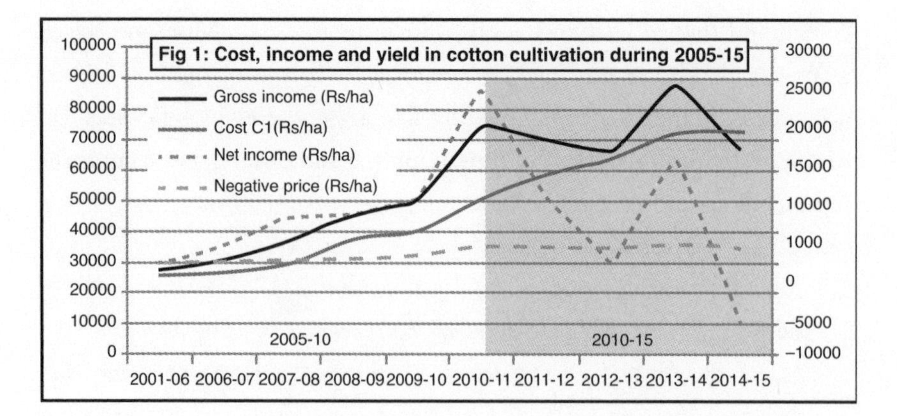

Monsanto has also made the false claim that the HC ruling was violative of TRIPS, trying to reduce India's standing in the international community.

The High Court judgment is not in violation of TRIPS. Both our Patent Act Amendment and the Plant Variety Protection and Farmers Rights Act are implementation of TRIPS, especially its Article 27.3(b) which gives parties the sovereign right to exclude plants and animals from patentability. TRIPS also gives the option to parties to protect plant varieties i.e., seeds of plants, either through patents, or a *sui generis* system. Article 3(j) of the Patents Act is an implementation of this option of exclusion and has been ruled as consistent with TRIPS by the WTO since the need for amending our patent laws arose from a TRIPS dispute initiated by the US. Once we had amended our law, and Section 3(j) was introduced to implement article 27.3(b), the dispute was settled.

The High Court ruling is therefore TRIPS consistent contrary to Monsanto's claim in its appeal. In a similar claim, the ABLE case challenged the Seed Price Control Order of the government, the HC dismissed it and the appeal in the Supreme Court will also likely be dismissed because the HC has clarified India's position on IPR issues as related to seeds and plants.

India's Laws are Sovereign Laws

India's patent laws are sovereign laws. Our laws differ from US laws in that we are a sovereign country. Being different from US laws, which are clearly Monsanto influenced laws, is not to be TRIPS inconsistent. In fact, for the protection of biodiversity, food security, farmers' rights, and real innovation, US laws need to learn from the Indian laws and the decisions on patents our courts have upheld.

This is why the Appellate Authority on Patents rejected Monsanto's Patent for Climate Resilient Plants on the basis of Article 3(d) and Article 3(j).

On July 5, Hon. Justice Prabha Sridevi, Chair of the Intellectual Property Appellate Board of India, and Hon Shri DPS Parmar, technical member, dismissed Monsanto's appeal against the rejection of their patent application to the Patent Office for "Methods of Enhancing Stress Tolerance in plants and methods thereof." The title of the patent was later amended to "a method of producing a transgenic plant, with increasing heat tolerance, salt tolerance, or drought tolerance."

The patent office refused to grant the patent for application filed in India (2407/DELNP/2006) on May 1, 2006 as it was found that "the application lacked an inventive step" in view of (i) Willimsky Gerald Journal of Bacteriology, Volume 174, No. 20, 1992,6326-6335,(ii) WO 90/0944, and US 5470971. (ii) Claims do not define any invention under section 2(1)(j.a) of the Patents Act, 1970 as the structure and function of cold shock protein was already known in cited prior art and it is obvious to a person skilled in plant [production] to make transgenic plants. (iii) It is a mere application of an already known cold shock protein in producing cold stress, heat, salt and drought condition tolerant plants, claims fall within the scope of Section 3(d) of The Patents Act, 1970. (iv) As is evident from the title, the application initially claimed (a) recombinant DNA (rDNA) molecule encoding a specific cold shock protein (CSP) (b) steps for inserting the rDNA into plant cells and (c) transgenic plants expressing CSP. Later, Monsanto restricted the scope of the application to 'a method of producing a transgenic plant with increased heat tolerance, salt tolerance, or drug tolerance'. The claims on proteins of the 'cold shock domain' responsible for the cold tolerant properties and the resultant stress resistant plants were excluded.

Since the cold tolerant properties of CSPs are recognized in the prior article, the Board concluded that the patent lacked the inventive step and was ineligible in terms of Section 3(d). The Controller held that the structure and function of cold shock protein responsible for climate resistance is 'known' and hence rejected the claim as obvious.

The Controller refused registration for lack of inventive step and that the subject matter is ineligible in terms of Sections 3(d) and 3(j). The Intellectual Property Appellate Board (IPAB) concurred with these findings, and reaffirming the Controller, stated:

> *"The claimed invention is related to production of transgenic plants by transformation with admittedly known cold shock proteins. Claims do not define any invention under section 2(1)(ja) of the Patents Act, 1970 as the structure and function of cold shock protein was already known in cited prior art and it is obvious to a person skilled in plant [production] to make transgenic plants."*

On Section 3(d), Monsanto argued that the invention does not claim any 'new' use of known substance (i.e., CSP) instead, it submitted that the invention relates to a 'method' of producing a 'new product' (i.e., stress resistant plants). Further, it adduced post-filing data which demonstrated 'superiority' of transgenic plants produced using the claimed method vis-à-vis wild plants.

The Board again rejected the arguments, reiterating that the cold tolerant properties of CSPs were already known. The Board rightly concluded that the application in essence claims 'new use' of specific proteins from 'cold shock domain' for producing desired traits and therefore ineligible under Section 3(d).

The patent office found that it is not patentable under 3(j) as claims also include essential biological processes of regeneration and selection, which includes growing of plants in specific stress conditions.

The ground of the High Court decision of dismissal on the Monsanto case, in which I intervened, is similar to the ground of the rejection of the Monsanto application for Climate Resistant Seeds by the Controller and the Board.

Again, while the Indian patent office rejected a Monsanto patent on climate resilience, in the US Supreme Court case Bowman vs. Monsanto Co., the US ruled on behalf of Monsanto. This ruling interpreted the seed to be 'self-replicating machines' invented by Monsanto, and therefore created intellectual property in future generations of a grain or seed. Again, as was treated earlier: adding a resistance gene does not amount to 'inventing' or 'creating' a seed, nor its future generations.

In addition to suing farmers like Vernon Bowman, Monsanto has sued farmers like Percy Schmeiser of Canada whose fields were contaminated with Monsanto's Roundup-Ready canola. Instead of the principle of *polluter pays*, patents allow Monsanto to work on the principle of *polluter gets paid*. This has recently happened in Australia in the case of Steve Marsh.

We should not allow pressure on India to undo Section 3(d) and Section 3(j), and instead the US should take lessons from India about how to respect the integrity of living systems and processes, and the rights of farmers and citizens.

Over the last two decades, patent laws in the US have taken a perverse direction under the influence of corporations who want to own life and establish monopolies over seed and medicine. Such monopolies are in violation of Article 21 of the Indian Constitution which guarantees all citizens the right to life. India needs to defend her sovereign laws and spread her ethical and ecological civilizational values embodied in her laws and constitution to the world. That is what is at stake in the case on 3(j).

The protection of indigenous knowledge systems as systems of innovation and the prevention of piracy needs a widening of legal regimes beyond the existing IPR regimes such as patents. In this context, it becomes clear that what are referred to as 'strong IPR regimes' from the perspective of economically powerful corporations of western countries, are actually weak regimes from the perspective of people of countries like India with a rich biodiversity heritage and an ancient intellectual heritage of indigenous knowledge systems. What we need to evolve is a strong legal framework for biodiversity production, and the protection of our intellectual heritage.

'Strong' and 'weak' are, therefore, not absolute qualifications for IPR regimes but are relative to the social and economic objectives.

Most Indians live in a biodiversity-based economy. Biodiversity and indigenous knowledge are, therefore, central to the economic security of the country, with the economic security of the people of the country being central to the national security of the country.

National security = economic security = prevention of piracy of intellectual resources

This stance has been adopted in the US in the form of the Economic Espionage Act, which will be discussed in the following section.

The difference between the US and India is that for US, economic security is the interest of US corporations while for us in India, economic security must be the economic security of the two-third poor and marginalized communities. The sharing and exchange of biodiversity and knowledge of its properties and use has been the norm in all indigenous societies and it continues to be the norm in most communities, including the modern scientific community.

Sharing and exchange gets converted to 'piracy' when individuals, organizations, or corporations who freely receive biodiversity and knowledge from indigenous communities convert the freely received gifts into private property through IPR claims. This blocks the continuity of free exchange, thus leading to an 'enclosure of the commons.'

Biopiracy refers to the process in which the rights of indigenous cultures to these resources and knowledge is erased and replaced by monopoly rights for those who have exploited indigenous knowledge and biodiversity.

The mistake of granting patents on seeds and life forms in some countries needs to be corrected to protect biodiversity globally, as well as scientific and ecological integrity. We are no longer living in a colonial era. Fair and just agreements between sovereign countries protecting the rights of sovereign communities are necessary to protect biodiversity, people's rights, and the sovereignty of countries recognized in both the TRIPS Agreement and the CBD.

In June 2018 there was an international conference[18] on TRIPS and CBD issues for charting a clear roadmap for pursuing this issue at the WTO.

This continues to be the challenge for the future.

US PATENT 214436

No.	Claims Category	# of claims made in application	# of claims objected in First Examination Report (FER)	Reply to FER	# of claims objected in Second Examination Report (SER)	Reply to SER	# of claims granted		
				# of claims deleted	# of claims added		# of claims deleted	# of claims added	
1	Nucleic Acid Sequence ("NAS") Also referred as artificial gene sequence or chemical	4 (Claim # 44 – 47)	1 (Claim # 44)	1 (Claim # 45)	Nil	Nil	NA	NA	3 (Claim Nos. 25 – 27)
2	Biotechnology Methods of creating Transgenic Plant i.e. plant with NAS	Nil	NA	NA	24 (Claim # 1 – 3 and 5 – 25)	Nil	NA	NA	24 (Claim Nos. 1 – 24)
3	Transgenic Plant i.e. plant with NAS	41 (Claim # 1 – 40 & 57)	41 (Claim # 1 – 40 & 57)	41 (Claim # 1 – 40 & 57)	Nil	NA	NA	NA	Nil
4	Parts of Transgenic Plant i.e. plant cell, plant tissue, seed etc. with NAS	10 (Claim # 48 – 56 & 58)	10 (Claim # 48 – 56 & 58)	10 (Claim # 48 – 56 & 58)	5 (Claim # 32 – 36)	5 (Claim # 32 – 36)	5 (Claim # 32 – 36)	Nil	Nil
6	Essential biological processes to produce Transgenic plants/seeds	4 (Claim # 41 – 43 & 59)	4 (Claim # 41 – 43 & 59)	1 (Claim # 59)	Nil	4 (Claim # 4, 26 – 28)	4 (Claim # 4, 26 – 28)	Nil	Nil
	Total Claims	59		-53	+30		-9		27

THREE

Agrobiodiversity, Seeds and India's Plant Variety Protection and Farmers' Rights Act

1. Farmers are the first breeders. The agrobiodiversity that is the basis of food, nutrition, and climate security has been collectively, cumulatively evolved by farming communities.
2. Farmers' rights include the rights to breed, use, sell, conserve, and freely exchange farmers' varieties.
3. Farmers' rights as buyers of seed include the right to safe and affordable seeds.
4. TRIPS states that all countries must either give patents for plants or implement an effective *sui generis* system. The UPOV model was promoted by the seed industry within industrialized countries as the most 'effective' system to be adopted by the lesser industrialized countries.
5. In the Indian reality, where most farmers are small peasants and 70% of seed suppliers, *sui generis* alternatives to UPOV were created based on farmers' rights taking into account farmers as breeders, conservators, and users of seeds.
6. Farmers' rights are legal rights that require formal recognition as a subcategory of biodiversity related regime. Agrobiodiversity is a subcategory of biodiversity. These legal rights have been recognized in the *sui generis* option of TRIPS.
7. Farmers rights include their rights to be recognized as breeders, and for access to their varieties to be governed by the access and benefit sharing clauses of the Biodiversity Act.

The Relationship between CIRs and IPRs Explained

The Protection of Agricultural Biodiversity and Farmers' Rights

Graine. *Seme.*
Samen. *Seed.*
Saad. *Bija.*
Semilla.

Just like the diversity of life we see all around us, we are surrounded by the diversity of the seed, reflected through the different names each culture has given to this sacred source of life. *Bija* is life, and life is *bija*. Seeds, like every other form of life are all evolving, self-organized, sovereign beings. They have intrinsic worth, value, and standing. This awareness is the reason that Indian civilization has evolved the deepest knowledge of Ayurveda and the richest biodiversity in agriculture. Its philosophy of *Vasudhaiva Kutumbhakam* (the Earth family) has always perceived the seed as the ultimate commons which we have nurtured and preserved since millennia.

However, over the past few decades, in spite of national laws prohibiting patents on seed, the seed commons are under attack. Illegal claims to patents on life are hijacking biodiversity and indigenous knowledge. They are unleashing a new epidemic of biopiracy and an enclosure of the biological and intellectual commons. But seeds are not an invention. Seeds are life forms. Seeds are our kin members. Seeds are our earth family.

Reminiscent of the imperialistic narrative of Columbus "discovering" the American Continent and claiming it as *terra nullius,* which implied a brutal erasure of the indigenous people who had been living there before him, the patenting of life forms and seeds also creates an erasure. An erasure of the farmers' breeding, their knowledge, and the biodiversity they have gifted us.

It is an erasure and enclosure of the source of the seed; the culture of the seed, and the commons of the seed.

The ecological vulnerability of agricultural monocultures has made the conservation of agricultural biodiversity an environmental imperative. The Convention on Biodiversity Conservation (CBD) has been one of the responses of the world community to conserve the ecological basis of biological production through biodiversity conservation.

There are two political conditions that the CBD gave rise to. Firstly, it recognized the national sovereign right of countries to their biological wealth. Secondly, it recognized the contribution of indigenous communities to knowledge about the utilization of biodiversity. The recognition of sovereignty and indigenous knowledge create a major shift in the political context of the ownership, use and control of generic resources, especially in the area of agricultural biodiversity, including seeds and plant genetic resources. The seeds of the Third World could no longer be treated as the "common heritage of mankind," freely accessible to all, including northern seed corporations. The seeds sold by transnational seed corporations could no longer be regarded as the only ones embodying an intellectual contribution. Farmers' seed got recognized as embodying significant intellectual contribution by Third World farmers.

A third major shift was the recognition that "improvement" of seed is not absolute and context independent. Improvement is a contextual category. "Improvement" of crops from the viewpoint of agribusiness is often a regression and loss from the point of view of farmers. Thus agribusiness "improves" crops for industrial processing, or for increased use of chemical inputs, whereas farmers need crops that are easy to process at home and crops that decrease the dependence on external inputs.

Conventional breeding only looks at yield potential which is defined as "the yield of a crop when growth is not limited by water or nutrients, pests, diseases, or weeds." In the realities of farmers' fields these are precisely the limitations that farmers face, and their breeding is responsive to the environmental stress and ecological diversity within which they must practice agriculture.

Thirty years of Navdanya's work in biodiversity conservation in agriculture has shown that diversity, nutrition, and resilience are the breeding objectives for farmers' communities.[1] We have also shown that in the context of hunger, malnutrition, and poverty "yield" of a partial commodity that goes for biofuel and animal feed is not scientifically adequate as it does not take into account the nutrition nor the costs. We have evolved the metrics of "Health per Acre" to reflect nutrition, and "Wealth per Acre" to reflect true costs and benefits.[2] "Improvement" needs to be guided by ecological benefits, health benefits to society, and economic benefits in terms of higher net incomes to farmers.

Corporate breeding strategies therefore cannot be treated as the only direction of evolution in breeding and research, and "improvement" from the perspective of TNC interests cannot be translated into an overall societal benefit. The TNC's monopoly on seed through IPRs is therefore neither desirable nor necessary from the public interest perspective.

Farmers have been the original breeders and seed supply has been based on farmers' contribution to conservation, breeding, and utilization of diverse species and crop varieties. In India, 80% of the seed supply was from farmers' seed supply until the 1990s. In most industrialized countries, most farmers depend on the seed industry for their seed; however, there was a time when they were able to save and exchange seeds amongst each other, under what was called the "farmers' privilege." Changes in plant legislation in Europe and the US have, however, allowed the seed industry to take away the last remnants of farmers' freedom and enslave them to the seed industry. Farmers have been pushed to a situation of total lack of freedom to exercise their role as breeders or as members of the community of producers, freely saving and exchanging plant material.

Today farmers are under siege, with their lives and rights being under real threat. In the 1990s, Intellectual Property Rights (IPRs) legislation was introduced in the area of Plant Genetic Resources (PGR) under pressure from the United States government. While the WTO gave a five-year transition period to introduce PGR legislation, the US demanded monopoly protection for Transnational

Corporations (TNCs) which controlled the seed industry. On the other hand, people's organizations started fighting to protect farmers' rights to their biodiversity on their right to survival as well as the freedom of scientists to work for the removal of hunger rather than corporate profits.

Farmers' organizations, biodiversity conservation groups, sustainable agriculture networks, and public interest-oriented scientists were trying to ensure that farmers' rights were protected, and through the protection of farmers' rights, sovereign control over biological wealth and its sustainable use in agricultural production would be ensured. The conflict over PGR legislation was a conflict between farmers and the seed industry; between the public domain and private profits; between an agriculture that produces and reproduces diversity; and one that consumes diversity and produces uniformity, monocultures, and monopolies.

The Monopoly Control Over Seeds

> *"We are facing problems because people are concentrating only on their short-term selfish interests, not thinking of the entire human family. They are not thinking of the earth and the long-term effects on the universal life as a whole."*
>
> – The Dalai Lama XIV, A New Approach to Global problems

On January 29, 1996 at an address at the Indian Institute of Agricultural Research, the United States Secretary of Agriculture, Mr. Daniel Glickman, directly addressed the issue of the protection of seed multinationals (MNCs). He said, *"I hope your new legislation will provide a responsible and reasonable protection to private seed companies, which will encourage them to provide the best seeds available for your farmers. There would be very few inventions of anything particularly in agriculture, without patent protection because it is the fundamental fact of new ideas just for the altruistic benefit of the human race."*

The US IPR orthodoxy was based, and continues to be based, on the fallacious idea that people do not innovate or generate knowledge unless they can derive private profit. However, greed is not a "fundamental fact of human nature" but a dominant tendency in societies that reward it. In the area of seeds and plant genetic resources, innovation of both the 'formal' and 'informal' systems have so far been guided by the larger human good. Norman Borlaug, the scientist behind the Green Revolution and the recipient of the Nobel Peace Prize, made this clear in his statement at a Press Conference at the Indian Agricultural Research Institute, New Delhi on February 8, 1996. He expressed concern against private companies and TNCs gaining control of plant genetic resources and seeds, subsequently patenting plants. Professor Borlaug stated:

"We battled against patenting. I and late Glen Anderson (of International Wheat and Maize Research Institutes) went on record in India as well as other fora against patenting and always stood for free exchange of germplasm."

He saw IPRs in PGRs as a prescription for famine, commenting on the US demand for patents he reflected:

"God help us if that were to happen, we would all starve."

The concern about plant patents is therefore a deep and widespread concern.

Besides using a fallacious essentialist argument about human nature, Mr. Glickman also stressed the inevitability of farmers' dependence on MNCs for seeds due to trade liberalization and its impact on agriculture. According to him:

"As income increases throughout Indian society, food needs will change– higher vegetable oil consumption, a shift from rice to wheat in urban areas and some shifting from grain to poultry and livestock products. Also, the needs of the new food processing industries will change the types of crops demanded. Therefore, farmers must have access to new crop varieties in order to meet changing consumer preferences."

In other words, what the US government wanted to coerce the Indian government to do was introduce unhealthy fat and meat rich diets through the expansion of US agribusiness, agro-processing, and fast food industry. The proposal was to replace the small peasant and farmer based agricultural economy of India with agribusiness controlled industrial agriculture. This shift was associated with a transformation of farmers as breeders and reproducers of their own seed supply to farmers as consumers of propriety seed from the seed industry for globalized, industrialized agriculture. It was also a shift from a food economy based on millions of farmers as autonomous producers to a food system controlled by a handful of TNCs which control both inputs and outputs. This was a recipe for food insecurity, biodiversity erosion, and the uprooting of farmers from the land. We have seen the emergence of farmers' suicides, of the increase in malnutrition and hunger, and the epidemic of chronic diseases related to the shift to unhealthy industrial diets.

The Constitution of India under *Article 47* guarantees that:
"The State shall regard the raising of the level of nutrition and the standard of living of its people and improvement of public health as among its primary duties."

This duty of the State is in fact a reflection of the fundamental right of citizens to have access to health and nutrition.

It is often stated that IPRs will not stop traditional farmers using native seeds. However, when it is recognized that IPRs are an essential part of a package of agribusiness controlled agriculture in which farmers no longer grow native seeds, but instead seeds supplied by the TNC seed industry, IPRs become a means of monopoly that wipe out farmers' rights to save and exchange seed. This leads to TNC totalitarianism in agriculture. TNCs will decide what is grown by farmers, what they are able to use as inputs, and when they sell their produce, to whom and at what price, with what content and how much information is made available to them about the nature of food commodities. We have watched this scenario emerge in the case of the cotton seed supply.

IPRs are a significant instrument for the establishment of this TNC totalitarianism. The protection of the rights of citizens as producers and consumers need the forging of new concepts and categories, new instruments and mechanisms to counter and limit the monopoly power of TNCs in agriculture.

This is where community rights come in as an important balancing concept for protecting the public interest in the context of IPR protection from corporations. In the field of food and agriculture, farmers' rights are the countervailing force to breeders' rights and patents on seed and plant material. Farmers' rights in the context of monopoly control of the food system become relevant not just for farming communities, but also for consumers.

These rights are necessary not just for the survival of the people but also for the survival of the country. Without sovereign rights of farming communities to their seed and plant genetic resources, there can be no sovereignty of the country.

Patents on plants raise serious concerns about monopolies over food and agriculture systems. In March 1994, the European Patent Office granted an extraordinarily broad patent to Agracetus Corporation, a subsidiary of W.B. Grace. The patent covered all transgenic soya bean varieties and seeds, regardless of the genes used and all methods of transformation. Dr. Geoffrey Hawtin, Director General of the International Plant Genetic Resources Institute in Rome, Italy expressed his concern at such patenting:

> *"The granting of patents covering all genetically engineered varieties of a species, irrespective of the genes concerned or how they were transferred, puts in the hands of a single inventor the possibility to control what we grow on our farms and in our gardens. At a stroke of the pen, the research of countless farmers and scientists has potentially been negated in a single, legal act of economic hijack."*

Unlike Plant Breeders' Rights (PBRs) the utility patents were very broad-based, allowing monopoly rights over individual genes and even over characteristics. PBRs did not entail ownership of the germplasm in the seeds, they only granted a monopoly right over the selling and marketing of a specific variety. Patents, on the other hand, allowed for multiple claims that may cover not only whole plants, but plant parts and processes as well.

According to attorney Anthony Diepenbrock:

"You could file for the protection of a few varieties of crops, their macro-parts (flowers, fruits, seeds and so on), their micro-parts (cells, gene, plasmids and the like), and whatever novel processes you develop to work these parts, all using one multiple claim."

Patent protection implied the exclusion of farmers' right over resources having these genes and characteristics. And it undermined, and continues to undermine, the very foundations of agriculture. For example, a patent was granted in the US to a biotechnology company, Sungene, for a sunflower variety with very high oleic acid content. The claim allowed was for the characteristic (i.e., high oleic acid) and not just for the genes producing the characteristic. Sungene had notified others involved in sunflower breeding that the development of any variety high in oleic acid would be considered an infringement of its patent.

The landmark event for the patenting of plants was the 1985 judgment in the US; now famous as *ex parte 'Hibberd,'* in which 'molecular genetics' scientist Kenneth Hibberd and his co-inventors were granted patents on the tissue culture, seed, and whole plant of a corn line selected from tissue culture. The Hibberd application included over 260 separate claims, which gave the molecular genetics scientists the right to exclude others from use of all 260 aspects. While *Hibberd* apparently provided a new legal context for corporate competition, the most profound impact was felt in the competition between farmers and the seed industry.

As Kloppenburg has indicated, with *Hibberd*, a juridical framework came in place that allowed the seed industry to realize one of its longest held and most cherished goals, that of forcing all farmers of any crop to buy seed every year instead of obtaining it through reproduction. Industrial patents allowed the right to use the product, not to make it. Since seed makes itself, a strong utility patent for seed implied that a farmer purchasing patented seed would have the right to use (to grow) the seed, but not to make seed (to save and replant).

Since the last few decades, the US has been pushing for patent regimes in the area of agriculture. However, our current Patent Act holds its ground and does not allow patenting in the field of agriculture. It excludes patents on seeds and plants (Chapter 2).

The 1970 Act excludes all methods of agriculture and horticulture from patentability. In addition, the exclusion of product patents in the area of agro-chemicals was also ensured through Section 5(a). The Patent (Amendment) Act 2005 does not allow the patenting of seeds, plants, or animals.

The TRIPS Agreement in its original corporate form militated against people's human right to food and health by conferring unrestricted monopoly rights to corporations in the vital sectors of health and agriculture.

Looking back in history, another decision on plant patent infringement suits set a precedent for interpreting plant patent coverage.

Dennis and Becky Winterboer were farmers owning a 500-acre farm in Iowa. Since 1987, the Winterboers had derived a sizable portion of their income from "brown-bagging" sales of their crops to other farmers to use as seed. A "brown bag" sale occurs when a farmer plants seeds in his own field, and then sells the harvest as seed to other farmers. Asgrow (which had plant variety protection for its soybean seeds–A1957 and A2234) started a court case against the Winterboers on grounds that its property rights were being violated. The Winterboers argued that they had acted within the law since according to the Plant Variety Act, farmers had the right to sell seeds, provided that both the buyer and the seller were farmers.

The federal circuit board interpreted "marketing" as requiring "extensive or coordinated selling activities such as advertising using an intervening sales representative or similar merchandising or retail activities." On appeal, the Supreme Court disagreed and interpreted "marketing" as holding forth property for sale, and hence ruled against the Winterboers.[3]

This was the case of Imagio Nursery vs. Daina Greenhouse, where Judge Spence Williams, for the US District Court for the Northern District of California, ruled that a plant patent could be infringed by a plant that merely had similar characteristics to the patented plant. When combined with the reversal of burden of proof clauses, this kind of precedence was disastrous for countries from where the biodiversity that gave rise to those properties was first taken. It was even more disastrous where the original donors of the biodiversity were accused of 'piracy' through such legal precedence in the absence of the prior existence of biodiversity laws that prevented the misuse of such legal precedence.

In 1994 in the US, the Plant Variety Act was amended and the farmers' privilege to save and exchange seed was amended through statutes 3136 and 3142, establishing absolute monopoly of the seed industry by making farmer-to-farmer exchange and sales illegal.

Asgrow is now owned by Monsanto which, in turn, is owned by Bayer. While farmers rights are eroded, corporate concentration and control over seeds continues to grow.

Not only is the seed/chemical/biotechnology industry gaining total control over seed supply, it is also becoming increasingly concentrated. As Robert Farley of Monsanto has stated:

> *"What you are seeing is not just a consolidation of seed companies, it's really a consolidation of the entire food chain."*

The absolute rights of the seed industry and the absolute lack of rights for farmers have been further established in Monsanto's "Roundup Ready Gene Agreement" for "Roundup Ready Soybeans." The agreement is meant to enforce US patents 4,535,060, 4,040,835, and 532,505, preventing the grower from selling or supplying the seed or material derived from it, to any other person or entity. It also prevents saving any of the seed.

The agreement requires a payment of five dollars per pound of 'technology fee' over and above the price of seed and royalties. If any clause is violated, the grower has to pay one hundred times the damages and this is not deemed to limit the amount of damages. Monsanto has a right to visit the fields of the farmer at any time even without the farmers' presence or permission for three years after the agreement. Thus, the right to property of the farmer is not respected. This clause has made farmers extremely outraged.

The agreement is binding even to family heirs and personal representatives of successors of growers, but growers' rights cannot be transferred without Monsanto's permission. Thus, Monsanto's rights exist over others related to the farmer, but the farmer is denied his/her rights to transfer the agreement.

In addition, the agreement has no liability clause. It has no reference on the performance of Roundup Ready soya beans, and Monsanto has no responsibility in case the crops fail to perform as promised nor if there is ecological damage caused by Roundup. This is especially relevant given the failure of Monsanto's genetically engineered cotton called 'Bollgard' in the 1996 season in the US and its failure in India to protect the cotton crop from bollworm, despite promotional material that had stated that bollworms could cause no damage to Bollgard.

The Roundup Ready Gene Agreement is thus: the latest step in the seed industry claiming far reaching monopoly rights over seeds and farmers, bearing no ecological or social responsibility associated with the introduction of the herbicide resistant or pest resistant genes into crops. This one-sided system–in which seed/chemical companies have all the rights and bear no social or environmental responsibility, and farmers and citizens have no rights but bear all the risks and costs–can neither protect biodiversity nor provide food security.

Even though Monsanto does not have a patent on seed because of Section 3(j) of the Patent Act it continues desperately to claim a patent while constantly changing its claim as to what it has "invented."

Beginning with the seed, shifting to microorganism, it has now shifted to a chemical.

Science is not based on such shifting sands. Nor is law.

In countries where plant patents are not allowed, patenting genes was available as an opening for patenting properties and characteristics of the plant which created a door to having exclusive rights to those properties and characteristics.

Further, patents for plant-based products, such as patents for *azadirachtin* derivative insecticides from the neem, taken out by transnational corporations like W.R. Grace would have also had a major impact on the access to raw material and market for neem products if we had not challenged and won the case against the biopiracy of neem.

Besides patents, corporations use seed legislation to prohibit distribution of farmers' varieties.

Furthermore, seed legislations push out farmers' varieties and make farmers' breeding an illegal activity. The case of farmer Joseph Albrecht in Germany and potato seed farmers in Scotland were examples of how seed acts prevented farmers from engaging in their own seed production.

Joseph Albrecht was an organic farmer in the village of Oberding, Bavaria. Not satisfied with commercially available seed, he developed his own ecological varieties of wheat. Ten other organic farmers from neighboring villages took his wheat seeds. Albrecht was fined by the government of upper Bavaria because he traded in "uncertified" seed. He challenged the fine and the seed act because he felt restricted in freely exercising his occupation as an organic farmer by this law.

During the Leipzig conference on plant genetic resources, I joined Joseph Albrecht to initiate a non-cooperation movement (Seed Satyagraha) against seed legislation that denied the farmers the right to freely breed and exchange their seeds. The movement started in the same church from which the democracy movement against the erstwhile communist state of GDR was organized in Leipzig.[4]

In Scotland, there were a large number of farmers who grew and sold seed potatoes to other farmers. They could, until the early 1990s, freely sell the reproductive material on to other seed potato growers, to merchants, or to farmers. In the 1990s, holders of plant breeders' rights started to issue notices to potato growers through the British society of plant breeders and made selling of seed potatoes by farmers to other farmers illegal. Seed potato growers had to grow varieties under contract to the seed industry which specified the price at which the contracting company would take back the crop, and barred growers from selling the crop to anyone. The companies started to reduce the acreage and reduce the prices. In 1994, seed potato bought from Scottish farmers for 140 pounds sterling, was sold for more than double that price to English farmers. When the two sets of farmers were prevented from dealing directly with each other, the seed potato growers signed a petition complaining about the stranglehold of a few companies acting as a "cartel."

They also started to sell non-certified seed directly to English farmers. The seed industry claimed they were losing 4-million-pound sterling in seed sales through the direct sale of uncertified seed potato between farmers.[5]

In February 1995, the British Society for Plant Breeders decided to proceed with the high-profile court case against the farmer from Aberdeenshire. The farmer was forced to pay £30,000 pounds sterling compensation to cover royalties lost to the seed industry by direct farmer-to-farmer exchange.

UK and European Union laws, thus, prevented farmers from exchanging uncertified seed as well as protected varieties. In the US also, farmer-to-farmer exchange was made illegal, as reflected in the case filed by the Asgrow Seed Company–now owned by Monsanto–against the Winterboers.

In practical terms, allowing patenting or other seed monopolies in the field of agriculture has the following adverse consequences:

- It encourages monopoly control of plant material by Western transnational corporations as has already happened in the case of Bt cotton through Monsanto's false claim that it had a patent.

The CCI has already found *prima facie* evidence in the case on Monsanto's Bt cotton monopoly. In reference case number 02/2015 and case number 107/2015, The CCI has already passed an interim order on 10/02/2016–that Monsanto's control of Bt cotton is *prima facie* a monopoly.

- This in turn makes farmers dependent on corporations for the most critical input in agriculture, i.e., seed. This monopoly control is more far-reaching given the takeover of seed companies by the large chemical and agribusiness corporations which control other inputs into agriculture such as fertilizers, pesticides, and herbicides.
- Monopoly control on seed, linked with corporate control over agriculture, leads to large scale disappearance of farmers' varieties, thus threatening biodiversity conservation as well as farmers' survival. Biodiversity erosion in turn leads to the erosion of the rich cultural diversity of a country.
- Due to royalty payments the prices of seeds go up. This is why the Government of India had to introduce the Seed Price Control Order 2015.
- The changed economics, resulting from corporate IPRs, leads to the displacement of small farmers, who get into debt and destitution and are driven to suicide.
- Large-scale uprooting of agricultural society without equivalent absorption in new industrial opportunities leads to social disintegration, spurts in crime, and the breakdown of law and order.
- Intellectual Property protection in the area of agriculture and plant variety undermines food security since the protected and patented varieties are not linked to food needs, but to the processing and marketing requirements of agribusiness.
- The shift to the control of agriculture through the control of seed also contributes to secondary impacts of other natural resources like land and water into the control of TNCs.
- IPRs in the area of seeds and plants could increase the national debt ten-fold.

- The undermining of food security will increase food imports, and hence the foreign exchange burdens, thus inviting deeper conditionality from institutions like the IMF and World Bank.
- The erosion of food security will create food dependency, turning food into a weapon in the hands of industrialized countries, thus leading to total slavery and recolonization.

Farmers' Rights therefore need to be safeguarded as positive rights in all laws related to biodiversity and IPRs not just Plant Variety Legislation as has already been done in India.

TRIPS and a *sui generis* regime for plants

TRIPS states that all countries must either give patents for plants or have effective *sui generis* system.[6] While it had not been explicitly stated, the seed industry wanted to see UPOV and the framework of breeders' rights implemented in every country. In India, we ensured that the *sui generis* system is a legal system centered on farmers' rights and on the conservation of biodiversity, in accordance with the principles of the convention on biological diversity.

Accordingly, to TRIPS, countries may provide a *sui generis* regime for IPRs in plant genetic resources. The TRIPS Agreement does not oblige countries to adopt the UPOV Convention, the Convention on Breeders' Rights. However, it has often been interpreted that the term 'effective *sui generis*' would be taken to implement only UPOV. We were successful in establishing that 'effective' is not determined solely in the context of corporate profits and market monopolies, but in the context of 'effective' for biodiversity conservation objectives of the CBD and the Biodiversity Act, and effective for farmers' rights.

The word 'effective' was inserted by the US in the Biodiversity Convention and in the TRIPS Agreements. The first sentence of the draft referred to the need to "promote" effective and adequate protection of intellectual property rights. The same phrase was in Section

301 of the Trade and Competitiveness Act of 1988, which has been used to retaliate against countries whose IPR laws do not conform to US standards. The term was defined by the office of the US Trade Representative.

The use of the term 'effective' in all negotiations related to IPRs and biodiversity is a result of US attempts to globalize its IPR regimes, which allow patenting of all life, including plants and animals. In the WTO text, the phrase 'effective *sui generis* system' was also introduced with the same intention.

However, countries can create alternatives to the UPOV Convention under a *sui generis* regime, especially in the context of the Convention on Biological Diversity which creates obligations for states to protect biodiversity and indigenous knowledge and practices. The term effective can be defined vis-à-vis CBD. This would enable countries to base their *sui generis* legislation on the protection of community rights and farmers' rights and the conservation of agricultural biodiversity as required by CBD.

For both these objectives UPOV is an inadequate instrument.

The UPOV Convention, Breeders' Rights and Farmers' Rights

The existing international agreement that covers Plant Breeders' Rights is the International Convention for the Protection of New Varieties of Plants–the UPOV Convention. The UPOV Convention was initially adopted by five European countries and membership was restricted to European countries until 1968. At the time the Convention was revised, and membership opened to all countries.

UPOV currently has seventy-five member states including several European countries, Japan, and the US amongst others. However, it has evolved as plant variety legislation suitable only to the socio-economic context of industrialized countries where farmers are no longer a large part of the population and do not have any control over plant breeding or seed supply. This situation is very different from contexts like

India's where the majority of the population continues to be engaged in farming and farmers' seed production and supply system is still the main source of seed.

The UPOV Convention is rigid, requiring that members adopt its standards and scope of protection as national law. The UPOV Convention has resulted in a high degree of standardization and goes against the reality of biological diversity and the socio-economic diversity of different countries. It is therefore inappropriate as a *sui generis* system evolved to protect plants, people and creativity in diverse realities.

This standardization is built into the way plant varieties are defined. To be eligible for protection, a variety must be:

- *New* - the variety must not have been exploited commercially
- *Distinct* - it must be clearly distinguishable from all other varieties known at the date of application for protection
- *Uniform* - all plants of the variety must be sufficiently uniform to allow it to be distinguished from other varieties taking into account the method of reproduction of the species
- *Stable* - it must be possible for the variety to be reproduced unchanged

The definition by its very nature rules out farmers' varieties, destroying biodiversity and producing uniformity as necessity. Such Plant Breeders' Rights (PBR) systems do not reward breeding to maintain and enhance diversity and substantiality, but instead reward the destruction of biodiversity and the creation of uniformity, hence creating ecologically vulnerable agricultural systems.

Therefore, the PBR legislation like UPOV is inherently incapable of protecting farmers' rights as arising from the role of the farmers as breeders who innovate and produce diverse farmers' varieties which form the basis for all other breeding systems.

While UPOV 1961 and 1972 failed to recognize and therefore protect farmers' rights as positive rights, UPOV 1978 did have a farmers' exemption which gave farmers the right to save seeds of protected varieties. Similarly, the breeders' exemption allowed researchers and breeders free access to a protected variety to use for breeding other varieties.

However, UPOV 1991 removed these exemptions, and now, breeders and researchers have to pay royalties to the PBR holder to use the protected variety of breeding other varieties. The farmers' exemption was also made optional. Article 15 of UPOV 1991 stated:

> *"Each contracting party may within reasonable limits and subject to the safeguarding of the legitimate interests of the breeder restrict the breeders right in relation to any variety in order to permit farmers to use for propagating purposes on their own holdings the product of the harvest which they have obtained by planting, on their holdings, the protected variety."*

Ultimately, it is the breeders who decide their legitimate interests and enforce this upon the state. Since the breeders are multinational seed companies in this case, more powerful than most Third World governments, 'reasonable limits' started being set by these corporations and not by individual governments. Breeders' authorization became the final determinant in respect to sale and marketing of harvested material. UPOV 1991 was therefore as monopolistic as patent regimes.

While most Third World governments were not considering the adoption of UPOV 1991, they had an option of joining UPOV 1978 until December 1995.

To avoid the more restricted 1991 Convention, most governments rushed to become members of the 1978 Convention, in order to base their *sui generis* system on it. India has successfully held its ground and has hitherto not joined UPOV. It has also shown that the *sui generis* systems can be evolved independent of UPOV, which for Third World countries is the best option.

UPOV 1991 threatened to infringe on farmers' rights by the removal of the clause pertaining to farmers as privileges and enforcing seed savers and exchangers to pay royalties.

Plant breeders have pushed for changes in plant breeders' rights in the US and in Europe. These changes, as discussed earlier, involve the successful attempts by the seed industry to reduce and restrict the acreage under farm saved seed (FSS), as well as ban the use of FSS in the case of crops which have commercial value, such as potatoes in Europe. Commercial seed processors, who process FSS in cottage industry operations, have been threatened with closure if they do not cooperate with the seed industry in disclosing which farmer is using how much FSS and of which variety.

In the US, the seed industry pressured the house of representatives and the senate to pass laws banning over-the-fence seed sales (earlier referred to as brown-bagging) between farmers under the charge that such sales erode the commercial market of the seed industry.

Protection of plant varieties in Europe extended the meaning of 'selling' to include 'delivery of seed by one person to another under a contract whereby the other will grow further reproductive material of other crops, regardless of who owns the resulting crop.' In the US and Europe, laws were passed in 1995 making the informal exchange of seed between farmers illegal.

In addition, farmers in Europe used to give their seeds to small seed cleaning and processing firms. In relation to farm saved seed of protected varieties of potatoes, contracts between an owner of seed, certified or farm saved, and a grower were apparently entered into whereby the seed was planted to produce 'small ware' for replanting by the original owner. This reproductive material was first made over in pursuance of a contract under which the grower would use the reproductive material for growing further reproductive material. A 'sale' would take place and the resulting infringement of plant breeders' rights would make the owner liable to legal proceedings.

The subsequent return of the resultant crop from the grower to the original owner would then be termed a 'transaction effected in the course of business under which the property in the reproductive material passes from one person to another' and so is also a sale. This would, in turn, be called an infringement on plant breeders' rights.

Accordingly, it was not possible for a grower to contract to take the seed of a protected variety of potato or any other species belonging to a third party and produce 'farm saved seed' for the third party. Delivery of the original seed and the subsequent return of the resulting crop were both infringements of plant breeders' rights.

When party A gets access to a resource owned and controlled by party B, party A shares benefits with B. In case of seeds, these issues are complicated because of a number of factors:

Parties A and B are a combination of farmers, governments and seed industry. They are not merely governments. National sovereignty over biodiversity necessitates a partnership between farming communities and governments. IPR regimes are based on governments acting on behalf of industry to enforce rights.

The TRIPS Agreement of WTO and Indian Legislation: The Plant Variety Protection and Farmers Rights Act

The Trade Related Intellectual Property Rights Agreement of the WTO provides a framework for the implementation of IPR laws. The section of TRIPS that most directly affects farmers' rights and agricultural biodiversity is Article 27.5.3(b). The article allows two forms of IPRs in plants: patents and a *sui generis* system.

(a) Plant Patents

The first part of this article requires that parties allow patenting of plants and animals produced through "non-biological and microbiological processes." This is a reference to the biotechnologies of genetic engineering. However, while the moving of species across species barriers through genetic engineering techniques can be defined as 'non-biological' in the sense that such mixing of genetic material would not happen in nature, the moment the genes become part of the production of plants and animals with genes introduced from other species there is an essentially biological process of reproduction taking place. This was the subject matter of the Monsanto claim to patents to Bt which was dismissed by the High Court of Delhi.

There are two other grounds in TRIPS which allow countries to exclude the patenting of plants and animals. These are in Article 27.2 referring to public morality and Articles 7 and 8 referring to public interest.

The decision in European Parliament against the Patent Directive, and the debates in Indian Parliament on the Patent (Amendment) Act were strongly guided by the ethical concerns arising from patenting of life. These debates have shaped the Amendments which include Section 3(j).

In 1993, a draft legislation entitled the Plant Varieties Act was prepared by the Government of India. However, the draft legislation could not be passed because of severe criticisms from people's organizations, especially those representing farmers and those involved in biodiversity conservation programs. The most significant inadequacy was the failure to articulate farmers' rights as ownership rights. The draft legislation restrained the definition of farmers' rights as a fund to be operated by the government.

The Research Foundation for Science Technology and Natural Resource Policy (RFSTNRP) and the M.S. Swaminathan Foundation were two organizations invited to give comments on the draft legislation. The Research Foundation took representatives of farmers' organizations for its consultations with the Agricultural Ministry since none of the farmers are consulted for drafting the legislation itself. The amendments proposed by the RFTNRP are contained in the Foundation's publication, "*Plants, Patents, and People.*"

The two main proposals made were that farmers' intellectual contribution be recognized as a basis of farmers' rights (since farmers' innovations are collective innovations) and seed is a shared resource. Farmers' rights should be community rights in the field of agricultural biodiversity. Farmers' rights set the boundary conditions for the free space for farmers to continue practicing agriculture with full freedom with respect to plant genetic resources. They also set the boundary condition for the operation of intellectual property rights monopolies of the seed industry.

The main proposal of the M.S. Swaminathan Foundation was the setting up of the National Community Gene Fund as a mechanism for compensating farmers. 'Farmers' Rights' in this proposal were not a juridical concept but merely a financial mechanism. However, rights cannot be reduced to mere funding mechanisms.

As a result of critiques of the draft legislation of 1993 from farmers, conservation groups, as well as the seed industry, the legislation was withdrawn, and new legislation was drafted.

The M.S. Swaminathan Foundation had organized a Technical Consultation on an Implementation Framework for Farmers' Rights in Madras in January 1996 to provide an input to the drafting of a new legislation. One of the issues addressed at the Technical Consultation was the definition of a farmer. Unfortunately, the definition adopted at the Consultation treated agribusiness and corporations as 'farmers' also, thus undermining all the unique rights of small traditional farmers who have provided and conserved agricultural biodiversity. A second discussion at the Technical Consultation was whether there should be separate legislation for plant variety protection and farmers' rights or if there should be a common legislation. It was then decided that there should be a single legislation with the title 'Plant Variety Protection and Farmers' Rights Act.'

The Research Foundation organized a seminar in New Delhi on February 20, 1996 on "IPRs, Community Rights and Biodiversity" to further develop the idea of farmers' rights as community rights having a juridical equivalence to IPRs. Justice Krishna Iyer, who closed the Seminar, laid the agenda for future action:

> *"The intellectual community of this country has been showing an amount of apathy, inactivity or conviction that they cannot change the 'irreversible' course of events which would end up in the recolonization of this country. The most important point here is community rights. All of us have been progressing on the Anglo-Saxon jurisprudential assumption that only individuals had any rights, and that communities*

do not matter. But in this ancient country a culture has evolved a certain way of cohesive living. They have always remembered that apart from individuals, communities have rights. These rights have been enjoyed from time immemorial, invisible in text, but real in terms of wealth. We have to revise our notions about community wealth, community rights and community property. The village communities in India have rights, they have legal persona, they can go to court, and they can fight for defense of what they have as a community. Collectivity itself is the persona. It is time that we introduce this into the jurisprudence that is being taught. Indian legal thought tells you there are community rights. And communities are fluctuating bodies, but they have a certain identity."

This right is embellished in the hierarchy of democratic institutions where the Gram Sabha is above all, even the Parliament. It is a natural right. Such a community right has already been recognized by the highest court of Australia which has held that the occupation and colonization of Australia by England, did not take away the rights of the aboriginals as no compensation was given. "The White Man in Australia had assumed everything was his. The White Man in America assumes the whole globe is his. The White Indian is willing to surrender. The pity of it, Oh God! The pity of it. You White Indian you are prostrating before the White American."

Justice Iyer emphasized that community rights are a reality of Indian law. He stressed that there was a need to return to ancient Indian legal literature which recognizes the reality of those rights. "It was never as relevant as today when we are being expropriated of all rights." The imposition, particularly, of IPR regimes is an arbitrary and unreasonable procedure by which people's rights are being forcibly taken away.

Community rights are sacrosanct because the Preamble of the Indian Constitution speaks of 'We, the People of India' individually and collectively. Article 38 of the Indian Constitution speaks of the social order and not of individual rights and imposes on the state "the burden of duty to guarantee the preservation of a social order that is just."

Furthermore, Article 51-A(g) of the Constitution states: "It shall be the duty of every citizen of India to value, cherish and preserve the rich heritage of our composite culture." India has an agricultural culture, a medical culture, an herbal culture, a curative culture, a pharmaceutical culture, a therapeutic culture, a psychic culture, a national culture. "It is impossible therefore to conceive of Indians abdicating the fundamental duty of not fighting to preserve their culture, their herbal culture, and allowing it to be patented away by trivial modifications. It is obligatory as our fundamental duty. Let there be no sense of weakness, no sense of importance."

Justice Iyer emphasized the need for national pride: "We speak with the pride and patriotism of 950 million Indians who together constitute the Shakti that is India, the India that is Bharat. It is this that we must realize."

This democratic process led to Shri Chaturan Mishra, the then agriculture Minister to set up an expert group to create a *sui generis* alternative to UPOV, allowed under Article 27.3(b) of TRIPS. I was invited to be part of the expert group which formulated the Plant Variety Protection and Farmers Rights Act 2002.

> This law on Plant Varieties has a clause on Farmers' Rights:
> *"A farmer shall be deemed to be entitled to save, use, sow, resow, exchange, share or sell his farm produce including seed of a variety protected under this Act in the same manner as he was entitled before the coming into force of this Act."*

After Monsanto's defeat in the HC on its false claims to patents on Bt cotton in violation of Section 3(j), the HC also made it clear the Plant Variety Act is the appropriate act for claiming IPRs on Plant Varieties since patents on plants and seeds are not allowed under the patent act of India.

The corporations are already misusing the Plant Variety Act as Professor NS Gopalkrishnan has pointed out in his two-part paper "Problems with the Indian Plant Varieties Regime."[8]

As Shalini Butani, a former colleague at Navdanya points out, the Monsanto Group already holds nineteen plant variety certificates (PVCs) granted by the PPV&FR Authority (see Table 1, compiled by Shalini Bhutani from data on the PPV&FR Authority website).[8] The economic rights granted under the law on the breeder (or his successor, his agent or licensee), upon grant of PVC include exclusive right to produce, sell, market, distribute, as well as import or export the variety during the fifteen year term for crops.

Monsanto Group's Cotton Varieties with IPR under the PPV&FR Act

No.	Company	Extant (VCK)	New Variety	PVP	Until
1	Monsanto Genetics India Pvt Ltd		G 9650798	2014	2029
2	Monsanto Holding Pvt Ltd		G 6882644	2015	2030
3	Monsanto Holding Pvt Ltd		G 4568960	2016	2031
4	Monsanto Holding Pvt Ltd	SO7H878 BGII		2016	2031
5	Monsanto Holding Pvt Ltd		G 9663905	2017	2032
6	Monsanto Holding Pvt Ltd		G 0898516	2017	2032
7	Maharashtra Hybrid Seeds Co Ltd		MRC 7160	2012	2027
8	Maharashtra Hybrid Seeds Co Ltd		MRC 7918	2013	2028

9	Maharashtra Hybrid Seeds Co Ltd		MRC 7041	2013	2028
10	Maharashtra Hybrid Seeds Co Ltd	MECH 12Bt		2013	2028
11	Maharashtra Hybrid Seeds Co Ltd	MRC 6301 Bt		2013	2028
12	Maharashtra Hybrid Seeds Co Ltd	MRC 6025 Bt		2013	2028
13	Maharashtra Hybrid Seeds Co Ltd	MRC 7326		2013	2028
14	Maharashtra Hybrid Seeds Co Ltd		C 5171	2013	2028
15	Maharashtra Hybrid Seeds Co Ltd		C 5197	2014	2029
16	Maharashtra Hybrid Seeds Co Ltd	MRDC 223		2016	2031
17	Maharashtra Hybrid Seeds Co Ltd	MRDC 222		2016	2031
18	Maharashtra Hybrid Seeds Co Ltd	MRC 6304 Bt		2017	2032
19	Maharashtra Hybrid Seeds Co Ltd	C 5710		2017	2032

The PPVFRA Act was designed for farmers' rights, not for corporate monopoly. It cannot be allowed to become an instrument of undermining farmer's rights,violating the obligations of access and benefit sharing under the Biodiversity Act.

The ownership and control governing access has two different legal frameworks:

The first is the legal framework of the CBD and the Biodiversity Act and the farmers' rights obligations in the PPVFRA recognizing ownership and control as based on national sovereignty and community rights. The other being the legal framework being imposed by the corporations, restricting ownership concept to IPRs of private industry.

The provider of seed is also the buyer of seed from industry. The strengthening of rights for the seed industry is directly in conflict with the rights of farmers. The seed industry's profits grow by draining incomes from farmers.

It is not just biological material that is being exchanged, but knowledge and technology too. Farmers' seeds have embodied knowledge and technology. Technology transfer thus takes place from the farmer to industry and from the biodiversity rich south to the biodiversity poor north.

These flows of access and benefit sharing at the biological and the knowledge level are schematized in diagram 1.

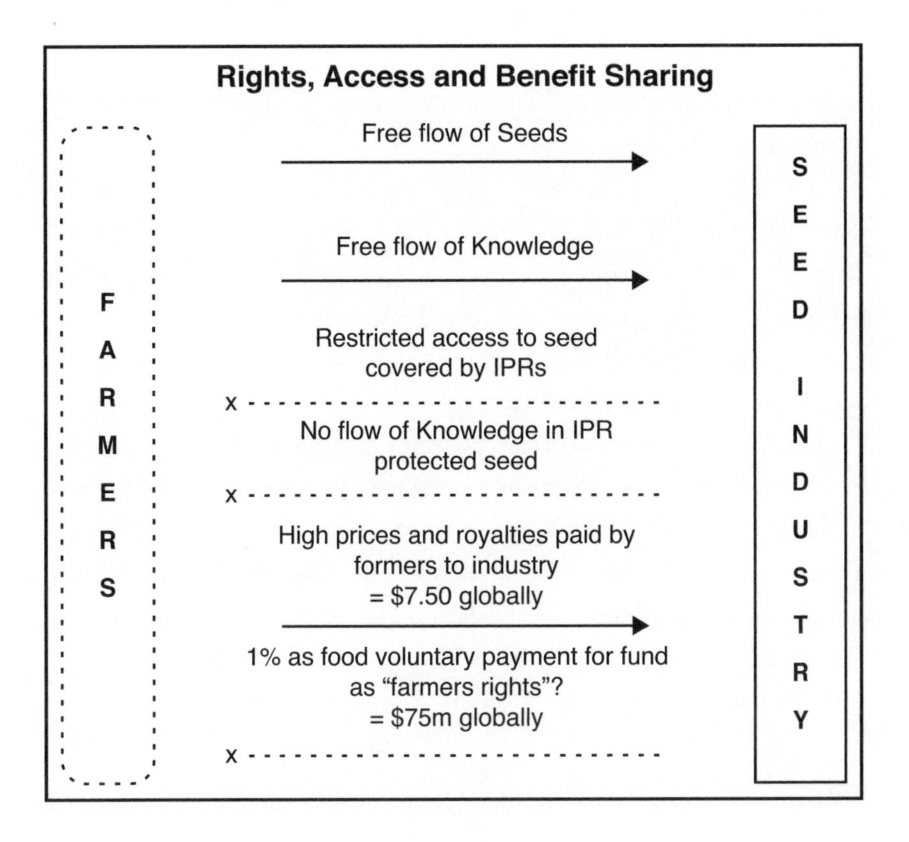

The corporate IPR regimes are based on:

- Free access to farmers' seeds and knowledge
- Restricted access to seeds from industry
- Increased burden of royalties on seed which is what has led to farmers' debt and farmers' suicides

If bioprospecting contracts, and free unregulated access to our biodiversity had been allowed to be the norm, industry would have had unregulated access to rich biodiversity and farmers varieties, they would have taken IPRs, the industry would have prevented the farming community from free sharing in the material and cognitive benefits of agricultural biodiversity and breeding. The seed industry would have also prevented farmer-to-farmer exchange.

That is why the exclusion of plants and seeds from patentability, the regulation for access and benefit sharing under the Biodiversity Act, and the positive recognition of Farmers' Rights in our act are important milestones in the evolution of the legal framework related to biodiversity, including agrobiodiversity and seeds.

Since its implementation in 2001, the Plant Variety Protection and Farmers' Rights Act faced its biggest test when PepsiCo India initiated legal proceedings against four farmers in Gujarat for 'illegally' growing its potato variety registered under the PPV&FRA.

The company applied for the registration of two hybrid potato varieties FL 1867 and FL 2027 in February 2011. These varieties were registered under the PPVFRA in February 2016 for a period of 15 years. PepsiCo marketed the latter variety under the trademark FC-5 and filed a 4.2 *crore* (10 million rupees) lawsuit against farmers of Gujarat. However, PepsiCo then withdrew its claims with the raising of Section 39 of the PPV&FRA.

Section 39: Farmers' rights indicate that–notwithstanding anything contained in this act–a farmer shall be deemed to be entitled to save, use, sow, resow, exchange, share or sell his farm produce including seed of a variety protected under this act in the same manner as he was entitled before the coming into force of this act.

Once again, PepsiCo in April 2019, sued a total of 4 farmers for 10 million rupees each in Gujarat for growing a variety of potatoes, claiming infringement of intellectual property rights under the Protection of Plant Varieties and Farmers Rights Act, 2001 for cultivating their proprietary FC5 variety of potatoes that are used to make Lay's chips. However, on May 2, 2019, again, due to Section 39 and having no ground in law to sue the farmers, PepsiCo withdrew its lawsuit against the farmers in Gujarat.

Under Indian legislation, the exclusion of patents on seeds, the laws on access and benefit sharing, and farmers rights combine to create a different "biodiversity and people centered access and benefit sharing framework."

We now have to ensure that the access and benefit sharing clauses of our Biodiversity Act apply to the Plant Variety Protection and Farmers' Rights Act.

Sharing of benefits is an important principle of the CBD and our Biodiversity Act. There are three kinds of benefits that need sharing:

- Material/biological
- Cognitive
- Financial

This sharing can take place between:

- Farmer to farmer
- Farmer to scientist
- Farmer to industry
- Scientist to scientist
- Scientist to industry

New models of participatory breeding and evolutionary breeding are evolving to breed seeds for nutrition, and climate resilience. Farmers' rights are key to the future of our seeds and the future of agriculture.

Farmers Rights': The Key to the Future of Our Seeds, Future of Our Farmers, Future of Our Farming

Farmer's rights are an ecological, economic, cultural, and political imperative. Without community rights, agricultural communities cannot protect agricultural biodiversity. This biodiversity is necessary not just for the ecological insurance of agriculture. Rights to agricultural biodiversity are also an economic imperative because, without it, our farmers will lose their freedom and options for survival. Since biodiversity and cultural diversity are intimately linked, conservation of agricultural biodiversity is a cultural imperative also. Finally, without farmers' rights, there is no political mechanism to limit monopolies in agriculture and the inevitable consequence of displacement, hunger, and famine that will follow total monopoly control over food production and consumption through the monopoly ownership over seed, the first link in the food chain.

That is why we need to question the assumptions of the US Secretary of State who said that the Government of India should produce legislation to protect US seed corporations so that they can provide the "best seeds for Indian farmers." What is good for Pepsi, Cargill, Monsanto, Bayer, Pioneer, and Dow is not necessarily good for Indian farmers and Indian consumers.

Pepsi needs tomatoes and potatoes for processing into tomato ketchup and potato chips for its fast food chains like KFC and Pizza Hut. For them, crops are raw materials, not food; consequently, nutrition, taste, and health are inconsequential. Cargill needs corn and soya for its feed industry, not for humans. Monsanto is interested in selling more of its failed Bt cotton and its herbicide Roundup through illegal herbicide resistant Bt cotton. These are the characteristics that have driven farmers to suicide and led to pesticide poisoning. These are not the characteristics of seed that Indian farmers would choose in their breeding strategies or characteristics of food that Indian consumers would choose for cooking qualities in their diverse food systems.

Farmers' rights reflect the breeding by farmers as well as alternative breeding strategies for protection of the biodiversity base of agriculture. Without farmers' rights biodiversity rich Third World countries cannot assert their sovereign rights to their agricultural biodiversity or in their agricultural policy. Further without the ownership rights of farming communities, biodiversity cannot be conserved. Without Farmers Rights a transition to sustainable agriculture is not possible.

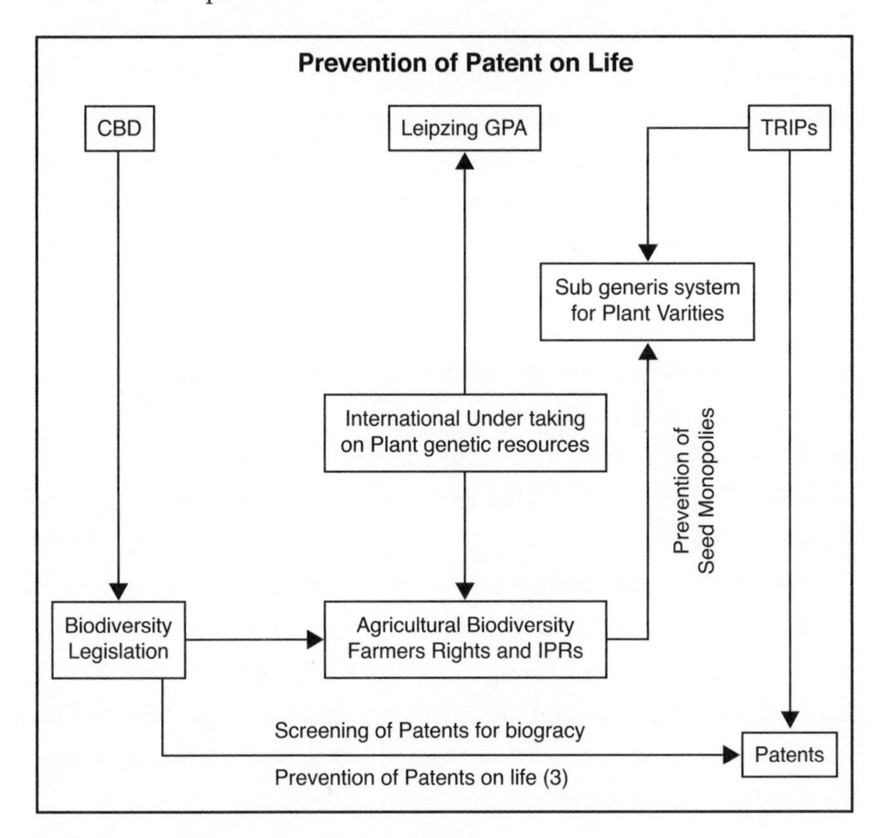

Farmers' Rights as Community Rights

No model yet exists which recognizes these rights of farmers and other producer communities who derive their livelihood from biodiversity. The rights of farmers, tribals, pastoralists, herbalists and fisher-folk to the biodiversity that they have conserved and used from time immemorial can be effectively granted only if they are allowed to participate actively, not passively, in decisions that have an impact on the status of their rights and the status of biodiversity. It is to fill this gap that I started Navdanya. We need a concept of farmers' rights as a subcategory of community rights.

On the one hand, community rights recognize the creativity and protect the livelihoods of diverse communities and on the other, they set limits and boundaries on the domain of monopoly protection shaped by IPRs. In the case of agricultural biodiversity these community rights are farmers' rights. They recognize the creativity of farmers; they protect farmers' livelihoods, and they restrict IPR monopolies.

The dominant model of the free unprotected flow of knowledge and resources from the gene rich south to the capital rich north, and the protected flow of knowledge and resources in the reverse direction is brazenly unjust and non-sustainable, desperately needing to be changed. It can only change through a political process which recognizes the original contributors of knowledge and genetic resources and respects their value system. Community rights are a way of balancing resources and respecting this value system. Community rights are a balancing mechanism for IPRs and a crucial part of building such a political process.

A world in which market values are the only values will impoverish us all–nature, the Third World, and the international community. To keep non-market monetary systems of value of biodiversity and knowledge alive and to subject the logic of the market to these higher value systems is the real political task for establishing rights to knowledge and biological resources.

Community Rights in a *sui generis* Regime

We used ample legal ground to go beyond UPOV in evolving a *sui generis* framework for protecting biodiversity–including plant diversity–especially in light of the Biodiversity Convention. Without it, we would not be able to protect community intellectual rights.

People's contribution to the development of an adequate *sui generis* system for plants therefore needs to focus on the three imperatives: ethics and ecology, recognition of creativity by communities, and economic equity.

- The ethical and ecological imperative to recognize the intrinsic worth of all species.

Countries need to have strong legislations to allow exclusion of patents on life on grounds of public morality. This is a possibility allowed in Article 25 of the TRIPS Agreement. Areas excluded from patentability need to be governed by non-monopoly regimes which protect people's right to creativity and innovation.

- The imperative for equal recognition of creativity in diverse cultures.

Diverse cultures have evolved different traditions of knowledge and innovation which need to be treated with equal respect and significance. This is also needed for cultural diversity. In the area of biodiversity, indigenous knowledge of farmers, tribals, and herbalists is the primary source of knowledge of properties of plants.

A *sui generis* system thus needs to:

Recognize this indigenous innovation, even though in structure, process and motivation it differs from the innovation in industrial systems

Through this recognition, prevent the piracy of indigenous knowledge and biodiversity in which it is embodied (e.g., patents on neem, colored cotton, etc.)

The economic imperative to provide all members of societies with health and nutrition

Monopolies in areas crucial to survival have to be prevented through various mechanisms that exclude vital areas from such monopoly control. Thus, because food and health are central to survival, national patent laws have prevented the monopolization of patents in these areas. For example, the Indian Patent Laws do not allow patents for living resources. The Indian Patent Act 1970 states that "patents cannot be given for a method of agriculture, of horticulture, or for any process for the medicinal, surgical, curative, prophylactic, or other treatment of human beings or any process for a similar treatment of animals or plants to render them free of disease or to increase their economic value or of their products [Section 3(h) and 3(i)]."

While protecting the legislations that have evolved over the last two decades which have ensured that the ethical and economic imperatives are fulfilled and our laws allow us to protect our biodiversity and our indigenous knowledge in this era of biopiracy, we have to continue to be vigilant against renewed efforts by the pirates to undermine our sovereign laws and impose US corporate style IPR models.

The word 'property', by its very design, has always been excluded in describing the knowledge systems of communities. Property rights in the term 'intellectual property rights' as presently understood, connotes commoditization and ownership in private hands aimed at commercial exchange. The integral element of the relationship of the community to its knowledge is that it is communally 'owned' and shared. The sum total of knowledge which is of value (though not necessarily priced) in communal control (and not privatized) and cumulative is more aptly described by the term 'community intellectual rights'.

It was, therefore, suggested that the governments exercise their sovereign rights over genetic diversity jointly with the owners of diversity–the farming communities to prevent piracy of genetic material, to strengthen the negotiating capacity of the country by having state sovereignty backed by people's sovereignty, and to ensure just returns for allowing access to genetic material.

In order to protect farmers' rights, it is essential that access to such genetic material be made conditional to negotiations between the parties interested in acquiring the material, the communities concerned, and their governments. This is why we have Article 3 and 6 in our Biodiversity Act.

Farmers varieties need to be protected in perpetuity because they are perennial, perpetual, and always useful–by contrast to breeders' varieties, whose usefulness is time bound. It is necessary to ensure that the right exists in perpetuity and cannot be extinguished. Such a prohibition to advance public policy is common in domestic legislation. Farmers have a right for the continuation of free exchange and access emanating from whole communities to other reciprocating communities. It is predicated upon the non-exclusive holding in common of knowledge innovations and practices of indigenous and local communities in respect of genetic resources and biological diversity. The free sharing does not apply if there is commercial utilization of the variety of innovation. It should be assured that communities retain control over their resources, emphasizing the non-monopolistic facet of community innovation. This is reflected in the provision of the Biodiversity Convention to "encourage the equitable sharing of the benefits" arising from the utilization of such varieties, knowledge, innovations, and practices of indigenous and local communities.

To prevent prolonged dispute as to whether the variety, knowledge, practice, or technology relating to the innovation is in the custodianship of a community there is a need for a declaration to be made by the duly constituted representatives of the community that they have been using the variety or innovation. 'Them' being the custodians of the variety or innovation also suffices to vest the variety or the innovation in the community.

This reflects back to why we started Community Biodiversity Registers to document indigenous biodiversity and knowledge. The declaration will be in a manner which accords with their custom or practices. Legal burden is defined as the ultimate and main duty of proving the issue when all is said and done, failing to do so would mean the case is lost. Evidentiary burden is the duty of producing sufficient evidence to raise a particular issue.

More than one community may have contemporaneously created the genetic resource and the technologies or accumulated the knowledge. The innovation will, in such circumstances, vest jointly in all these communities, and each will have complete rights and duties in relation to it–save that any payments will be apportioned accordingly. Communities may be weak in enforcing their rights and asking the state to protect their community's interests in negotiations for access with foreign/commercial interests. As this obligation of the state emerges from joint ownership with communities, the state cannot take unilateral decisions but has to consult the community before taking action.

The right to pursue, present and develop innovation and enforce rights in relation to it is vested not only in the community but also in anybody, governmental or otherwise. This recognizes the lack of capacity in some communities to mount any kind of action to pursue, defend, and enforce their intellectual rights. However, the communities' right to do so always takes precedence.

Declaration of parent lines with their passport data in breeder rights claims is essential to guarantee that the farming communities that have contributed the varieties can be identified and given just compensation. Declaration of parent lines will also help other researchers use these varieties to develop new and/or improved varieties.

Farmers' rights include the right to breed new varieties and to sell seed. Farmers' seed sales account for over 70 percent of the seed supply in India, helping maintain both the price of the seed as well as the quality. Eliminating the farmer as a seed seller places him at the mercy of seed corporations and endangers the food security of the entire country.

Farmers' Rights are Rights to Seed in the Past, Present, and Future

The discussion of farmers' rights as merely a fund was based on 1 percent of voluntary payments/taxes. Back then, the total seed industry potential was estimated at $7.5 billion. This was a benefit forcefully taken from the farmers by the seed industry, since farmers had to give up farmers' rights of free-exchange, free sale, and free saving within their communities to cater to markets protected by IPRs. Low cost, royalty free seed economies for the farmer were thus substituted by a high cost, royalty burdened economy controlled by the seed industry. Instead of focusing on the $7.5 billion benefit provided by farmers to the said industry, all discussion on benefit sharing ended up focusing on the remote possibility of a 1 percent fund, based on voluntary contributions. This non-existent fund was then equated with 'farmers' rights.'

The real issue of farmers' rights, and access and benefit sharing in agricultural biodiversity is to ensure that the public good is not sacrificed for the private interests and the profits of the seed industry. The fundamental conflict between corporate IPRs and farmers' rights is a conflict between private interest and the public good, between private property and the commons. Farmers' rights are, in fact, rights of farming communities and should therefore be implemented as a subcategory of biodiversity related common intellectual rights for the domain of agricultural biodiversity.

Seeds of Suicide: Enclosure of the Seed Commons, Seed Monopolies, Undermining of Farmers' Rights through IPRs Leading to Farmer Suicides

A consequence of the enclosure of seeds is being reflected in the thousands of farmer suicides we are witnessing. Since the legalization of Bt cotton in 2002, after its illegal introduction in 1998, Monsanto has looted Rs 7,000 crores from the poor Indian cotton farmers and is directly responsible for pushing Indian farmers into debt, and ultimately suicide. 318,000 farmers have committed suicide since 1995 when the globalization of agriculture flagged off the hijack of our seeds, our agriculture, and our food systems. The suicides continue. Nearly 85% of these are in the cotton areas where Monsanto established a 99% monopoly, as recognized by the Cotton Commission of India.

Datta Chauhan, of Bhamb village, swallowed poison on November 5, 2013 because his Bt cotton crop did not survive the heavy rains in July that year.

Shankar Raut and TatyajiVarlu, from Varud village committed suicide due to the failure of their Bt cotton. Tatyaji Varlu was unable to repay the Rs. 50,000 credit through which he received seeds.

Ganesh, in Chikni village, left behind a family of 7 after the repeated failure of his Bt cotton crop. Ganesh had no option but to buy more Bt cotton and try his luck multiple times because Bt cotton was the only cotton seed in the market.

Thus, these are not just numbers but real people and real lives being destroyed.

It is crucial to note that wherever farmers have reclaimed native seeds as a commons; they have reduced costs, increased incomes, become debt-free, and have not been driven to suicide. The indigenous seeds are bred by farmers for renewability, diversity, nutrition, taste, and resilience. On the other hand, corporate seeds are based on the theft of farmers' varieties which are turned into 'genetic raw material', then modified to be uniform to sell more chemicals.

Seed, the ultimate symbol of renewability, is made non-renewable 'intellectual property' which farmers are forced to buy every season at a very high cost. This shift from renewable,organic seed to non-renewable, chemical, corporate seed creates a system in which farmers spend more and earn less. This is the primary cause for farmers' debt, distress, and suicides.

There are three interconnected issues at the root of the enclosure of the seed commons:

- First is the farmers' right to reliable and affordable seed and with it the duty of the government to protect farmers' right to livelihood and right to life. It is the government's duty under Article 21 of the constitution to protect the life of all its citizens.

- Second is the issue of IPRs, patents, royalty, and technology fees in the context of false claims and a failing technology, and the duty of the government to act to revoke a patent according to Article 64 and Article 66 of the Indian Patent Act.
- The third is the issue of monopoly on seed. The government has a duty to prevent monopolies being established. This is why we had the MRTP commission earlier, and now the Competition Commission.

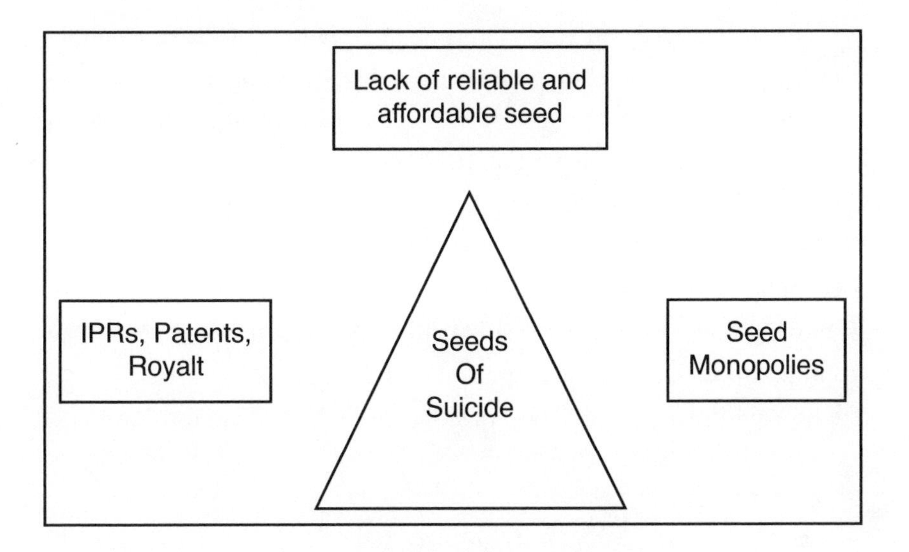

Why are Indian Farmers Committing Suicide Today?

Rapid increase in indebtedness is at the root of farmers' taking their lives. Debt is a reflection of a negative economy. Two factors have transformed agriculture from a positive economy into a negative economy for peasants: the rising costs of production and the falling prices of farm commodities. Both of these factors are rooted in policies of trade liberalization and corporate globalization.

In 1998, the World Bank's structural adjustment policies forced India to open up its seed sector to global corporations like Cargill, Monsanto, and Syngenta. The global corporations changed the input economy overnight. Farm saved seeds were replaced by corporate seeds which couldn't be saved,needing fertilizers and pesticides to survive.

Corporations prevent seed savings through patents and by engineering seeds with non-renewable traits. As a result, poor peasants have to buy new seeds for every planting season and what was traditionally a free resource, available through putting aside a small portion of the crop, becomes a commodity. This new expense increases poverty and leads to indebtedness.

The shift from saved seed to corporate monopoly of the seed supply also represents a shift from biodiversity to monoculture in agriculture.

Therefore, the root cause is the separation of agriculture from nutrition, and from ecology. For 10,000 years we have farmed to produce nourishment for the soil and society. The combination of the "Green Revolution" and corporate globalization 'reforms' have created policies that undermine our 10,000-year civilizational heritage of bowing down to the earth and farmers in humility and respect. The dominant policies of agriculture today, driven by global corporations, are bowing down to corporate profits, while destroying our land and its farmers.

Green Revolution: The Beginning of the End

We are witnessing a massive death right now. The death of our soils. Our land. Our farmers. And the roots of this contemporary crisis lie in fifty years of the chemical intensive, capital intensive, monoculture-based "Green Revolution," and two years of corporate globalization which has transformed Indian Agriculture into a market for costly seed, chemical inputs, and a supplier of cheap commodities.

In the 2 percent cultivated area, Punjab uses 10 percent of the synthetic fertilizers used in the country. Between 1970-71 and 2010-2011, the overall fertilizer use has jumped from 213,000 tons to 1,911,000 tons. Since synthetic fertilizers do not return organic matter to the soil, Punjab soils are diseased and dying owing to their use. The replacement of the rich diversity of Punjab, with monocultures of rice in the kharif season, and wheat in the rabi season, has also contributed to the impoverishment of the soil and the farmers of Punjab.

There was violence in this Green Revolution rooted in violent agriculture, with this violence being responded to with a militarized violence of Operation Blue Star. The army was sent into the Golden Temple, the most sacred shrine of the Sikhs. he vicious cycle of violence only deepened, with Indira Gandhi's assassination, and with the brutal killing of 3,000 Sikhs that followed.

If in the 1980s the crisis led to militancy, today it is expressed in epidemics of farmers' suicides and cancers. Instead of learning lessons from 1984, and the continuing legacy of a violent and toxic Green Revolution, our governments continue to sign MOU's with Monsanto, along with an intention to spread the poisonous legacy of the Green Revolution eastward.

Albert Howard reminded us that: "The birthright of all living things is health. This law is true for soil, plant, animal, and man; and health for these four is one connected chain."

Completely ignorant of this interconnectedness, the high cost external input agriculture has turned farming into a negative economy. While costs of production in 2011-12 were Rs 1,700 for rice and Rs 1,500 for wheat, the MSP was lower: at Rs 1,285 and Rs 1110 respectively. Between 1995-2001 and 2001-2005, net income of Punjab farmers dropped from Rs 77/- to Rs 7/- for rice, and Rs 67/- to Rs 34/- for wheat.

As a consequence, the farmers are in deep debt, with an average of Rs 41,576/acre. 17% having debts of Rs 80,000/acre. Debt for purchase of costly, non-renewable seeds and unnecessary toxic inputs is the primary reason for farmers' suicides and farmers' protests. The government–driven and controlled by MNCs–is planning to deepen this debt trap by creating wider markets for costly seeds and chemicals. The 2017 budget has Rs 100,000 crores allocated for agricultural credit, making it conducive for farmers to get into more debt for more chemicals, more hybrid, and GMO seeds from multinationals. This is a recipe for a deeper debt trap and an increase in the resulting suicides.

Continuing on the path shaped by global corporations and US interests will only make the crisis worse. Getting rid of small farmers has been the intention of industrial agriculture and the consequent aim of every government since globalization was forced upon us. It continues to be the main call after the farmers' protests started in June 2017. "Farming without farmers" is the new slogan of industry. But this inevitably means farming with more fossil fuels and chemicals. The end of farmers is the end of real food.

Myths and Frauds

Over the two decades since Monsanto entered India, it has violated laws, deceived Indian farmers by making unscientific and fraudulent claims, extracted super profits through illegal royalty collection by violating India's Patent and Intellectual Property laws, pushed farmers into debt; and, as a consequence of the debt trap, to suicide.

Fraud No. 1: Claiming that its Bt cotton will control the bollworm

The technology has been proven false with the emergence of resistant pests. In 1996, 2 million acres in the US were planted with Monsanto's Bt transgenic cotton called Bollgard, which had genes from the bacteria *Bacillus thuringiensis* (Bt). However, cotton bollworms were found to have infested thousands of acres planted with the new breed of cotton in Texas.[9] Not only did the genetically engineered cotton not survive the cotton bollworm attack, there were also fears that the strategy will create superbugs by inducing Bt resistance in pests. The Texas failure shows that Monsanto knew that its Bt cotton did not control pests when it lied to Indian farmers and the Indian government. The bollworm has evolved resistance to the Bt toxin, and not only was this emergence of resistance known back then, but it has since amassed substantial scientific evidence to support it.[10]

The problem with both the Bt and HT GMO technologies is that they exert intense selection pressure on pest populations to evolve resistance, (the bollworm/rootworm for cotton and weeds through HT crops), bringing on resistance much faster than would have otherwise occurred. Both Bt and HT crops are as a result unsustainable GMO technology in agriculture.

Furthermore, since the Bt toxin in Bt cotton is released in every cell and every part of the plant it has the impact of making pests resistant to the Bt and hence creating 'superpests,' which will require more pesticide use instead of reducing pesticide use. Insects were found to develop resistance rapidly to the transgenic plants with built-in biopesticide, when exposed to the toxin.

The Central government admits to the failure of Bt technology

In an affidavit filed on January 23, 2016, the central government told the Delhi High Court that the efficacy of genetically modified Bt cotton in resisting pest attacks has declined over the years. The government's response came in a dispute over an order to regulate cotton seed prices and fix royalties. It clearly stated in its affidavit:

> *"Pink bollworm, a major pest to the cotton crop, has already developed resistance in the last 2-3 years; farmers are a worried lot having sown Bt cotton seeds purchased at a high price… The crop is getting damaged due to pink bollworm incidence. It is a natural phenomenon that over the years efficacy of the technology goes down, hence the royalty on technology should also be reduced…cotton seeds are now unaffordable to farmers due to high royalties charged by MMBL*

(Mahyco Monsanto Biotech Ltd) which has a near monopoly on Bt cotton seeds and that this has led to a market failure." [11]

Despite this knowledge, NITI Aayog is still pushing GMO seeds as the future of India's agriculture; additionally, farmers continue to be forced to use pesticides which result in pesticide exposure, and ultimately, in their deaths.

Fraud No. 2: GMO Bt crops are safe for biodiversity and the environment, in spite of the scientific knowledge that GMO Bt is not the same as natural Bt. A recent review by Latham et. al. in the *Journal of Biotechnology and Genetic Engineering Reviews* clearly states:[12]

"The biotech industry claims that its Bt toxins are natural and as safe as those used by organic farmers. GMO regulators around the world share this view. Indeed, they make it the baseline assumption of their risk assessments for food safety and environmental toxicology. As we show in a new peer reviewed publication, however, assumptions of similarity of any GMO Bt with its natural ancestor are very wide off the mark. More than that, we show that the differences between natural and GMO Bt toxins are such as to make the latter much more toxic."

The GEAC clearance for commercial planting of Bt cotton in 2002 was given on the ground that it leads to pest control. The Bt technology has failed as a pest control strategy.

Monsanto's fraud, and government failure to stop the fraud, first trapped farmers in debt and then forced them to suicide.

Indian farmers are paying with their lives for Monsanto's fraud. They are being forced to spray pesticides because Bt cotton is failing to control the bollworm and is leading to the emergence of new pests. Pollinators have been killed because of high dose super toxins in Bt crops. This has also led to poisoning of the soil and the killing of soil organisms, threatening the very foundation of agriculture and future food security.

Vidarbha and Yavatmal: Death by pesticide poisoning

Twenty-one farmers and farm laborers died and around 1,000 others were infected in Yavatmal, in Vidarbha region, between the months of August to November in 2017, after they sprayed pesticide on the cotton crop. However, the figures shared by the agriculture ministry in the Lok Sabha show that this larger malaise with there being 272 deaths in the past four years due to pesticide poisoning.

The Special Investigation Team (SIT) blamed the farmers and farm laborers for "their failure to follow safety measures." However, the order of Bombay High Court dated February 22, 2018 clearly stated that the "deaths due to spraying of insecticides are not in dispute" and concluded that the insecticide companies were responsible for these deaths. Later, a challenge to the said order was defeated when a division bench consisting of Justice Bhushan Dharmadhikari and Justice Swapna Joshi refused to modify February 2018 order and reiterated that these unfortunate deaths, mostly in Yavatmal districts were due to spray of insecticides. The SIT report blamed the farmers, while the innocence of companies was brutally brushed aside by the Court. These deaths by pesticide poisoning reflect another ugly side of the corporate driven agriculture.

Farmers' Rights in the FAO: Evolution of Legal Exclusions

There was almost complete silence until the 1960s in international law with regards to plant genetic resources. Apart from a few exceptions of national governments issuing orders for the export of genetic plant material, these sets of resources were absent from the spectrum of national laws as well.[13] The shift started in the 1960s when we got the UPOV Convention 1961 with its revisions in 1972, 1978, and 1991. It aimed to align all approaches in various laws concerning the protection of plant variety.

In 1983 came the non-binding instrument adopted by the FAO council called the International Undertaking on Plant Genetic Resources which put forth the idea of these plant genetic resources "being a common heritage of mankind" and so should be freely available without restrictions. Multiple countries did not support the undertaking in lieu of their pro-privatization plans to appropriate various parts of Plant and Genetic Resources for Food and Agriculture (PGRFA). In response to this opposition, in the year 1989, the FAO council adopted Resolution 5/89 which prioritized laws for plant variety protection over the "common heritage" doctrine.

This Resolution still caused some discontent among the countries bent towards privatization. The Uruguay Round of GATT, along with the unpleasantness caused after the compromise in Resolution May 1989, formed the context in 1991 to FAO's Resolution April 1991 where it fully proclaimed the idea of states having complete sovereignty over their genetic resources.

This was reaffirmed with even more strength in the year 1992 with the creation of the Convention on Biological Diversity (discussed in more depth in subsequent sections).

Similarly, in the realm of national laws and regional laws, from the 1980s until today, the world has seen a massive sprouting of laws governing PGRFA in the form of various IPR regimes and Access and Benefit Sharing laws (ABS) which allow various stakeholders (governments, communities, and owner companies) to exclude access to PGRFA.[14] These laws for exclusions have taken the following major forms:[15]

- Patent laws: use of PGRFA is restricted completely if patent owners' consent is absent.
- Plant variety protection laws: PGRFA cannot be commercialized without the right holder (provided it is not 'essentially derived' from the protected material). Some national laws also include exemptions so that farmers can save seeds and use them on their own cultivation. However, there is also an obligation on the farmer to pay a royalty to the company in such cases.

- Contractual restrictions pertaining to seed sales: many companies sell seed with enhanced restrictions (beyond those in PVP or patent laws). These contracts can have clauses where farmers agree to a forfeiture of their rights existing under national law to save and reuse seed.
- Bilateral laws on access and benefit sharing: most national laws that were designed to give effect to ABS provisions of the Convention on Biological Diversity do not allow access to genetic resources in the country concerned without the prior informed consent of authority/community/legal persons handling the resources.

Though these techno-legal developments took the world ahead on a path away from the free sharing of genetic resources, a part of the international community kept striving for finding mechanisms which facilitated sharing of at least some PGRFA which are essential for livelihood and food security. After the Nairobi Final Act of 1992, the FAO undertook a renegotiation of the international undertaking on plant genetic resources (which had claimed the common heritage of mankind principle) through the FAO Commission on Plant Genetic Resources with the aim of harmonizing this undertaking with the Convention on Biological Diversity (which claims the sovereignty of states over their genetic resources). These efforts to align the two frameworks led to the adoption of the International Treaty on Plant and Genetic Resources for Food and Agriculture (ITPGRFA) which took effect in 2004.

Until recent times it was the local communities that have used, developed, and conserved biological diversity who have been custodians of the biological wealth of this planet. It is their control, their knowledge, and their rights that need to be strengthened if the foundations of biodiversity conservation are to be strong and deep.

However, instead of being treated as common property of local communities or as national property of sovereign states, the Third World's biodiversity has been treated as the common heritage of humankind.

By contrast, the modified biodiversity is sold back to the Third World as priced and patented seeds and drugs. As Jack Kloppenberg has observed, "whereas germplasm flows out of the south as the 'common heritage of mankind' it returns as a commodity."

After centuries of the gene-rich south having contributed biological resources freely to the north, Third World governments are no longer willing to have biological wealth taken for free and sold back at exorbitant prices as 'improved' seeds and packaged drugs. From the Third World viewpoint, it is considered highly unjust that the south's biodiversity be treated as the 'common heritage of mankind' and the return flow of biological commodities by patents are priced and treated as private property of northern corporations.

It was this unequal exchange of biological resources between the north and south that was finally challenged in the FAO in the mid 1980s. FAO discussions led to what has been called the "seed wars." The attempt of the south to treat all genetic resources as common heritage to be freely shared including the 'improved' and 'elite' lines was not successful. Breeders' rights prevented seeds from the seed industry to be viewed as "common heritage." However, the seeds from farmers' fields in the Third World were defined as "common heritage."

This is why the introduction of the concept of "farmers' rights" in the undertaking of plant genetic resources was a major opening. In the March 1987, in the meeting of the FAO Commission on Plant Genetic Resources, Third World delegates argued that if plant breeders had rights of ownership control and compensation by virtue of laboring for a decade to develop a new variety from Third World genetic resources; then Third World farmers also had rights since they had domesticated our important agricultural crops-observed, developed, and safeguarded the tremendous biodiversity that breeders and seed industry used as 'raw material.'

'Farmers rights' at the FAO were observed through the creation of an 'international gene fund' for the conservation and utilization of plant genetic resources. Such a fund, it was felt, would make 'farmers' rights' concrete.

Administered by the commission and thus indirectly by the international community it was to 'reward' farmers with programs beneficial to all. Farmers' rights, as defined in the text of the International Undertaking on Plant Genetic Resources of the FAO, meant "rights arising from the past, present, and future contributions of farmers in conserving, improving, and making available plant genetic resources–particularly those in the centers of origin/diversity. Those rights are vested in the International Community as a trustee for present and future generations of farmers and supporting the continuation of their contributions as well as attainment of overall purposes of the International Undertaking."

The main problem with 'farmers' rights,' as construed in the FAO commission, was that farmers did not have a place for negotiating biodiversity rights and determining patterns of biodiversity utilization. As Abdul Qawr Yusuf had stated, the right did not accrue to individual farmers but became a right for governments to receive assistance in the maintenance of genetic resources.

This system of compensation through aid or assistance for the exploitation of these resources by the north was inappropriate, insufficient, and undignified. In addition, the contributions to the gene fund were *voluntary* unlike the *mandatory* royalty payments under IPRs.

The idea of farmers' rights as a fund had the basic deficiency that farmers and local communities were pegged as not engaging in decisions about biodiversity and transactions of knowledge and biological resources. The idea was that government and non-government agencies involved in collection would receive the 'compensation' for information and resource transfer while the local communities remain excluded. Therefore, in principle the FAO model recognized the contribution of farmers but in practice farmers' rights needed to be realized by finding ways to reward farmers' innovations without discrimination (under which the farmers would be treated as inferiors just because they ran farms and not multi-million-dollar labs.)

It was recognized that informal innovations of farmers contribute to increased and sustainable production. However, these innovations were discriminated against by policy instruments that had evolved to support the diffusion of the formal innovation system in the private and public sectors both under the Green Revolution phase as well as in the biotechnology phase.

If innovations by farmers have to be recognized and rewarded, pluralism in agricultural development strategies becomes essential. Farmers' rights then become real, effective, and active rights to influence decisions related to the use of biological resources which are their 'means of production.' These decisions include basic questions of ownership and control over genetic resources, patterns, and criteria for their development and use.

The concept of farmers' rights as embodying sovereignty and creativity is different from the concept of 'farmers' rights' without sovereignty. In fact, it is because during the 1980s the issue of "ownership" was restricted to ownership of the seed corporations derived from 'breeders rights' and IPRs, combined with the fact that Third World resources were treated as a free access resource, that the concept of farmers' rights in the FAO Undertaking on Plant Genetic did not evolve as an ownership right but merely as a fund for compensation.

However, with the recognition of sovereign ownership in the CBD, farmers' rights can be re-conceptualized as ownership rights and creativity can be linked to sovereignty. This articulation of farmer's rights becomes particularly urgent given the concentration and expansion of the seed/chemical industry which is becoming a major threat to biodiversity food security and farmers' livelihoods.

What Farmers' Rights Are Not:

Farmers' rights are not a privilege or concession.

The impact of the 'Seed Satyagraha', the movement for the protection of farmers' rights and indigenous seeds can best be gauged from the fact that the Director General of GATT, Peter Sutherland himself had to intervene in the debate with his article "Seeds of Doubt."[16] However, nowhere in his article did Sutherland refer to farmers' rights. All he offered was an assurance on "farmers' privilege," which is not the same as "farmers' rights."

Farmers' privilege is not a right. It is a mere concession given to farmers by seed corporations, who alone have proprietary rights derived from innovation with biological resources. Besides failing to recognize farmers' innovation, the concept of "farmers' privilege" is also misleading because it falsely gives the impression that farmers can save seed as a right. However, IPRs in plant material are primarily based on the denial by multinational seed companies of the fundamental right of our farmers to conserve, use and produce seed as they see farmers' rights to their own seeds as an obstacle to their market expansion.

The shift from 'farmers' rights' to 'farmers' privilege' is a shift to the worldview that intellectual and economic value is only created by capital in the north, and that only northern corporations have rights that need protection. The pass allows the control and ownership of biological resources to shift into the hands of multinational corporations (MNCs) of the industrialized world.

Farmers' rights are not merely a fund

Farmers' rights have often been interpreted as funds run by international or national agencies. However, a fund cannot be a right. Rights guarantee protection, a fund provides compensation. Rights are available to all farmers. Compensation can only flow to some farmers. Rights put limits on IPR regimes and monopolies. A fund is based on the acceptance of unlimited monopolies and corporate rights. In this sense both the FAO interpretation and proposals in the Indian draft legislation were narrow in establishing farmers' rights as legal rights. Recognizing farmers' rights as legitimate legal rights has to be done over and above working out mechanisms for ensuring returns to farmers for their roles as original innovators and custodians of agricultural biodiversity.

Protection of Agricultural Biodiversity and Farmers' Rights through the Biodiversity Convention

The Biodiversity Convention provides an opportunity for governments to protect agricultural biodiversity, farmer's livelihoods, and sovereign rights to biodiversity. The Convention goes beyond the FAO Treaty on Plant Genetic Resources and recognizes the rights of biodiversity as the sovereign rights of nation states (Article 3). These need to be built on the prior rights of communities, who have conserved and protected biodiversity within national territories. Governments of the south can only be strengthened by standing behind their people, their biodiversity, supporting and protecting the democratic rights of diverse species to exist, and diverse communities to co-exist with them. If states in the south join the global move to deny rights and to take away control over biodiversity from local communities, they too will be weakened and will lose their sovereign rights and control over biodiversity to economic powers in the north–whose global empires in the globalization era are built on the destruction and colonization of the south's biodiversity.

In the preamble, the Convention states that contracting parties recognize "the close and traditional dependence of many indigenous and local communities embodying traditional lifestyles on biological resources, and the desirability of sharing equitable benefits arising from the use of traditional knowledge, innovations and practices, relevant to the conservation of biological diversity and sustainable use of its components."

However, no article in the Convention directly addresses farmers' rights or mechanisms for the compensation of indigenous knowledge. Articles 10(c) and 18.4 refer to indigenous practices, but not to the rights of farmers or local communities. Article 10(c) states:

> *"Each contracting party shall as far as possible and as appropriate protect and encourage customary use of biological resources in accordance with traditional cultural practices that are compatible with conservation or sustainable use requirements."*

Article 18.4 states:

"The contracting parties shall in accordance with national legislation and policies, encourage and develop methods of cooperation for the development and use of technologies, including indigenous and traditional technologies in pursuance of the objective of this Convention."

The Biodiversity Convention thus offers avenues for the protection of farmers' rights and national rights to biodiversity.

An important issue for government agencies is to explore ways in which the Biodiversity Convention can be used in the future of TRIPS negotiations. This is already happening under India's leadership. An International Conference on TRIPS-CBD Linkage was organized in Geneva in June 2018.

The Doha Ministerial Declaration in 2001 had tasked the TRIPS Council of the WTO to examine the relationship between the TRIPS Agreement and the Convention on Biological Diversity, and the protection of traditional knowledge and folklore.[17]

Government and non-government bodies also need to explore mechanisms for the recognition and implementation of farmers' rights vs. corporate IPRs.

In situ conservation of cultivated biodiversity makes it imperative that the concept of farmers' rights be evolved and implemented to enable farm communities to effectively conserve local biodiversity. However, IPRs as being defined in other negotiations such as the GATT are based on a denial of farmers' rights and their intellectual and material contribution to the global production and knowledge systems.

Making it clear that the rights of local communities are a right and not a concession, the Minister of Environment, Rajesh Pilot, in his speech at the Second Conference of Parties of the CBD had stated:

"The Convention has very importantly recognized the rights of local communities to a share in the benefits accruing from the use of genetic resources. This entitlement, and I emphasize the word 'entitlement', has been recognized not by way of any concession to these people, but by way

of a right, earned through building up traditional knowledge, innovating, sustainably using and conserving the biological resources.

It is a well-known fact that this vast wealth of traditional knowledge, uses and practices has been and is being exploited commercially in the areas of medicine, agriculture, and nutrition, etc. While the rights of the modern sector have been protected under the intellectual property rights regime, these regimes do not show the same respect for the knowledge and contribution of the local communities. What is urgently needed is a transparent and easily implementable system of recognizing and rewarding these informal knowledge systems with due place to them in IPR systems."

The challenge for operationalizing farmers' rights is therefore to give them due place in the implementation of IPR legislation.

The Seed Satyagraha for Protection of Farmers' Rights

Since 1991, when the Dunkel Draft Texts of the WTO agreement were leaked, Navdanya has organized awareness campaigns and rallies to alert farmers across the country about the emerging seed monopoly through patents. Navdanya spearheaded the movement to protect the farmers' rights to biodiversity, rights of seed saving and seed exchange. We have been organizing several seminars, yatras, signature campaigns to create awareness amongst the farmers and also to sensitize the policy makers and politicians of the country to defend seed freedom.

We started organizing farmers through the Bija Satyagraha Movement to keep the seed in farmer's hands. We refused to cooperate with the unjust IPRs and seed laws that make seed a corporate monopoly and seed saving and seed sharing a crime. In 1993, half a million farmers participated in a historic Bija Satyagraha rally at Bangalore's Cubbon Park. This was the first international protest against WTO.

Bija Satyagraha is:

- A grass-roots campaign on patent issues
- An assertion to people's rights to biodiversity
- A determination not to co-operate with IPR systems that make seed saving and seed exchange a crime

In February 1992, Navdanya organized a National Conference on GATT and Agriculture with the Karnataka Rajya Ryota Sangha (KRRS), this was followed by a massive farmers rally in Hospet which was organized by Navdanya in association with the KRRS in October 1992. The Seed Satyagraha was launched following Gandhi's Swaraj as a fight for truth, based on non-cooperation with unjust regimes.

In March 1993, we held a national rally in Delhi at the historic Red Fort under the leadership of the national farmers' organizations, the Bharatiya Kisan Union.

August 15, 1993 (Independence Day), was celebrated by farmers asserting their Collective Intellectual Property Rights' (Samuhik Gyan Sanad). According to the farmers any company which used their local knowledge or local resources without the permission of local communities was engaging intellectual piracy, as in the case of the patents of "neem."

On October 2, 1993, one year of the seed Satyagraha was celebrated in Bangalore with a gathering of 500,000 farmers, where farmers from other Third World countries, as well as scientists who worked on farmers' rights and sustainable agriculture, participated in an expression of solidarity.

On March 5, 1999, Navdanya reasserted the Bija Satyagraha Movement against the immoral and illegitimate laws with over 2,500 groups to defend farmers' rights and seed freedom in the face of biopiracy and seed monopolies. The movement was part of the Campaign for *Bija Swaraj*–Seed/Biodiversity Sovereignty. The Bija Satyagraha was launched to defend biodiversity and people's rights to biodiversity; a new freedom movement against the new colonization of our lives, livelihoods, and living resources.

The internationalization of the Seed Satyagraha, within one year, gave the word "globalization" a new meaning. From representing global markets (as in the parlance of free trade) it came to mean the globalization of people's rights and seed freedom through resistance to centralized control over all aspects of people's lives.

Navdanya with its network 'Diverse Women for Diversity' and its partner International Forum on Globalization was also active at the WTO protest in Seattle.

In September 2000, over 400 farmers from all over the world came together at the unique *Bija Panchayat* (People's Seed Tribunal) to give evidence of the crisis of seed and agriculture in the wake of globalization, which is pushing small farmers to suicide.

Today, the Bija Satyagraha has spread through a large number of communities and groups across the country. In response to the deepening crisis, RFSTE and Navdanya took the initiative to organize a *Bija Yatra* in India in the year 2000 with a focus on seed rights, seed conservation, and sustainable agriculture. The Yatra was jointly organized by Vidarbha Organic Farmers Association, Maharashtra Organic farmers Association, Andhra Pradesh Ryotu Sangham, MAR, All India Kisan Sabha, Karnataka Ryota Rajya Sangh, Bharat Krishak Samaj, Navdanya, and other activists and organizations.

Navdanya's Seed Tribunal and Bija Yatras (Seed March) have created awareness through seed fairs, seed exchange programs, and initiation of new community seed banks.

We have been organizing Bija Panchayats in different parts of the country in opposition to the existing IPRs laws; i.e., the Patent Act, Seed Act, the PVP Act, and Biodiversity Act to articulate the peoples' collective voice so that the entire discussion and policy on the seed is not solely determined by the corporate sector and interests driven by profit motives.

Navdanya, RFSTE, and the West Bengal Institute of Juridical Sciences also drafted an alternative IPR law, which provided sovereign rights to the nation over its genetic resources and recognized the rights of the local community over its biodiversity.

To counter the globalized industrial IPR system, Navdanya conceptualized the idea of Common Property Rights in Knowledge as early as in 1993 in order to counter the private IPRs system and to prevent biopiracy.

RFSTE/Navdanya has also drafted model laws which were later used and further developed by the Third World Network and the Organization of African Unity for creating *sui generis* options based on community rights to TRIPS.

From January to March 2005, Navdanya with its partners undertook Bija Satyagraha campaigns to declare non-cooperation with the new Patent Laws, which allowed patents on life and the proposed Seed Act, which would have criminalized our farmers. In the spirit of Gandhi's salt Satyagraha, more than 100,000 people committed themselves to participate in a seed Satyagraha if a Seed Act was brought into force. The declarations were handed over to the Prime Minister.

After the introduction of Bt cotton in India, it was witnessed that across the country, farmers were taking the desperate step of ending their lives because of the new pressure building upon them as a result of globalization and corporate hijack of seed supply. More than 20,000 farmers had committed suicide in Andhra Pradesh alone. The lure of huge profits linked with clever advertising strategies evolved by the seed and chemical industries, and easy credit for purchase of costly inputs such as pesticides was forcing farmers onto a chemical treadmill and a debt trap.

In response to the passage of Seed Act and growing suicide among farmers, Navdanya undertook Seed Pilgrimages (Bija Yatras) to stop farmers suicides and create an agriculture of hope using heritage seeds and farmers agroecological knowledge. Hence, the Bija Yatra 2006-2007 was launched on May 9 to mark 150 years of our struggle for freedom by building a movement to stop the genocide of our farmers and reclaim our food sovereignty. The Yatra started from Sevagram, District Wardha in Maharashtra. The Yatra was concluded on May 26 in Bangalore, Karnataka. The yatra covered: Amravati, Yavatmal, Nagpur, the Vidarbha region of Maharashtra, Adilabad, Warangal, Karimnagar and Hyderabad in Andhra Pradesh, Bidar, Gulbarga, Raichur, Hospet, Chitradurg and Bangalore in Karnataka. These were the regions where farmers had become locked into dependence on corporate seed supply for growing cash crops integrated to world markets, which was leading to a collapse in farm prices due to 400 billion dollars subsidies in rich countries. Awareness was also created through the medium of music and street play to convey the message of organic agriculture, resistance to corporate monopoly of seeds, the harms of mono-cropping, and the benefits of multi cropping systems.

Navdanya also organized a public hearing on the issue of farmers' suicide in Bhatinda, Punjab. The Diwan Hall of Gurudwara Haaji Rattan overflowed with the sea of widows and family members of suicide victims.

Apart from providing guidance and help to the farmers for the revival of agriculture, Navdanya, under the "Asha ke Beej" (Seeds of Hope) program, distributed the indigenous variety of seeds to the farmers and encouraged them to shift to organic and sustainable agriculture. More than 6,000 farmers were distributed indigenous seeds. Various posters conveying messages on Bt cotton failure, farmers' suicides, and sustainable agriculture were distributed among the farmer communities.

As a part of the yatra, over 250 village communities were covered and more than 5,000 farmers affirmed their rights to biodiversity by taking a pledge to conserve, rejuvenate, and protect their biodiversity. The awareness campaign reached areas of farmer's suicide and distributed indigenous seeds by covering around 75 villages in Maharashtra, 85 villages in Andhra Pradesh, and 90 villages in Karnataka. The

College of Agriculture in Bijapur, Karnataka gave its full support to our endeavor to promote awareness on the native seeds.

More than 10,000 people were reached through the yatra and more than 10 million populations were covered in Karnataka alone through electronic media. The Bija Yatra created awareness among farmers on GMOs, corporate farming, and seed monopolies. The yatris burnt Bt cotton throughout the journey of hope to encourage farmers to boycott Bt cotton, give up seeds of suicide, and seeds of slavery; and instead adopt the seeds of life, the seeds of freedom, and of hope. A truck full of seeds traveled with the Bija Yatra and there was a hunger for seeds among farmers whose seed supply had been destroyed by the seed monopolies of Monsanto and its Indian subsidiary/licensees.

Navdanya also organized a Bija Rally in the regions of Uttar Pradesh in October 2006 with a reach of more than 10,000 farmers. In each village, farmers signed the copy of the memorandum for cancellation of Seed Act 2004 and discussed drawbacks of the Seed Act, patent laws, and privatization of water. During the yatra, 200kg of wheat variety was distributed to farmers. The Seed Act of 2004 was designed to enclose the free economy of farmers alongside the free economy of seed varieties. Once farmers' seed supply was destroyed through compulsory registration by making it illegal to plant unlicensed varieties, farmers were (and still are being) pushed into dependency on corporate monopoly of patented seeds. The 2004 Seed Act had nothing positive to offer to farmers of India except a promise of a monopoly for private seed industries which had already pushed thousands of our farmers to suicide through dependency and debt caused by unreliable, high dependency, and non-renewable seeds. The Seed Act has not yet been passed.

Farmers' Rights: A People's Charter

- Farmers' Rights arise from their past, present, and future contribution to the conservation, modification, and exchange of plant genetic resources.
- Farmers' innovation in plant breeding takes place collectively and cumulatively. Therefore, farmers' rights arising from their role as conservers and breeders have to be vested in farming communities, not in individual farmers.
- Farmers' rights are rights derived from intellectual contributions to the breeding of seeds and plant genetic resources. Farmers are breeders even though their breeding objectives and methods might differ from the objectives and methods of the seed industry. Farmers breed for diversity while the seed industry breeds for uniformity. The recognition of farmers' breeding strategies is necessary to stop the practice of using farmers' seeds as "raw material" with no intellectual contribution of farming communities.
- Farmers' rights are a necessary component for the conservation of biodiversity since the breeding strategies based on the production and reproduction of diversity have to be protected if agriculture biodiversity has to be conserved *in situ*. The intellectual rights and capacities of farmers have a central role in the conservation of agricultural biodiversity and need to be protected under CBD.
- Seed is not the private property of individual farmers nor is it the "common heritage of mankind" which can be appropriated freely by the seed industry and then converted into proprietary commodities, being sold back at high costs with heavy royalties to the same farming communities. Seed is a common resource of local farming communities who have evolved and conserved it. Farmers are not merely "care takers" for the "raw material" that the seed industry needs for its industrial breeding. Farmers are the original breeders, custodians, and owners of seed material

and plant genetic resources–Farmers' rights are community ownership rights not mere caretaker rights.

- Farmers' rights include their right to ecological security. This includes their right to cultivate diverse crops and crop varieties to avoid ecological risk and vulnerability. The globalized economic system dominated by TNCs in which TRIPS is embedded, and which TRIPS consolidates even further, creates conditions for the spread of uniformity and the destruction of diversity. This violates farmers' rights to ecological security.
- Farmers' rights also include the rights of farmers as consumers. This includes the right to choose seed from the seed industry on the basis of criteria of sustainability of farmers' livelihoods and the agricultural ecosystem. Farmers have a right to full environmental impact assessment of commercial seed, especially hybrids and genetically engineered seeds. Farmers have a right to the full information about the risk of chemical pollution and biological pollution caused by seeds tailored to the increased use of herbicide and the risk of transfer of herbicide resistance through pollination across large distances. Farmer's rights therefore require that seed sales and distribution be covered by biosafety regulations.
- Since farmers' choice of seed is limited by the disappearance of farmers' varieties, the erosion of public sector research, and by the establishment of seed monopolies through exclusive rights in the form of IPRs; farmers' rights also involve limits on monopolies and the rights of farmers to challenge seed monopolies as consumers of seed.
- Farmers' rights also include the right to food security of agricultural producers. Rural communities have been the ones most vulnerable to food security, hunger, and famine. Farmers' rights to food security therefore include the freedom to produce food

for their subsistence and survival, as well as the right to exclude certain crops from IPRs so that IPRs do not become an aggravating factor for the generation of scarcity and famine.

- Farmers' rights include the right to produce diverse and nutritious foods for healthy consumption. Safe and healthy food is an essential element of food security, and farmers' rights are necessary for ensuring food security for all.

FOUR

Biopiracy: The Patenting of Indigenous Knowledge and Biodiversity

Biological and Intellectual Piracy

While the IPR debate during the Uruguay round of GATT negotiations was framed on the grounds that stricter, western style IPR regimes were needed globally to prevent piracy, it has now become evident that the piracy is in fact being undertaken by corporations of the North, which are appropriating both the biodiversity and indigenous knowledge from the South. The issue of IPRs is closely related to the issue of biopiracy and intellectual piracy engrained in the western modeled IPR regimes. The lack of legal protection for our biological and cultural heritage has made the indigenous communities of the Third World vulnerable to 'biopiracy' and 'intellectual piracy' as illustrated by the cases of patents for products from *Phyllanthus niruri*, neem, basmati, wheat and others.

Biopiracy of Phyllanthus Niruri

The plant is called *Bhudharti* in Sanskrit, *Jar Amla* in Hindi and *BhuinAmla* in Bengali. It is common throughout the hotter parts of India, growing both in fallow land and in shade. An annual herb, 10–30 cm high, its leaves are elliptic-oblong like the Amla, hence the name; it flowers and fruits from April to September.

The whole plant–its leaves, shots, and roots–are used for treating jaundice. In India it has also been a traditional treatment for various forms of hepatitis and other liver disorders for centuries. Its use is household knowledge and well documented. Its chemical has also been investigated and reported in numerous scientific journals, including a publication by the Indian Council of Medical Research (ICMR), in as early as 1969.

Western allopathic systems have no medical cure for jaundice or viral hepatitis. Jaundice in medical terms is basically the presence of certain signs and symptoms associated with liver dysfunction, e.g., yellowing of the eyes, nausea, loss of appetite, pain in the liver region, etc.

On the other hand, Indian systems of medicine–Ayurveda, Unani, and Siddha–and folk traditions have used various plants for the treatment of Jaundice. *Phyllanthus niruri* is one such medicinal plant used widely in India from North to South, from East to West. It is as much a part of the formal health care system of Ayurveda as of local health care practice, folk medicine, and traditional indigenous collective knowledge.

Thus, while one can see that the use of *Phyllanthus niruri* for the treatment of jaundice has been an ancient and well recorded innovation in the Indian systems of medicine, one still finds patents being applied for this knowledge and claims of 'novel' invention being made.

The Fox Chase Cancer Center of Philadelphia (US) had applied for a patent to the European Patent Office for its use in curing hepatitis. The patent claim was for the manufacture of a medicine for treating viral hepatitis B.[1]

The patent application referred to Dr. K.M. Nadkarni's *Indian Materia Medica* which reports the formulations based on '*Phyllanthus niruri* for treatment for jaundice in classical and folk tradition.' In spite of this prior knowledge of the use of *Phyllanthus Niruri* for cure for ***all*** forms of hepatitis, including hepatitis B, the Fox Chase Cancer claim stated that:

> *"In so far as is known Phyllanthus niruri has not been proposed for the treatment of viral hepatitis infection prior to the work done by the inventors of the present invention."*

In an allopathic system–where no specific treatment for jaundice exists–in cases of viral hepatitis, an attempt is made to provide systematic treatment by giving glucose, vitamin B complex, and avoiding both fatty and fried foods which cause nausea and vomiting. In Ayurveda, and in traditional systems of medicine, there are products which are known to help in the regeneration of the liver tissue. This treatment is, therefore, addressing a more deeply rooted cause of the health problem, not merely the symptoms.

Since, in traditional systems of medicine, the diagnosis of jaundice is made on the basis of it being a problem with liver function, it is *immaterial* whether the infective hepatitis is due to hepatitis A, B, C, D, etc., since the management of *all infective hepatitis* is essentially the same.

By isolating the application of *Phyllanthus niruri* for the treatment of jaundice to one form of infective hepatitis (hepatitis B) and treating this as novel application, even though medicines derived from *Phyllanthus niruri* have been used for treating all forms of hepatitis in the traditional systems of medicine, the scientists of the Fox Chase Cancer Center falsely presented an act of piracy as an act of invention.

This is blatant intellectual piracy of the local communities' traditional and cultural knowledge, coupled with arrogance in assuming that these resources gained 'additional value' when processed in western laboratories. Such a patent also adversely impacted the potential export market for drugs developed by Indian pharmaceutical companies which met the requirements of the holistic Indian medicine systems.

Biopiracy of Turmeric

Turmeric Patent Table

US Patent	Patent	Patentee	Assignee	Date
US 5,401,504	A method of promoting healing of a wound in a patient	Suman K. Das, Hari Har P. Cohly	Cohly Hari Har Parshad Das Suman Kumar Mississippi Medical Center, The, University of Mississippi Medical Center	12-28-1993

(Continue)

US 6,521,271	Compositions and Methods of Treatment for Skin Conditions Using Extracts of Turmeric	Dung Phan, 1101 Saddlewood Dr., San Jose, CA(US)95121	Dung Phan, San Jose, CA (US)	2-18-2003
US 64,97,908	Turmeric-Containing Cooking Oils and Fats	Seiri Oshiro, 27-21 Kyohara-cho, Naha-shi, Okinawa 901-0151(JP)	Seiri Oshiro, 27-21Kyohara-cho, Naha-shi, Okinawa 901-0151 (JP)	12-24-2002

The Indian biodiversity and its nurturers: its farmers, tribals, and local communities are under constant threat from the North (through its governments and TNCs) which is vigorously seeking to extend their IPR regime to plants, animals, and microorganisms. This was reflected in the patent claims for turmeric (*haldi)*, yet another example of biopiracy. For centuries, Indians have cured wounds by applying a pinch of yellow turmeric powder or by applying turmeric paste on bruises, wounds, and inflammation. Women apply turmeric as a daily routine for preserving and improving their facial complexion. Thus, one can easily see that the collective wisdom that has accumulated over generations in India was being claimed as something 'novel' and 'inventive'.

US Patent 5,401,504, which was granted to Suman K. Das and Harihar P. Cohly of Mississippi Medical Center, in Jackson (US), conferred exclusive rights to a specific formulation of *Curcuma Longa* – or turmeric. The right to exploit this patent rested with the Mississippi Medical Center. The other three turmeric patent holders were from

Germany, Indonesia, and the US. The German patent application was on the use of preparation of turmeric plants, the Indonesian patent had combinations of compounds isolated from turmeric which were used as anti-inflammatory agents, and the US Patent claim was on the turmeric's cooking process and turmeric's composition for food and beverages. The patent application for the use of turmeric as a wound healer admitted that although it is primarily a dietary agent, turmeric has long been used in India as a traditional medicine to treat various sprains and inflammatory conditions. The active ingredient in turmeric powder is curcumin.

The summary of US parent 5,401,504 stated:

"The present invention is directed to the use of turmeric to promote wound healing. The Present inventors have found that the use of turmeric at the site of injury by topical application and/ or oral intake of turmeric, Will promote healing of wounds."

The claim also added:

"Turmeric can be used in form of a powder, such as obtained from the food store. It can be orally ingested, for example, with drinking water. The powder can also be directly administered topically to the wound. The turmeric can be administered to mammals, including humans, to promote wound healing."

The patent on turmeric did not fulfill two of the most important requisites of patentability: 'novelty' and 'non-obviousness'. However, the US Patent and Trademark Office defended the claim by arguing that while turmeric as a wound healing ointment had been in public use, its application in the powder form had not.

Yet, as most of our grandmothers in India can vouch, this is absolutely incorrect.

The fact that Haldi's use had been *unknown to the US's medical establishment* permitted the piracy of the *common knowledge of India* by a medical center of an American University.

Liberating the 'Free Tree': Challenging the Neem Biopiracy Patent

The botanical name of the neem tree is *Azadirachtaindica*, which is taken from the Persian name for the tree, Azad-Darakth, meaning "the free tree." India has freely shared its "free tree" and knowledge of its myriad uses with the world community which is why it now flourishes in the many countries of Africa, Central and South America, the Caribbean, and Asia. Neem has been used for diverse purposes over centuries in India, having been used both in medicine and in agriculture. Research has shown that neem extracts can influence nearly 200 species of insects, many of which are resistant to pesticides.

Neem has long been known to cure all kinds of diseases afflicting humankind. The medicinal properties of neem have been described in the ancient Indian medicinal literature, e.g., Atharvaveda, the *Ghthyasutras,* and the Sutragranthas. In fact, the Sanskrit name, *Nimba* is a derivative of the term *Nimbatisyasthyamdadati* (to give good health). It is called *SarvaRogaNivarini* (the curer of all ailments) in our religious and other ancient texts. Ancient Indian medical texts state that neem is *kushtaghna* (removes skin disorders including leprosy), *krimighna* (anti-microbial), *vrnapacaka* (anti-ulcer), *vranas' odhaka* (purifier of ulcers), *putihara* (removing pus), *dahapras'amaka* (anti-burning), *kandaughna* (against clotting), *vrnaropaka* (healing effect), *vedonasthapaka* (anodyne), *rocaka* (appetizer), *grahi* (constipation), *yakrtuttejaka* (liver stimulant), *amlapittahara* (gastric demulsant), *rakta'sodhaka* (blood purifier), *raktavikakajanyas' othara* (anti-inflammatory), and *kaphaghna* (anti-phlegm).

Unani texts detail the pharmacological action and the therapeutic efficiency of neem as resolvement action (anti-inflammatory), concoctive, strong blood purifying, anti-leprosy, anti-vitiligo, anti-bile/phlegm, and anti-arthritic, anti-flatulent, wound healing, anti-septic, anti-purulent, anti-pyretic, anti-microbial, and possessing anthelminthic actions. Unani scholars consider that neem can take care of nearly all aspects of human health and recommend its widespread use as it is available free of cost.

But the product gifted by neem almost became the 'intellectual property' of western scientists and large corporations by being patented. In as early as the 1970s, scientists in the US and in Japan filed patents in their countries on the various properties of neem and their extraction processes. These principles and properties of the neem have been known and used for centuries in India. Even the processes that were claimed to be patented were only minor modifications of processes that have been used for centuries to prepare extracts.

There has been considerable research conducted on the properties of neem carried out in multiple institutions ranging from the Indian Agriculture Research Institute and the Khadi and Village Industries Commission (KVIC). Much of this research was fostered by Gandhian movements such as the *Boycott of Foreign Goods Movement*, which encouraged the development and manufacture of local Indian products.

For centuries the West ignored the neem tree and its properties. The practices of Indian peasants and doctors were not deemed worthy of attention by the majority of British, French, and Portuguese colonialists. It was the growing opposition to chemical products in the West which led to a sudden enthusiasm for the pharmaceutical properties of neem.

In 1971, US timber importer Robert Larson observed the tree's usefulness in India and began importing neem seeds to his company headquarters in Wisconsin. Throughout the following decade he conducted safety and performance tests upon a pesticidal neem extract called *Margosan-O,* and in 1985 he received clearance for the product from the US Environmental Protection Agency (EPA). Three years later he sold the patent to the multinational chemical corporation, Race and Company.

Since 1985, multiple US Patents had been filed by US and Japanese firms on the formulae for stable neem-based solutions, emulsions, and neem-based toothpaste. At least four of these patents were owned by

W.R. Grace, three by another US company (the Native Plant Institute), and two by the Japanese Terumo Corporation (before they were revoked in the court of law). When they had their patents, they had set about manufacturing and commercializing the products by establishing a base in India. They then approached several Indian manufacturers with proposals to buy up their technology or to convince them to stop producing value-added products and instead supply the company with raw materials.

In many cases, Grace was met with a rebuff. MN Sukhatme, Director of Herringer Bright Chemicals Pvt. Ltd. which manufactured the neem-based insecticide Indiara, was put under pressure by Grace to sell the technology for a storage-stable neem extract, which did not require heating or any chemical change. Sukhatme refused the offers. Eventually W.R. Grace managed to arrange a joint venture with a firm called PJ Margo Pvt. Ltd. They set up a plant in India which processed up to 20 tons of seeds in a day.

In 1992, the US National Research Council published a report designed to "open up the Western World's corporate eyes to the seemingly endless variety of products the tree might offer". According to one of the members of the NRC panel: "in this day and age, when we're not very happy about synthetic pesticides, neem has great appeal."

This appeal to "open their eyes" was blatantly commercial. Back then, the US pesticides market was worth about $2 billion. And bio-pesticides, such as pyrethrum, together with their synthetic mimics, constituted about $450 million of that market. The commercial aspects of this venture were even observed by Science Magazine, which stated that "squeezing bucks out of the neem ought to be relatively easy."

Grace's aggressive interest in Indian neem production provoked a chorus of objections from Indian scientists, farmers, and political activists who asserted that multinational companies had no right to expropriate something which had evolved through centuries of indigenous experimentation and several decades of Indian scientific research. This stimulated a bitter transcontinental debate about the ethics of intellectual property and patent rights. In April 1993, a Congressional Research Service (CRS) report to the US Congress set out some of the arguments which had been used to justify patenting:

> *"Azadirachtin itself is a natural product found in the seeds of the neem tree and it is the significant active component. There is no patent on it, perhaps because everyone recognizes it as a product of nature. But... a synthetic form of a naturally occurring compound may be patentable, because the synthetic form is not technically a product of nature, and the process by which the compound is synthesized may be patentable."*

These patents were only applicable to methods of extracting the natural chemical in the form of a stable emulsion or solution, methods which were simply an extension of the traditional processes used for millennia for making neem-based products in India. The biologically active polar chemicals could be extracted using technology already available to villages in developing countries. W.R. Grace's justification for patents, however, pivoted on the claim that these modernized extraction processes constituted a genuine innovation:

> *"Although traditional knowledge inspired the research and development that led to these patented compositions and processes, they were considered sufficiently novel and different from the original product of nature and the traditional method of use to be patentable."*

The processes which were supposedly 'novel' were directly drawn from Indian techniques. This *novelty* seemed to exist because of a single reason: the ignorance of the West. Over the 2,000 years that neem-based biopesticides and medicines have been used in India, many complex processes were developed to make them available for specific use, though the active ingredients were not given Latinized 'scientific' names. Common knowledge and common use of neem was one of the primary reasons given by the Indian Central Insecticide Board for not registering neem products under the Insecticide Act, 1968. The Board argued that neem materials had been in extensive use in India for various purposes since time immemorial, without any known deleterious effects.

PJ Margo, Grace's Indian partner had claimed:

"Azadirachtin, which was being destroyed during conventional processing of neem oil/neem cake, is being additionally extracted in the form of water-soluble neem extract and hence it is an add-on rather than a substitute to the current neem industry in India."

The allegation that Azadirachtin ended up being destroyed during traditional processing was inaccurate. The extracts were subject to degradation, but this was never a problem for farmers, as they put such extracts to use as and when they needed to be packaged for longer periods in order to be marketed commercially.

Moreover, stabilization and other advances attributable to modern technology had already been developed by Indian scientists in the 1960s and 1970s, well before the US and Japanese companies expressed an interest in them.

Dr. R.P. Singh of the Indian Agricultural Research Institute attests: "Margosan-O is a simple ethanolic extract of neem seed kernel. In the late sixties we discovered the potency of not only ethanolic extract, but also other extracts of neem... Work on the neem pesticide originated from this division as early as 1962. Extraction techniques were also developed in a couple of years. The Azadirachtin-rich dust was developed by me."

The reluctance of Indian scientists to patent their inventions and leaving their work vulnerable to piracy may in part have derived from recognition that the bulk of the work had already been accomplished by generations of anonymous experimenters. This debt has yet to be acknowledged by the US Patentees and their apologists.

The CR report claimed that "the method of scattering ground neem seeds as a pesticide would not be a patentable process, because this process . . . would be deemed obvious"–a statement that betrayed either lamentable misjudgment or a racist dismissal of indigenous knowledge. The discovery of neem's pesticidal properties and of how to process it was by no means 'obvious'. It had evolved through extended and systematic knowledge development in non-western cultures.

Consequently, Grace Company's aggressive interest in Indian neem production provoked a chorus of objections from Indian scientists, farmers, and political activists, who asserted that traditional companies have no right to expropriate the fruits of centuries of indigenous experimentation and several decades of Indian scientific research. This also stimulated a bitter transcontinental debate about the ethics of intellectual property and patent rights. In April 1993, a Congressional Research Service (CRS) report to the US Congress set out some of the arguments used to justify patenting:

> *"Azadirachtin itself is a natural product found in the seeds of the neem tree and it is the significant active component. There is no patent on it, perhaps because everyone recognizes it as a product of nature. But a synthetic form of a naturally occurring compound may be patentable because the synthetic form is not technically a product of nature, and the process by which the product is synthesized may be patentable."*

However, neither Azadirachtin (a relatively complex chemical extract from neem) nor any of the other active principles had been synthesized in laboratories. Those patents applied only to methods of extracting the chemical in the form of a stable emulsion or solution, methods which were straightforward applications of conventional organic chemistry and an extension of the traditional processes used for millennia for preparing neem-based products. "The biologically active polar (water) chemicals can be extracted using technology already available to villagers in developing countries," said Eugene Schultz, chair of the NRC panel. Thus, the claims were neither 'novel' nor 'non-obvious', and therefore undeserving of patent protection.

The Resistance

In response to all of the above, in June of 1995, the Research Foundation for Science, Technology, and Natural Resource Policy in conjunction with the International Federation of Organic Agriculture Movements (IFOAM) and 200 other associates legally challenged two of the neem patents held by W.R. Grace, one in the US and one in the European Patent Office.

The sole objective was to highlight the issue of biopiracy and emphasize the need to create a legal system that takes full cognizance of the innovation in indigenous systems of knowledge and treats the developments built on this knowledge as obvious steps given that the knowledge of the utilization of biodiversity already exists.

The challenge to the patent at the Munich office of the EPO was made by Dr. Vandana Shiva, Director of the Research Foundation for Science, Technology and Natural Resource Policy (RFSTNRP), now renamed as Research Foundation for Science, Technology and Ecology (RFSTE), along with Ms. Magda Alvoet on behalf of the Green Party in the European Parliament, Brussels, and the International Federation of Organic Agriculture Movements (IFOAM), based in Germany, through their counsel Dr. Fritz Dolder of Switzerland.

Besides these three groups, several other European groups supported the Neem Challenge in EPO. These were the Schweisfurth Stiftung (Germany), Kein Patent auf Leben (Munich, Germany), The European Coordination No Patents on Life! (Switzerland), A-SEED International (based in Amsterdam), GAIA International (based in UK), Oxfam-Wereldwinkels (Belgium), Oxfam-Solidarity (Belgium), Ecoropa (France), Erklarung von Bern (Switzerland), KeinePatente auf Leben (Koordination Schweiz), Actionaid (UK), Five Year Freeze (UK), and The Edmonds Institute (US) among many others.

There was a rich and vibrant background of protections and resistance which led to the filing of this opposition in the patent office. This movement was collectively called the 'The Neem Campaign'. It was launched by RFSTNRP along with farm groups and NGOs in 1993 in India to mobilize worldwide support to protect indigenous knowledge systems and resources of the Third World from piracy by the West, particularly in light of emerging threats from intellectual property rights regimes under WTO and TRIPS.

As part of the Neem Campaign, a massive signature campaign was also launched in India demanding that the patents on Neem be withdrawn. More than a hundred thousand people–children, students, housewives, professional workers, doctors, lawyers, teachers, farmers, engineers, environmentalists, artists, etc., joined the signature campaign to protest the neem patents. The signatures collected were finally submitted on May 9, 2000 in Munich, Germany (a day before the revocation of the neem patent) to the EPO by Dr. Vandana Shiva and Afsar H. Jafri of Research Foundation for Science, Technology, and Ecology along with Mr. Nammalwar, an Indian farmer, Prof. Udai Pratap Singh, and Dr. Abhay D. Phadke–Indian scientists.

The Opponents submitted evidence to the EPO that the fungicidal effect of hydrophobic extracts of neem seeds was known and used for centuries on a broad scale in India, both in Ayurvedic medicine to cure dermatological diseases, and in traditional Indian agricultural practice to protect crops from being destroyed by fungal infections. Since this traditional Indian knowledge was in public use for centuries, it would seem that the patent application in question lacked two basic statutory requirements for the grant of a European patent, namely novelty and inventive step (in the US non-obviousness).

In addition, the Opponents charged that the fungicidal method claimed in the patent was based on one single plant variety (Azadirachtaindica) and hence resulted in at least partially monopolizing this single plant variety. Since the European Patent Convention (EPC) explicitly prohibited the patenting of plant varieties, the patent should therefore be revoked.

What is more, the Opponents also charged that even the claimed method to produce the hydrophobic extracted neem oil was a standard method which has been state of the art for many decades. Hence there can be no doubt that the method for producing the formulation was not new at the time when the patent was granted.

On the day of oral hearing, May 10, 2002, Dr. Vandana Shiva briefed the court on the importance of neem in Indian culture and agriculture while Dr. Phadke gave extensive evidence detailing the entire process of manufacturing neem oil-based fungicide.

For example, in the case of US Patent 5,124,349, the processes described by W.R. Grace, to effect stable formulations, were well known at the time of patenting. As one reviewer of the patent commented, "I find it incomprehensible that W.R. Grace could have been granted a patent... claiming novelty on a process the whole world has known for years." Solvents mentioned in the patent, and solvents similar to them, have been used on neem seeds and described in publications long before the company's application.

The primary reason that such obvious processes were treated as 'novel' was that the basic knowledge existed in non-western traditions but was not known to the patent offices of the West. While the knowledge of indigenous systems was used, it was not recognized. But the use of that same knowledge by tinkering in western labs was accorded recognition by adapting the definitions in ways that were in accordance with western science and western practitioners.

The Victory of Biodiversity and People Against Corporate Piracy of Neem

On May 10, at 2:30 pm
History was made.

Mr. Tzschoppe, the Chairman of the Opposition Division of the EPO declared that the "PATENT IS REVOKED AND THE PROCEEDING STANDS TERMINATED." The four-panel judge revoked, in its entirety, the patent 436,257, which had been granted to the United States of America and the multinational corporation W.R. Grace for a fungicide derived from seeds of neem.

The ruling upheld indigenous innovation by communities against false claims of innovation and novelty by corporations. The 4-person panel judged the oral evidence presented in court and declared that the evidence given on foliar spraying of the hexane extracted 85 percent emulsified Neem oil proves "Prior art" with regard to 'Inventive Step', which is a prerequisite to obtaining patent protection.

On the issue of "Novelty" and "Auxiliary Request" related to concentration of Neem oil, the court ruled that the USA/Grace Neem fungicide product was lacking in "novelty," another patent criterion, and established that its properties and use were "prior art" years before the "proprietors" applied for a patent.

And so on the May 10, the European Patent Office (EPO) revoked the patent 0436257 B1 relating to the 'method for controlling fungi on plants by the aid of hydroponic extracted neem oil (neem fungicide) which failed to meet the criteria of Article 53 (a), 54, 56, 83 and 84 of the European Patent Convention (EPC). These Articles asserted: "Contrary to morality, lack of novelty, lack of inventiveness, insufficient disclosure and lack of clarity."

In accepting the challenge and revoking the patent, the four-member panel of the EPO, headed by Mr. Tzschoppe at Munich, agreed that the patent amounted to biopiracy and that the process for which the patent had been granted had actually been in use in India from time immemorial.

Neem Patent

US Patent	Patent	Patentee	Assignee	Date
494-6681	Method to prevent an improved storage stable neem seed extract	James F. Walker	W.R. Grace and Co. (US corp.)	August 7, 1990
496-0791	Salannin derivative insect control agents	James A. klocke et al.	Native Plant Institute (NPI) (US corp.)	October 2, 1990
4,515,785	Neem Bark Extracts	Masaki Shimizu, TodashiSudo Takeo Nomura (Japan)	Terumo Corporation	May 7,1985
455-6562	Stable anti-pest neem seed extract	Robert Larson	Vilewood Ltd. (US corp.) Has since been taken over by W.R Grace and Co. (US)	December 3, 1985
4,902,713	Azadirachtin-like compounds, and insect destroying agents containing them.	Heinz Reimbold, et al.	Max-planc - Gesellschaft Zur	February 20, 1990
453-7774	Hot water extracts of neem	Masaki Shimizu, TodashiSudo Takeo Nomura of Japan	Terumo Corporation (Japanese)	August 27, 1985
494-3434	Insecticidal hydrogenated neem extracts	Zev Lidert	Rohm & Haas (US corp.)	July 24, 1990

500-1149	Azadirachtin derivative insecticide	James A. Klocke, et al.	NPI	March 19, 1991
500-1146	Storage stable Azadirachtin formulation	Charles G. Carter, et al.	W.R. Grace and Co. (US corp.)	March 19, 1991
5047242	Azadirachtin derivative insecticide	James A Klocke et al.	NPI	September 10, 1991
511-0591	Neem Oil Emulsifier		PPG Inc., Pennsylvania (US corp.)	May 5, 1992
512,449	Storage stable Azadirachtin formulation	Unknown	W.R. Grace and Co.	1992
436 257 B1	Methods for controlling fungi on plants by the aid of hydrophobic extracted neem oil	James Charles Locke Hiram Gordon Larew III	James Frederic Walter	September 14, 1994
500-9886	(Dentifrice)		Floss Product Corp Illinois (US corp.)	April 23, 1993

Biopiracy of Basmati by RiceTec

On July 8, 1994, RiceTec Inc., a Texas based company, filed a generic patent on basmati rice lines and grains in the United States Patent and Trademark Office (USPTO) with 20 broad claims designed to create a complete rice monopoly patent which included planting, harvesting collecting and even cooking. Though RiceTec claimed to have "invented" the basmati rice, they accepted the fact that it was derived from several rice accessions from India. It claimed a patent for inventing novel basmati lines and grains.

US Patent	Patent	Patentee	Assignee
56,63,484	Basmati rice lines And grains	Eugenio S. Sarreal, John A Mann, James E. Stroike, Robin D, Andrews	RiceTec Inc, Alvin, Taxas, USA

On September 2, 1997 US Patent 56,63,484 on basmati rice lines and grains was granted. xThe 'invention' relates to novel rice lines, plants, grains of these lines, and to a method for breeding these lines. The 'invention' is also related to a 'novel' means for determining the cooking and starch properties of rice grains and its use in identifying desirable rice lines. The 'invention' also provided a method for breeding novel rice lines. There were three forms of piracy in this patent:

- The piracy of unique cultural heritage embodied in the name of basmati
- The economic piracy of export markets from farmers and countries who have evolved this unique aromatic rice (claim 4, 15–17)
- The piracy of farmers innovation and nature's creativity in the claim of inventing a novel rice line (claims: 1, 5, 6–14, and 18– 20)

The Research Foundation for Science Technology and Ecology (RFSTE), along with others, filed a case in public interest in the Supreme Court of India on March 4, 1998 seeking the court's direction in urging the Government of India to challenge the USPTO's patent, primarily on the grounds that the patent by this foreign company was in violation of sovereign rights of India, which included the indigenous and inherent knowledge systems of our farmers.

In the same year, the campaign against the basmati patent was started with widespread protests in India. A memorandum on behalf of people's organizations against the basmati patent was sent to the US Ambassador to India at New Delhi. However, at that stage, the Government of India chose not to take any action in the matter.

On April 27, 2000, as a result of protests and a case filed by the RFSTE before the Supreme Court of India, the Government of India filed a petition in the USPTO for re-examination of the grant of patent to RiceTec in respect of its "claims from 15–17" which were related to the grain. The re-examination request was filed by the Government in the name of Agricultural and Processed Food Products Export Development Authority (APEDA) and no challenge was made to the remaining claims, thereby sidelining the issue of protection of farmer's rights. The government did not challenge claims related to basmati seeds and plants, and hence to farmers' rights and traditional knowledge even though the research done by the Central Food Technology Research Institute (CFTRI) and ICAR established that the basmati seed claims covered our traditional varieties. The research done by CFTRI and ICAR provided enough evidence of prior art to get a cancellation of all generic claims related to basmati seed & rice lines. These were broadly worded claims and encompassed all types of rice grains irrespective of their origin. RiceTec not only claimed to have invented novel rice line but also its cultivation and cooking method. This was a blatant attack on the innovations of Indian farmers who had developed basmati. By not challenging these claims, the Indian government compromised the rights of millions of Indian farmers to save the rights of a few basmati traders.

Even the claim by RiceTec on the use of the term "basmati" was not challenged and the Union of India accepted in its affidavit to the Supreme Court that its limited challenge–if successful–will not prevent RiceTec from continuing to call its strain "basmati-like" or "basmati strain" though the fact is that basmati is not a generic term; rather, it is associated only with a long grain rice of a unique aroma and flavor peculiar to the Indian subcontinent. The government, in a way, accepted that the patent as a whole (which would cover seed and plant) could not be challenged.

In November 1999, during the WTO Ministerial Meeting in Seattle, RFSTE with International Center for Technology Assessment, US, and other US and European organizations, launched the Global Campaign against biopiracy to fight the basmati piracy and other biopiracy cases.

As a result of the challenge from the government of India and pressure from international citizens movements, RiceTec withdrew four of its claims (15–17 and 4), which related to the grain quality. This meant that RiceTec could not exercise exclusive rights to the trading of basmati rice and hence India's export markets and traders' rights remained protected.

On January 25, 2001, the GOI represented by APEDA told the Supreme Court they were satisfied with the withdrawal of four claims by RiceTec and did not intend to fight the basmati patents any further because exporters' interests had been defended. There was no attempt to defend farmers' rights. Even in the debates in Parliament, the basmati issue was narrowed down to the issue of exports, and detracted from the large issue of biopiracy, traditional knowledge, and farmers' rights.

The continued use by RiceTec of the name "basmati" which embodied the unique cultural heritage and innovation was a form of intellectual piracy. "Basmati" is not a generic name for all aromatic varieties, but a particular aromatic variety evolved in the foothills of the Himalaya. The uniqueness of Basmati from South Asia had to be defended as an indicator of quality both in the interest of Indian and Pakistani farmers as well as in the interests of the consumer.

The basmati variety for which RiceTec had claimed a patent had been derived from Indian basmati crossed with semi-dwarf varieties–including Indica varieties. The basmati varieties were farmers' varieties bred over centuries by farmers of the Indian subcontinent. The method of crossing different varieties to mix traits–in this case the basmati characteristics from basmati and the semi dwarf characteristics–was also not novel. It was a very commonplace method of breeding, which everyone familiar in the art of breeding knew.

Again, the characteristics for which RiceTec had claimed a patent were derived from traditional basmati. However, the patent claim blatantly denied prior breeding by farmers; by denying the role of farmers as breeders, it falsely claimed a derivation as an invention.

Basmati Characteristics

Indian basmati Characteristics

Bas 370	Type-3 Basmati
Length of 6.75 mm;	Length of 6.87 mm;
Width of 1.85 mm;	Width of 1.93 mm;
Length/width ratio of 3.72;	Length/width ratio of 3.55;
82.33% elongation during cooking	113% elongation during cooking
Burst index of 3;	Burst index of 3;
Starch index of 30.1;	Starch index of 29.0;
2 acetyl-1-pyrroline value of 395 ppb; and	2-acetyl-1-pyrroline value of 869.5 ppb;
Whole grain index of 53%	Whole grain index of 59%

RiceTec's claims were:

Grain from Bas 867	Grain from RT1117
Length of 6.75 mm	Length of 3.92 mm;
Width of 1.85;	Width of 1.85 mm;
Length/width ratio of 3.65;	Length/width ratio of 3.92;
elongation during cooking;	75% elongation during cooking;
Burst index of 2;	Burst index of 3;
Starch index of 29.0;	Starch index of 29.1;
2-AP value of 360-600 ppb; and	2-AP value of 150; and
Whole grain index of 50%	Whole grain index 45%

The double denial of Nature's Creativity and Farmers' Creativity

The basmati patent claimed by RiceTec perfectly illustrated the problems inherent to patents on living resources. Patents on living resources, such as a rice variety, are based on false claims to invention. Claiming invention for plant varieties is based on a double denial of the creativity of nature on one hand and of farmers on the other. The patent claims stated:

> *"One aspect of the instant invention relates to novel rice lines and to the plants and grains of the said lines."*

This claim to *"instant invention"* on *"novel rice lines"* was (and is) ontologically false.

The Basmati variety for which RiceTec had claimed a patent had been derived from Indian basmati (Table: 1) crossed with semi-dwarf varieties including Indica varieties (Table: 2).

Thus, on the one hand, the patent was for rice derived from Indian basmati which had the essential characteristics of such and was hence a variety "essentially derived" from a farmers' variety. Therefore, it could not be treated as novel. On the other hand, the patent claimed the "invention" of a "novel line". RiceTec's Basmati 867 could not be '*like traditional basmati*' and '*novel*' at the same time. RiceTec's claim stated that:

> *"Although the invention is described in detail with reference to specific embodiments thereof, it will be understood that variations which are functionally equivalent are within the scope of this invention. Indeed, various modifications of the invention in addition to those shown and described herein will become apparent to those skilled in the art from the foregoing description and accompanying drawings. Such modifications are extended to fall within the scope of the appended claims.*

Farmers Rights for Prevention of Biopiracy

The most efficient mechanism for preventing biopiracy and protecting farmers is by creating a legal framework for farmers' rights. Farmers' rights recognize the collective, cumulative innovation of farmers embodied in distinctive varieties like basmati. It is based on innovation being a time continuum.

NO PATENTS ON SEED AND FOOD
NO PATENTS ON RICE
Rice is the heritage of Asian farmers who have evolved hundreds of thousands of varieties over millennia, and Asian consumers who have developed a million ways of storing, saving and processing rice and rice products to provide nourishment to over half the planet's people.
Now a handful of giant corporations are trying to own and control rice through patents and IPRs claims based on piracy and trivial tinkering – Golden Rice, Basmati Rice, Jasmine Rice, Basmati Rice powder to coat other rice, parboiling techniques, biryani, masala dosa, etc.
Monsanto and Syngenta have taken patents on the entire genome of rice.
Rice cannot be allowed to become a Corporate Monopoly.
Stop Rice Biopiracy.
Join the Movement
Against Patents on Seed and Food.
For more information on Campaign Against Rice Biopiracy and Campaign Against Patents on Seed and Food contact:
RFSTE / Navdanya
A-60, Hauz Khas, New Delhi-110016 Tel.: 26561868, 26968077, 26853772
Telefax: 26562093 E-mail: vshiva@vsnl.com Website: http://www.vshiva.net

Protest organized by Navdanya with farmers groups to prevent the signing of the GATT/WTO Agreement, 1993.

Over half a million farmers protested at this rally in Red Fort, 1994.

Seed Satyagraha in Bangalore, before burning of the effigy of Dunkel.

Burning the effigy of Dunkel, the Director General of GATT at the Seed Satyagraha Rally, 1994.

Burning the TRIPS Agreement draft at the 1993 rally in Bangalore.

Vandana Shiva on stage at the Seed Satyagraha, 1995.

Save our sovereignty.
Save our seeds.
Save our salt.
Boycott Cargill and other TNCs
NATIONAL ALLIANCE OF PEOPLE'S MOVEMENT

Protest at the European Patent Office during the Neem Biopiracy Hearing in 1994.

In November 2013, Prince Charles visited Navdanya's Earth University (Bija Vidyapeeth), a 47-acre biodiveristy conservation farm and learning center–storing, conserving, planting, and studying 1,500 seeds.

Vandana Shiva and Prince Charles have been associated since the BBC Reith Lectures in the year 2000.

Vasudhaiva Kutumbkam:
Seeding Freedom
No Patents on Seed

We are the children of *Vasudhaiva Kutumbkam,* the Earth Family.
We have a duty to protect our relatives, to protect the plant and animal diversity that enrich our lives with beauty and nourish us.
Humans do not invent and create life on Earth.
Humans cannot own plants and animals through patents.
We are proud citizens of a sovereign country which has laws that defend our seed, our land and our Mother Earth.

#NoPatentsonLife

Article 3(j) of our Patent Act excludes from patentability "plants and animals in whole or in any part thereof other than microorganisms but including seeds, varieties, and species, and essentially biological processes for production or propagation of plants and animals"

These laws protect our future and the future of our Earth Family
They protect the rights of our farmers who grow our food
Giant chemical corporations producing poisons have spread diseases, killed our bees, butterflies, earthworms and pushed **300,000 farmers to suicide** due to debt.

They are now challenging every law of India:
The Patent Act, Plant Variety & Farmers Act, Competition Commission, Essential Commodities Act.
Every one of these acts creates the framework for our security and freedom

It is our right to grow up in a Free Independent, Sovereign, Democratic Republic called India
#NoPatentsonSeed

Navdanya

navdanya@gmail.com
www.navdanya.org
@Navdanyabija

Table 1
Basmati Lines suitable for breeding Novel Rice Lines
Varities
BAS - 138
BAS - 203
BAS - 376
BAS - 427
BAS - 375 'A'
BAS - 10 - 123
BAS - 375
BAS - 122
BAS - 334
BAS - 213
BAS - 372
BAS - 397
BAS - 433
BAS - 242
BAS - 406
BAS - 443
BAS - 388

Table 2
Long grain varieties suitable for breeding Novel Rice Lines
Varities
CICA -6
L202
C8801G
LEBONNET
LEMONT
CB801
L201
LABBLLE
CB860
LC770AC38 -30
IR841-85-1-1
P33-C-19
LEAH
P33-C-30

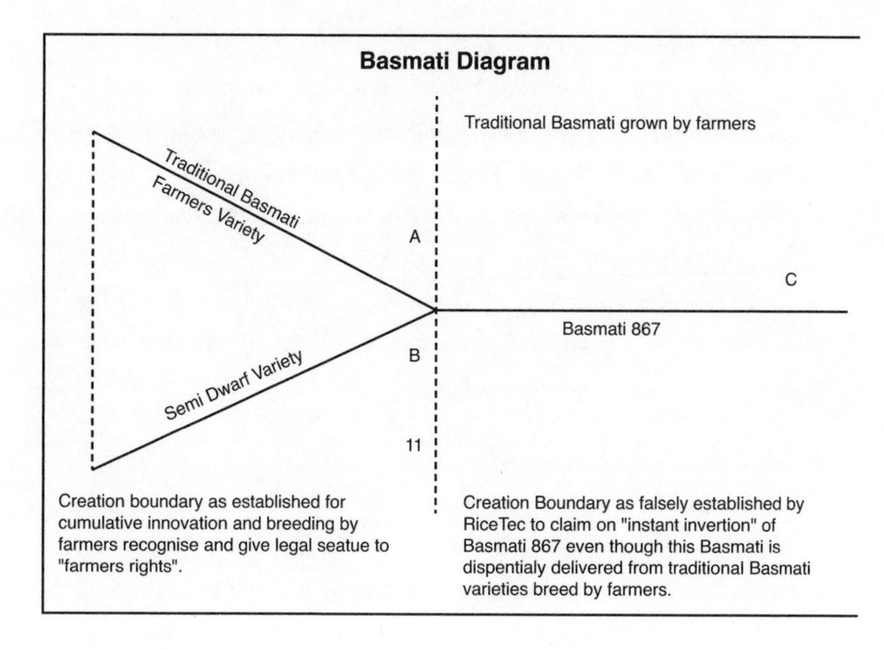

The attempted patent denied farmers' rights and instead of recognizing that the RiceTec basmati was derived from farmers' varieties, it created an artificial boundary at time t1 which allowed the false claim of "instant invention." Breeding rights in UPOV were also based on false "creation boundaries" which denied the prior art embodied in farmers' varieties. If farmers' rights were recognized, the false "invention" claim at time t1 did not hold, and an attempted patent claim by RiceTec could not be legitimately recognized.

Protest Letter from the Indian Farmers to the U.S. Ambassador

April 3, 1998

To,

The US Ambassador to India

American Embassy

New Delhi - 110 021

Dear Mr. Ambassador,
For several years now your government has been bullying India to accept the American doctrine of economic supremacy being forced through an unequal Intellectual Property Rights protection regime. Trying not to get into an unnecessary brawl, we have been ignoring the threats issued from time to time under what you call Special 301. What now comes as a shock is that bypassing all the norms associated with patenting, American companies are indulging in blatant loot of our indigenous resources and traditional knowledge.

You are familiar that patent is a very sensitive political issue in India because of the phenomenon of "biopiracy"–the patenting of indigenous knowledge as "inventions" by the Western scientists and companies, mainly from the United States. If newspaper reports are to be believed, even you have expressed surprise at the basmati patent drawn by an American trading company, RiceTec Inc.

The company now has the exclusive right to market aromatic rice and sell it under the trademark "basmati" rice. It will not only sell the branded "basmati" rice within the US, but also label all its rice exports. Needless to say, this will have a crippling impact on the basmati trade from India.

Today the wrath of the people of India, especially the farmers, has burst out against the laws and policies of the United States which have encouraged and perpetuated a trend of piracy of our biological resources, and intellectual property of Indian farmers, traditional health practitioner and tribal, etc. The phenomenon of biopiracy by the US corporations, institutions and organizations from the biodiversity rich countries particularly India has reached its pinnacle. One such wicked example is a patent given by USPTO on basmati rice lines and grains to Texas based RiceTec Inc. on September 2, 1997. This is obnoxious and can never be tolerated by the people of India.

The US have a history of robbing and plundering the biological and genetic wealth of the Third World countries and monopolizing the products made of them through their patent system. Your patent laws are made to facilitate biopiracy from the biodiversity rich countries and you, per organizations 'WTO' and 'World Bank', protect such piracy. In any car, American biotechnology, pharmaceutical, and seed industry is built upon systematic loot of Indian biological resources. Through a perfected system of steal, grab, and plunder, almost 90 percent of India's estimated 45,000 plant species and 75,000 animal species are being stored within the US. For your kind information, the US has not paid a single penny to India for the genetic resources misappropriated all these years.

United States accuse the people of India for pirating its intellectual property. Your Economic Espionage Act (1996), has, in effect, criminalized the natural development and exchange of knowledge between communities and countries. But the truth is that the US is pirating the intellectual property of the farmers, healers, tribals, fisher folk, etc., of Indian and other developing countries. The UNDP estimates that biological resources worth approximately US $5.4 billion are being stolen from the Third World countries every year. Considering that the US alone is taking 60 percent of the biological loot, aren't you stealing genetic wealth worth some US $3.2 billion every year? Do you pay on these resources? Isn't India one of the biggest free donors of genetic resources to America?

On the other hand, you claim a patent infringement, to the tune of US $120 million every year against India. But you will agree that the patent infringement is not even a fraction of the pirated biological resources which are now accepted to be a national property. America owes us and needs to start immediately paying us royalties on our resources.

Like all pirates do, the US government has also been dragging India at every given opportunity before the dispute settlement body of the World Trade Organization (WTO). This is a shameful act, and we strongly condemn the American behavior. More importantly, because you have been violating almost all international Conventions whether it is the ILO, Montreal Protocol, Climate Convention, or the Convention on Biological Diversity. Let us make it very clear that unless the United States first ratified the Convention on Biological Diversity, a bit that is held up with the Senate Foreign Relations Committee, we will ensure that India takes all democratic steps to protect its existing patent regime.

The moral and economic poverty of the US is being exhibited by the promotion and protection of piracy from the Third World. The WTO ruling against India and the persistent US pressure on the Indian government to change its patent laws is an assault on Indian democracy and an encouragement of all acts of biopiracy. It is the US Patent Law, and not Indian legislation, which is weak and needs to change. US Patent laws should recognize the traditional knowledge system of the biodiversity rich Third World countries in order to deny'novelty' and 'non obviousness' criterion to the patent claims based on such knowledge. We want to say, firmly, to change your patent laws first and stop exerting pressure on the government of India for changing its patent law. India is a sovereign country and the people of India will never tolerate such pressure tactics. They reject the ruling given by the WTO against India, which is criminal and protects the criminals.

The people of India have elected a sovereign government and we will not accept any sort of coercion and threat against this democratically elected government. If the US will not desist from such pressure tactics, the people of India will force the Indian government to exit the WTO.

We will never compromise on this great civilization, which has been based on the culture of sharing the abundance of the world and will continue to maintain this trend of sharing our biodiversity and knowledge. Bur we will never allow your culture impoverishment and greed to undermine our culture of abundance and sharing.

You and your colleagues have been using the official forums to brow-beat the Indian officials into submission. Since you believe in democratic traditions, at least you do it officially; we would like to tell you how we feel we are being wronged. We have had enough of your lies, lies, and damn lies. The peoples' protest today is a demonstration of the fact that the American and the WTO-TRIPS regime is biased and unequal, and is not suited to India's socio-economy, nor its national and public interests.

We all have gathered here in front of your Embassy to express our feelings and anguish on the patenting of basmati rice along with numerous other Indian plants and crops by the United States and its corporations. We request you that you persuade RiceTec Inc. to withdraw its basmati patent. We also request that you give instructions to your Patent and Trademark Office to avoid accepting patent claims based on the traditional heritage of the Third World countries in general and India in particular.

Research Foundation for Science, Technology and Ecology (RFSTE)
BharatiyaKisan Union (Ambavat)
Swadeshi JagaranManch

Navdanya
BharatiyaKisan Sangh
Hind Mazdoor Kisan Panchayats
Bharatya Janata KisanMorcha
Samajwadi Abhiyan
KisanAvam Swadeshi Chetna Abhiyan
Akhil Bharitya Gram PardhanSangthan
Gene Campaign
Forum of Biotechnology and food security
Bharatiya Mazdoor Sangh
Akhil BharaityaVidayarthi Parishad
Kisan Trust

Azadi BachaoAndolan
VidyaBharati
Swadeshi Science Movement
Laghu Udyog Bharati and others.

People's Victory

The citizens' movement against RiceTec had an impact as a result of which, on March 27, 2001, the USPTO initiated a full re-examination of RiceTec's patent and sent a 46-page letter to the RiceTec representatives rejecting all but three of the remaining 16 claims. RiceTec was also given a chance to respond. RiceTec sent its response to the USPTO on April 28, 2001 and reconsidered all the claims in light of the USPTO action and accepted the following:

- Cancel claims 1-3, 5–7, 10, 14, and 18–20;
- Amend Claim 12;
- Needless to mention that RiceTec had already withdrawn claims 4 and 15–17.

Therefore, only Claims 8, 9, and 11–13 of the basmati patent were left. RiceTec submitted that the remaining five satisfied all of the criteria for patentability and requested a quick response from USPTO in its favor. Quite surprisingly, RiceTec even renamed the title of the patent to: 'Rice Lines Bas 867', 'RT 1117', and 'RT 1121'.

On August 14, 2001, one day before India's Independence Day, history was made once more.

USPTO finally struck down Claims 1–7, 10, 14–20 of the basmati patent. USPTO also issued a 'Notice of Intent to Issue Re-examination Certificate' and (unfortunately) confirmed the patentability of the claims 8, 9, and 11 of the original patents relating to specific varieties bred by RiceTec, i.e., 'BAS 867', 'RT 1117', and 'RT 1121'. Claims 12 and 13 were also amended for a narrow scope.

We won the basmati biopiracy battle; and this victory was based more on citizens' actions than government action. It was the Indians in solidarity with the people worldwide who succeeded in freeing the Indian basmati from the clutches of monopoly, colonialism, and seed terrorism of corporations.

Notice Served by Jaiv Panchayats to Rice Tec in the Campaign Against Basmati Biopiracy

To,
CEO
Rice Tec Inc.
Schloss Vaduz
FL-9490 Vaduz
Liechtenstein

Dear Sir,
Your corporation, Rice Tec Inc., has pirated centuries of our indigenous knowledge and inventions by falsely claiming our collective, cumulative knowledge of basmati to be your invention in US Patent 5,663,484.

This patent is illegal, unethical, and immoral.

The patent violates our ethical fabric and ordre public since it treats the gifts from our venerated plants and our ancient knowledge systems as your creation and invention and hence your property. Our plants are sacred to us. Our plants are members of our extended Earth Family, VasudhaivaKutumbkam. Your patent is therefore unethical and immoral.

Your patent is also illegal and unjust because you have pirated and stolen our indigenous knowledge and claimed it as your invention.

Our Jaiv Panchayat, the local community structures, is the highest competent authority in matters related to the utilization of biodiversity, including dispute settlement arising from misuse and abuse of our knowledge systems and resources. Our JaivMaha Panchayat herewith gives you notice of the cancellation of the US Patent 5,663,484 based on the piracy of our indigenous knowledge.

We also serve notice upon you to present yourself before our Panchayat to apologize to all of the Indian people and seek forgiveness for your act of piracy and theft.

Please inform us immediately about when you will present yourself to the Dispute Settlement Panel of our Jaiv Panchayat. Your failure to appear before our community will force us to launch a campaign to boycott all products of your company.

We hope that you will withdraw your patent immediately and avoid both the trade and cultural war that you have unleashed.

The CBR, which is documented by all who use biodiversity, especially women and children, is owned by the community and maintained by the village community –Gram Sabha along with the Jaiv Panchayat Declaration. This ownership by the community gives the community the right to set the ethics and laws for biodiversity governance and management; including making the community the site of settling disputes (even the international disputes). In addition, since community needs and community rights also need to be recognized and taken into account in national policy formulation, the CBRs serve as the basis for building a national community biodiversity register.

All communities that have declared themselves as Jaiv Panchayats are in the process of preparing their Community Biodiversity Registers, with over 100 registers completed presently.

Syngenta's attempt at Rice Biopiracy of India's Rich Rice Heritage

Syngenta, the biotech giant which has now merged with ChemChina (2017), made an attempt to grab the precious collections of 22,972 varieties of paddy, which were part of India's rice diversity from Chhattisgarh in 2002. It had signed an MoU with the Indira Gandhi Agricultural University (IGAU) for access to Dr. Richaria's priceless collection of rice diversity which he had looked after as if the rice varieties were his own children.

Dr. Richharia was the rice sage of India. He is the inspiration behind all agricultural biodiversity conservation movements in India, including Navdanya. He had collected thousands of rice varieties first in the Cuttack Rice Research Institute (which is older than IRRI) and then the Raipur Research Institute (now called the Indira Gandhi Agricultural University).

This news (Dainik Bhasker, November 11, 2002) came soon after the news that Syngenta was going to be on the board of the Consultative Group on International Agricultural Research (CGIAR).

Syngenta on the Board of Global Gene Banks: A Recipe for Biopiracy

The Consultative Group for International Agriculture Research (CGIAR) is a body based in the World Bank which controls a network of 16 international agriculture research centers which coordinates National Agriculture Research Systems and gene banks. At a meeting in the Philippines chaired by Ian John of the World Bank, who was also the chair of CGIAR, Syngenta Foundation was co-opted as a Board Member. A biopirate now had full access to the biodiversity held in the gene banks of the world. This is an excellent example of Public-Private partnerships promoted by the World Bank.

The gene banks and research centers under the CGIAR include:

- CIMMYT (International Maize and Wheat Improvement Center) in Mexico City, Mexico
- IRRI (International Rice Research Institute) in Los Banos, Philippines
- CIP (International Potato Research Institute) in Lima, Peru.
- ICRISAT (International Crops Research Institute for the Semi-
  arid Tropics) in Patancheru, India
- CIAT (International Center for Tropical Agriculture) in Coli, Columbia
- IFPRI (International Food Policy Research Institute) in Washington, D.C., US

- ISNAR (International Service for Agricultural Research) in Hague, Netherlands
- IPGRI (International Plant Genetic Resources Institute) in Rome, Italy
- WARDA (West African Rice Development Association) in
Bonake, Cote d'Ivoire
- IITA (International Institute of Tropical Agriculture) Ibadan,
- Nigeria
- ILRI (International Livestock Research Institute) in Nairobi, Kenya
- ICARDA (International Center for Agricultural Research in Dry Areas) in Aleppo, Syria
- IWMI (International Water Management Institute) in Battaramulla, Sri Lanka
- ICLARM (World Fish Center) in Penang, Malaysia
- CIFOR (Center for International Forestry Research) in Bogor, Indonesia

The International Rice Research Institute (IRRI) was set up in 1960 by the Rockefeller and Ford Foundations, nine years after the establishment of a premier Indian Institute, the Central Rice Research Institute (CRRI) in Cuttack. The Cuttack Institute was working on rice research based on indigenous knowledge and genetic resources, a strategy clearly in conflict with the American-controlled strategy of IRRI.

Under international pressure, Dr. Richharia, then director of CRRI, was removed when he resisted handing over his collection of rice germplasm to IRRI, and when he asked for restraint in the hurried introduction of High Yield Varieties (HYV) from IRRI.

The Madhya Pradesh Government gave a small stipend to Dr. Richharia the ex-director of CRRI so that he could continue his work at the Madhya Pradesh Rice Research Institute (MPRRI) at Raipur. On this shoestring budget, he conserved nearly 20,000 indigenous rice varieties *in situ* in India's rice bowl in Chattisgarh. Later the MPRRI, which was doing pioneering work in developing a high yielding strategy based on the indigenous knowledge of the Chhattisgarh tribals, was also closed down due to pressure from the World Bank (which was linked to IRRI through CGIAR) because MPRRI had reservations about sending its collection of germplasm to IRRI.

Much of the rice germplasm had been painstakingly collected from local farmers by Dr. Richharia, who had devoted his lifetime to the conservation of local rice varieties. Dr. Richharia's vision was to disseminate all appropriate varieties selected from the collection to farmers across Chhattisgarh through decentralized research and extension networks with rice farmers and scientists as equal partners in development with the ownership of these varieties vesting with farmers.

Syngenta's getting access to Dr. Richharia's collections, and simultaneously controlling the World Bank run International Agricultural Research system (which was getting patents on rice), was part of the MNC's strategy for total control on rice which was most of Asia's staple food.

When this news became public several groups working on people's rights to natural resources from Chattisgarh and outside firmly opposed this deal between Syngenta and IGAU. Several peoples' organizations came together, and a mass-based agitation was started on December 3–the Bhopal Gas Tragedy Day.

In addition, the Chhattisgarh Seed Satyagarha was launched on December 10, 2002, the International Human Rights Day. Thousands of workers, peasants, women, and youth from all over Chhattisgarh began to protest to protect their sovereignty for survival, sustenance of human community, and to re-assert their rights over the rare varieties of rice seeds.

Peoples' victory and challenges

The mass agitation by the peoples' organization, farmers' unions and civil liberty groups, women's groups, students' groups and biodiversity conservation movements against Syngenta and IGAU bore result and Syngenta called off the deal. But this was just one of the many battles for the recovery of the commons.

News Article Excerpts

The Institute of Science in Society

Date: July 15, 2002

Patents on Life Patently Undermine Food Security

"...TRIPS has opened the floodgates to corporate patenting on life. In November 2000, according to research commissioned by *The Guardian*, patents were pending or granted on more than 500,000 genes and partial gene sequences in living organisms.

TRIPS has also facilitated patenting over plant varieties (varieties of plants developed by humans through traditional and non-traditional breeding), as Article 27.3 (b) stipulates that plant varieties should be protected, either by patents, a *sui generis* (unique) system, or a combination of both.

By 2001, just six corporations–Aventis, Dow, Du Pont, Mitsui, Monsanto and Syngenta–controlled 98% of the global market for patented GM crops, 70% of the global pesticide market and 30% of the global seed market. The same six corporations owned 60.8% of patents granted on rice, 70.8% of patents granted on wheat, 71% of patents granted on maize, 76% of patents granted on soybean, and 46.7% of patents granted on sorghum. These are all staples that supply most of the calories for the poor...."

The Hindu Business Line, New Delhi

Date: December 11, 2002

Syngenta Pulls out of Research Collaboration with IGaU

New Delhi, December 10 (PTI) –Stung by criticism, the seed giant Syngenta India Limited has pulled out of the controversial research collaboration with the Indira Gandhi Agricultural University (IGAU) in Raipur, a company official said today.

Pawan Malik, president of seeds division of Syngenta said the discussions with IGAU were inconclusive and the proposal has been dropped.

"We are very disappointed to see the misleading and false accusations that were made [against the collaboration]," he said.

The collaboration would have given the company commercial rights to over 19,000 strains of local rice cultivars held by the university.

The rice varieties had been painstakingly gathered by the agricultural scientist R. H. Richharia in the 1970s. In exchange, IGAU would have received an undisclosed amount of money and royalties from Syngenta.

Environmentalists and some scientists opposed the deal on the ground that Richharia's collection is a national wealth and not private property of the university and that opening the database to a multinational company is a sellout.

Malik made a statement that his company and the university were looking at a collaboration to work together to develop new rice hybrids that meet specific farmers' needs in that part of the country.

"We have collaborative research agreements with over 100 organizations and universities in different parts of the world," he said.

Though its deal with IGAU has fizzled out, Syngenta is already working in collaboration with many institutions in India including the Vasantdada Sugar Institute, Pune, G. B. Pant Institute of Agriculture and Technology, Pantnagar, and the KonkanKrishiVidyapeeth, Dapoli.

Malik pointed out that rice is one of the crops covered under the International Treaty on Plant Genetic Resources for Food and Agriculture, which "aims to facilitate access to genetic resources and benefit sharing."

He said Syngenta was committed to comply with the principles of this treaty, but it was too bad the deal with IGAU did not work out.

Ashok B. Sharma, *Indian Express*, New Delhi

Need to Learn Lesson From IGKV-Syngenta Deal

The proposed collaboration of the multinational Syngenta's subsidiary, Syngenta India, with the Raipur-based Indira Gandhi KrishiVishwavidyalaya (IGKV) for developing new rice hybrids from the collected local germplasms held in the University's gene bank was the center of controversy since last month. The controversy got finally defused when on December 10, Syngenta India president, Pawan Malik (seeds division), finally told the media that his company was no longer interested in the proposed collaboration.

Ten days later, Indian Council of Agricultural Research (ICAR) Director-General Dr. Panjab Singh said, "No such MoU was signed between IGKV and Syngenta India and there was no question of the company 'pulling out' of the collaboration." He also said, "Even if the IGKV intends to have any collaboration with Syngenta India, it cannot hand over the collected germplasm. The ownership of the collect germplasm rests with the National Biodiversity Board and the state biodiversity board.

What is clear from the news appearing in the language media from November 9 is that a fifteen-point MoU was drafted which was then reduced to a twelve-point MoU but was not signed by either of the parties.

There are reports that the local press in Raipur insisted IGKV vice chancellor Dr VK Patil, on many occasions, to divulge the details of the MoU which he did not oblige.

Dr. Patil may be right in the sense that an MoU cannot be made public before it is signed by the concerned parties. However, Dr. Patil should have taken care to address the concern raised by NGOs and civil rights activities over the possible handing over of 19,095 strains of local rice cultivars painstakingly collected by the late legendary agro-scientist, Dr. R. H. Richharia and his team.

This is definitely an issue of public concern as genetic resources held in gene banks are public property, rather the property of the local community.

Dr. Patil's way of handling the situation created several doubts in the media, which still remain unclear, as to what actually transpired between the two parties. However, Mr. Pawan Malik was frank in his statement that his company and the University were looking at a collaborative project to develop new rice hybrids that would meet specific needs of farmers in that part of the country. He also pointed out that rice is one of the crops covered under the International Treaty on Plant Genetic Resources for Food and Agriculture (ITPGRFA), which aims to facilitate access to genetic resources and benefit sharing.

Incidentally, this happened at a time when Parliament was gearing up to pass the Biodiversity Bill which is 'intended to protect bioresources' and stipulate benefit-sharing; and India is still negotiating with the European Union to gain access to UPOV without withdrawing the rights given to farmers to save seeds for the next season in the Plant Variety Protection & Farmers' Rights Act. The ITPGRA is also likely to come into force soon.

Now, it is necessary to discuss what lessons should be learnt from this mysterious fractured deal between IGKV and Syngenta India. ICAR DG Dr. Panjab Singh is curt in saying, "We should do adequate homework before entering into such a deal and see that our interests are not sacrificed." The UK-based Intermediate Technology Development Group (ITDG) food security policy advisor Patrick Mulvany, writing in AgBioIndia bulletin, said, "We must all remain on-guard–the ITPGRFA is threatened!" Adding later that ITPGRFA, to which India is a signatory, still has ambiguities in its agreed text and these can only be resolved once the governing body is formed after it comes into force.

Mr. Mulvany said that these ambiguities relate to whether or not IPRs can be taken on the genetic resources in the multi-lateral system (MLS) i.e., those thirty-five genera of food crops, including rice, wheat, maize, potato and twenty-nine forages covered by the MLS in its Annex 1.

He said that the UK government's Commission on IPRs took advantage of the ambiguity in words 'in the form received from MLS' in Article 12.3 (d) of the treaty and said that patents can be allowed on modifications to the materials received from MLS. "This ambiguity needs to be removed," he said.

Dr. Suman Sahai, of the Gene Campaign, has criticized the Biodiversity Bill recently passed by Parliament for the lack of clarity on IPRs.

Thus, it is clear that we need to learn lessons from the mysterious fractured deal between IGKV and Syngenta India and strengthen our laws to protect our valuable bioresources from any possible biopiracy.

ETC Group, News Release

March 12, 2001 & January 31, 2002

Syngenta having largest Arsenal of Terminator Patents

The ETC group (formerly RAFI) announced today that the biotechnology industry continues to aggressively pursue the development of genetically modified seeds that are engineered for sterility. "We have uncovered two new patents on Terminator technology," said Hope Shand, Research Director of ETC group. "One patent is held by Dupont (the world's largest seed corporation) and the other is held by Syngenta (the world's largest agrochemical corporation)," said Shand.

Syngenta, the world's largest agribusiness firm, was formed on November 13, 2000 with the merger of AstraZeneca and Novartis. The next day the company won its newest Terminator patent, US Patent 6,147,282 for "method of controlling the fertility of a plant." (The patent was issued to Novartis–but the company's intellectual property goes to Syngenta.) With *pro forma* 1999 sales of US $7 billion, Syngenta is the world's largest agrochemical enterprise, and the third largest seed corporation.

Syngenta holds the largest arsenal of Terminator patents and controls at least six Terminator patents and a host of new patents on genetically modified plants with defective immune systems.

In 1999, Zeneca's R&D director wrote that Terminator was "one piece of technology we did not want to take forward, and the project was stopped in 1992." Why, then, has the company continued to file for and win Terminator patents since 1992? (The newest Syngenta patent issued on May 8, 2001. The application date was March 22, 1997, long after Zeneca claims it stopped the project.)

Dupont (Pioneer Hi-Bred International), US Patent 6,297,426, issued October 2, 2001 with the title: 'Methods of Mediating Female Fertility in Plants'.

The patent describes the identification and inactivation of a native gene critical to female fertility. The gene is cloned, linked to an inducible promoter, and inserted into the plant. The result is a plant that is functionally female sterile with inducible female fertility. (Note: although the patent describes the use of this technology for facilitating production of hybrid seed, this approach involves chemical control of female fertility, and its extension to other seed lines. ETC group considers this a Terminator-type technology.)

Syngenta (Zeneca), US Patent 6,228,643 was issued on May 8, 2001 with title: Promoter. The patent describes a new promoter, isolated from rapeseed, and the control of plant traits (including fertility) that can be inactivated and restored by application of a chemical inducer. In one embodiment, the seeds will not germinate unless sprayed with a chemical inducer.

Syngenta's new 'Terminator Patent', US Patent 6,147,282, is the latest in a series of Terminator patents won by Novartis. The patent describes a complex system for chemical control of a plant's fertility. The application of a chemical inducer can be used to either abolish or restore a plant's fertility.

Norfolk Genetic Information Network (NGIN)

USAID & Syngenta

"... George Bush has increased the US aid budget specifically for the purpose of encouraging the uptake of biotechnology. Earlier this year, USAID launched a $100m program for bringing biotechnology to developing countries. USAID's 'training and awareness raising programs' will, its website reveals, provide companies such as Syngenta, Pioneer Hi-Bred, and Monsanto with opportunities for 'technology transfer'. Monsanto, in turn, provides financial support for USAID...."

Norfolk Genetic Information Network
July 2002

Welcome to the Revolving Door

Andrew Bennett, who was one of the leading critics of Prajateerpu within DFID, has joined the agri-chemical giant Syngenta–the world's second largest promoter of mechanized, high-input, anti-poor agriculture.

Until recently, he was Director of Rural Livelihoods and Environment for the British Department of International Development in London and a principal advisor to government ministers on policy and programs for the improvement of rural livelihoods, better natural resources management, environmental protection, sustainable development, and research in international development.

The revolving door between DFID and Syngenta, along with the British environment Minister Eliot Morley's recent admission that UK government policy was being heavily influenced by trans-national GM corporations such as Syngenta, raises questions as to the extent to which DFID policy on GM and their critique of Prajateerpu is being dictated by commercial interests rather than the priorities of the poor.

Syngenta provided a witness, Dr. Partha Dasgupta and observers at last year's Prajateerpu hearings. The marginal farmers were particularly critical of Dr. Dasgupta's claims for GM.

"...In an airless conference room, a woman called Anjamma was asked, through an interpreter: "If this project goes ahead, what does she think she will do?" "There will be nothing for us to do," Anjamma replied, "other than to drink pesticide and die."

In the West, leaving the land might sound like liberation, but to Anjamma it spells only destitution. ...Anjamma isn't speaking out of ignorance. She was one of 12 farmers who were chosen to be part of a citizens' jury set up by a couple of non-governmental organizations to scrutinize the development plans. That meant that she has sat through days of evidence from GM-seed company executives, from politicians, from academics, from aid donors. That was why her certainty was all the more impressive." [The report on Prajateerpu, the Indian Citizen's Jury process that rejected GM crops and the Vision 2020 development project for Andhra Pradesh–funded by DFID, the UK's Department for International Development is available online through the International Institute for Environment and Development].

Monsanto's Attempted Biopiracy of Indian Wheat

Monsanto's patent (EP 0445929 B1) claimed to have "invented" wheat plants derived from a traditional Indian Variety, and products made from the soft milling traits that the traditional Indian wheat provides. On August 5, 2003, Research Foundation for Science and Technology and Ecology (RFSTE) along with Greenpeace and Bread for the World (Germany) launched a campaign against Monsanto's biopiracy of Indian wheat.

Monsanto repeated the biopiracy pattern which was earlier attempted by RiceTec in its claim to have 'invented' Indian basmati.

In reply to a Parliamentary Question (dated July 21, 2003) on the Monsanto wheat Biopiracy, the Ministry of Agriculture replied:

> *"M/s plant Breeding International, a Unilever company which was acquired by Monsanto in 1998, has obtained a patent for a new variety of wheat designed for use in Europe. This variety incorporates some characteristics of the Nap Hal Land race of Wheat from India. The Neo Hal Land race is not covered by the European Patent and continues to be available to Indian farmers and researchers."*

The Minister's reply indicated that the Government of India was not planning to take any action against biopiracy and was in fact legitimizing it. The reply also accepted two flaws in the patent claim: firstly, European Law did not allow patenting of plant varieties. Secondly, the reply accepted "Nap Hal" as a name of a land race in India, even though no farmer in India would name a traditional variety 'Nap Hal'.

Naphal means 'no fruits' – no farmers variety would be named as such.

Plants claimed as inventions in Monsanto's patent were essentially derived varieties of traditional Indians wheat referred to in the patent as 'Nap Hal' available as accession number 1,362 from the AERC Institute of Plat Science Research, Norwich, UK. In Hindi the word would mean that which gives no fruit. Nap Hal was not an Indian name for an indigenous Wheat variety. It could have been a name of Monsanto's 'Terminator Seeds'. The vernacular names of wheat varieties are *khani, mundia, rotta, sita, kathia, jandi* and many others. Breeders gave the wheat variety names in accordance with the breeding centers where they worked. "Nap Hal" was evidently a distortion of Niphad. If the British could turn Hindus into "Gentoos" and Mumbai into "Bombay", Niphad could easily be distorted to Nap Hal. Niphad was a place in Maharastra, which had a crop breeding center. Varieties selected and bred at Pusa were called 'Pusa-4', 'Pusa-6', etc. Varieties were named New Pusa (NP) when the agriculture station shifted from Pusa (in Bihar) to IARI Delhi. Those bred at Niphad had the nomenclature Niphad; P-4 / NP-4 was an Indian Variety which is a selection from local "mundia" found in the UP hills (now the Uttaranchal State), Gujarat, and the Deccan.

According to Dr. B.P. Pal, one of India's leading wheat breeders, it was the government's duty to investigate which variety has been incorrectly recorded as Nap Hal and correct the nomenclature appropriately. Wheat was the most documented crop in India since formal breeding of wheat started more than a century ago in 1905.

NP-4 or Pusa-4 / Niphad 4 was a beardless variety with felted, white plumes with gains of an amber color. Sir Albert Howard (known as the founder of modern organic farming, the author of the *Agricultural Testament* in whose honor RFSTE/Navdanya had organized the annual Howard Memorial Lectures on Nonviolent Agriculture on Gandhi Jayanti on October 2, his wife G.L.C Howard and Habibur Rehman Khan selected pure lines NP-4 (Pusa-4) from the mundia land in 1905. "Mundia" combined higher yield potential, early maturity with superior grain quality features. As an ICAR report stated "it soon crossed the national boundaries and was adopted in many countries. The variety won prizes in several international grain exhibitions as one of the best grain quality wheat during 1916–1920." This was how it must have entered the UK collections and gotten recorded under the distorted name 'Nap Hal'.

Indian wheats have travelled widely since 1873, with the opening of the Suez Canal and removing export restrictions. Indian wheat was so important a crop for the British Empire that an important Resolution of the Government of India no. I-39-50 of March 14, 1877 was passed on the wheat question requiring the Governor General to provide all information on Indian wheat including "*local names for the varieties of wheat cultivated and three description in English.*" More than 1000 wheat samples in bags of two pounds each were sent to the India Office, examined by Forbes Watson, and a detailed report was provided to the Secretary of State. It was the traits, not the name which was the basis of our challenge of biopiracy.

Nap Hal was extremely unusual in lacking two high molecular weight (HMW) subunits of gluten coded by the 'x' and 'y' genes, which refers as the "Glu-D1 double null" trait. The HMW sub-units of glutenin, which make up only about 6–10 percent of the gluten (wheat protein) content of wheat was the key component in conferring elasticity and dough mixing stability. Due to the lack of HMW glutenin in Nap Hal, the dough became easily hydrable as compared to other wheat. It produced very weak inelastic dough which was highly extensible. This lent advantage in making of semi-sweet biscuits, non-fermented crackers, wafers, and food ingredients. They were made better as the flour formed dough with less water (when Sodium Metabisulphite or SMS was not used). The production of a strain of wheat variety Galahad-7 claimed by Monsanto compromised of crossing a commonly grown soft wheat variety "Galahad" with a "Sicco" line containing the "Nap Hal" Glu-D1 double null wheat strain (Nap-Hal-Sicco). The Galahad-7 was essentially derived from native Indian wheat. Crossing was an obvious step in breeding and violated the criteria of 'novelty' and 'non-obviousness' necessary for patentability.

Even though plants are not an invention, the first statement in Monsanto's patent stated that "this invention relates to plants and to products derived there from." In this case the plant was essentially derived from the plant which had collectively evolved and had been conserved over millennia. Just like in the cases of neem, haldi, and basmati; the patent, in effect, pirated the collective cumulative innovation of Indian farmers and claimed the piracy as an invention. The traits of India's wheat, which were being claimed by Monsanto as its invention were traits which had evolved through India's food culture and cuisine based on 'rotis' and 'chapattis'. The patent was thus a piracy not just of millennia of breeding by Indian farmers, but also of millennia of innovation in food qualities.

Gluten wheat protein plays an important role in the texture of chapattis and other food preparations made from wheat. The gluten content of wheat varies from about 9–13 percent. The hard-milling varieties contain more gluten than the soft milling one which is more suitable for chapattis. Soft Milling Wheat is not an Invention–it is our daily diet.

For thousands of years we have eaten soft milling wheat appropriate to our food culture. Ignoring the daily diet of one fifth of humanity, Monsanto arrogantly claimed:

> *"No wheat varieties are yet available commercially which are soft milling and from which dough with low or very low elasticity can be prepared without either chemical treatment or the use of carefully controlled conditions (e.g., low temperature) during the preparation of dough. The need to maintain critical conditions during dough preparation was obviously a serious constraint on manufacturers. The need for chemical free treatment of the flour usually conducted with sodium metabolism (SMS) would be avoided. If possible, especially in view of the current consumer pressure for foodstuffs that are 'chemically treated', it is generally recognized that the biscuit making industry would be an avid user of SMS unless there was any commercially viable alternative."*

This 'alternative' was available widely in India in our daily food. This was the alternative which Monsanto attempted to pirate. Monsanto's claim covered wheat plants derived from Indian wheat varieties and products made from soft milling wheat.

The patent had to be revoked because it was not an invention. Furthermore, it also needed to be revoked because with an exclusive right to grow wheat with low gluten and produce high value product with it, Monsanto could have extended those rights to India under the Patent Cooperation Treaty (PCT) and then charged royalties from farmers who grew traditional wheat varieties. Even if the patent was not recognized in India, Monsanto's biopiracy patent in Europe and the US prevented India from deriving benefits from the growing market in the US and Europe for chemical free and low gluten wheat products.

On January 27, 2004 The Research Foundation for Science, Technology and Ecology along with Greenpeace and Bharat Krishak Samaha filed a petition at the EPO challenging the patent rights given to Monsanto for revoking the patent.

Biopiracy Victory of Indian Wheat

The third victory against biopiracy for Navdanya came in 2004 when the European Patent Office in Munich revoked Monsanto's patent on the Indian wheat variety, 'Nap Hal'.

ConAgra and the Biopiracy of Atta (Flour)

After neem, turmeric, and basmati, the US corporations attempted to patent atta (wheat flour) chakkis through the US Patent 6,098,905, granted to ConAgra on August 8, 2000.

This "novel" patent was very broad and related to a "novel" method for producing wheat flour or atta. The patent covered all subsequent changes, variations, modifications, and other uses and applications which did not depart from the spirit and scope of the invention.

The method which has been patented was the familiar method used in thousands of attachakkis (roller flourmills) throughout South Asia.

ConAgra's method included:

"Passing an amount of wheat through a device designed to crack the wheat so as to produce an amount of cracked wheat, followed by passing the cracked wheat through at least two smooth rolls designed to grind the cracked wheat into flour, with the smooth roll importantly grinding the wheat to a smaller particle size and shearing the wheat to cause starch damage in the finished atta flour. The atta flour will have an amount of starch damage equal to between about 13% and about 18% and an amount of ash equal to at least 1%."

There was not much difference in the theft techniques or biopiracy methods of W. R. Grace, RiceTec, ConAgra, or any other multinational corporations. All these corporates simply copied indigenously developed processes and knowledge of the Third World communities and took monopoly rights through the biased patent system.

Since the ConAgra patent also covered the 'spirit and scope' of the invention, any modification and variation in the invention was also patented under the scope of the patent. ConAgra, in one broad sweep, ensured that the wheat flour mills in whole of South Asia came under its monopoly control over the technology. This was mainly to capture the mammoth atta market in India.

Additionally, they expected the market for wheat flour in India, Pakistan, Bangladesh, and Indonesia to grow. ConAgra clarified that its patent was not meant for India but for the US market, and so thousands of existing roller and stone grinding mills would have nothing to fear. This was exactly what RiceTec, which drew the controversial patent on basmati rice, had claimed. But the fact was, ConAgra had already established a chain of flour mills in India and had started the procurement of wheat which would only cater to the Indian market.

Atta is the most essential staple of millions of people of India. It nourishes the people and provides them livelihoods–from the crores of farmers who grow the wheat, to over 3,000,000 local, small chakkis who grind the wheat for the consumers to meet their special needs of quality and taste.

Wheat is traditionally processed in small chakkis–stone grinding mills. These may be small mills used by women in the house, or larger water or electrically run machines used by the local miller to meet the needs of the community. The selection of wheat to be ground, getting it ground to the exact specifications needed for the various preparations, storing and using wheat is still a major preoccupation even in many middle-class homes.

The local miller is one of the most important members of the community, advising on the qualities of various wheats, processing the wheat for the families, storing it, and selling it in smaller quantities to those who cannot afford to stock a large supply.

ConAgra's patent on chakkis would have had a disastrous impact on these small chakkis. Millions of people would have lost their livelihood.

Atta Monopoly: ConAgra to takeover small chakkis

ConAgra, was not a new multinational corporation for India. Before taking patent on attachakkis, ConAgra had already established its base with the help of Indian companies and Government agencies to capture the atta market, especially the packed atta market. With the help of the patent, ConAgra would have gotten rid of all the competitors including millions of small chakkis, which in effect would create a dent in the profit margin of the food giant.

ConAgra had an Indian subsidiary called Agro Tech Foods Ltd (ATFL), which was formerly known as ITC Agro-Tech Ltd (ITCA). ConAgra, a $24 billion food major, had acquired 51.3 percent stake in ITCA, through CAG-Tech Ltd, Mauritius, from ITC Ltd. (CAG- Tech was a joint venture between ConAgra and Tiger Oats, Africa). ITCA was incorporated in 1987, the name of the company was changed to Agro-Tech Foods Ltd (ATFL) with effect from June 29, 2000. The company entered into an agreement with ConAgra for supplying food ingredients. Subsequently ITCs stake in ITCA declined to 17 percent.

In 1995, ITCA acquired the edible oil brands from ITC for a consideration of Rs. 25 crore. In 2000–2001, the company made a turn-around and, for the first time since its acquisition, posted a net profit of Rs 1.9 crore. ConAgra was confident that its Indian subsidiary ATFL would become a $500-million company within the next five years and expected ATFL's sales to grow at a rate of 20 percent per annum.

ConAgra was also keen on exporting processed food ingredients from India. The multinational company had already identified a few Indian producers for a strategic alliance or a marketing tie-up in this regard.

ConAgra's President and Chief Operating Officer, Mr. Larry A. Carter, told *Business Line* that the US-based global player was looking at India as its "primary business opportunity in Asia over the next decade." He felt that India had a better climate than China for private enterprise.

According to him, the processing technology already existed in India. Hence, there was no need for ConAgra to bring in the technical knowhow. But the technology had to be adapted to the product that was privatized in different parts of the world.

With regard to Indian operations, he said that ConAgra was primarily looking at basic foods. ITCA had ventured into branded grocery product segment with the launch of new products under some of the leading brands in ConAgra's portfolio. Atta (wheat flour) and dried green peas had been launched under the Healthy World umbrella. Healthy World Atta was "successfully test marketed" in the South and had been extended to the rest of the country from January 2001. Apart from consumer packs, AFTL proposed to sell its Healthy World Atta (wheat flour) to bakeries in bags of 25 kg and 50 kg. The company had also been looking at opportunities in snacks business.[2]

To diversify into the trading of value-added wheat, ATFL entered into collaboration with the Madhya Pradesh State Agro Industries Development Corporation. ATFL had launched 'Healthy World Protein Power Atta', which was priced at a 10 percent premium over the regular product. The brand was test-marketed in Bangalore, before an all-India launch. The company was setting up ware houses in Indore, Bhopal, and Itarsi to grade and store at least 10,000 tons of locally grown durum wheat varieties like Sharbati. After getting permission from the state for direct procurement from farmers, Agro-Tech started buying sharbati wheat for trading in both local and in international markets.

Through ATFL, ConAgra set up a new 1,000 tons-per-month milling plant in Indore to cater to western India's markets of Maharashtra, Gujarat, and Rajasthan. The company already has plants in Chennai and Delhi for producing atta, and has identified their main areas of future operations: basic foods, edible oils, commodity sourcing, and exports.

Monsanto's Biopiracy of Indian Melons

In May 2011, the US company Monsanto was awarded a European patent on conventionally bred melons (EP 1 962 578). These melons, which originally stemmed from India, had a natural resistance to certain plant viruses. Using conventional breeding methods, this type of resistance was introduced to other melons and was patented as a Monsanto 'invention'. The actual plant disease, Cucurbit Yellow Stunting Disorder Virus (CYSDV), had been spreading through North America, Europe, and North Africa for several years. The Indian melon, which conferred resistance to this virus, was registered in international seed banks as PI 313970. With this new patent, Monsanto could block access to all breeding material inheriting the resistance derived from the Indian melon. The patent would also discourage future breeding efforts and the development of new melon varieties; needless to say, melon breeders and farmers would also be severely restricted by the patent. At the same time, it was already known that further breeding was necessary to produce melons that were actually protected against the plant virus.

DeRuiter, a well-known seed company in the Netherlands,

originally developed the melons using plants designated PI 313970–a non-sweet melon from India. Monsanto acquired DeRuiter in 2008 and came to own the patent. The patent was opposed by several organizations in 2012.

Stopping Monsanto's Piracy of Rajasthan's Agriculture

In 2012, a MoU was signed between Monsanto and the Rajasthan Government. Under the MoU, public resources would be given away freely to Monsanto at a subsidy and Monsanto's IPR monopolies would be protected. This was an MOU where Monsanto takes all and the public system gives all.

Under pressure from the Prime Minister's Office–which in turn was under the pressure of the White House because of signing the US-India Agriculture Agreement, on the board of which Monsanto sits–the States were signing MoUs with seed corporations to privatize our rich and diverse genetic heritage. The Government of Rajasthan signed seven MOU's with Monsanto, Advanta, DCM-Sriram, Kanchan Jyoti Agro Industries, PHI Seeds Pvt. Ltd, Krishidhan Seeds, and J.K. Agri Genetics. While what was being undertaken was a great seed robbery under the supervision of the State, it was being called a 'Private Public Partnership' (PPP).

The MoU, with Monsanto, focused on maize, cotton, and vegetables (including hot pepper, tomato, cabbage, cucumber, cauliflower, and watermelon). Monsanto bought up Seminis, the world's largest seed company. Monsanto controls the cotton seed market in India and globally. Monsanto controls 97 percent of the worldwide Maize market, and 63.5 percent of the GM cotton market. And Dupont has had to initiate antitrust investigations in the US because of Monsanto's growing seed monopoly. Thus, the MoU would have deepened Monsanto's monopoly over seed supply.

The MoU violated farmers' rights by handing over the genetic wealth of farmers to corporations without the consent of farmers. It stated:

"Monsanto's proprietary tools, techniques, technology, knowhow and intellectual property rights with respect to the crops shall remain the property of Monsanto although utilized in any of the activities outlined as part of the MOU."

While public resources would have been freely given away to Monsanto as a subsidy, Monsanto's IPR monopolies would have been protected. It was clearly an MOU for privatization of our seed and genetic wealth, our knowledge and a violation OF farmers' rights. The seed supplies that the agriculture universities were handing over to Monsanto were neither the property of the state, nor of Monsanto; rather, they were, and are, the common property of farming communities.

That is why Navdanya started the campaign for cancellation of the MoUs on August 9, 2011, also known as: "Quit India Day" (the day 13 years ago when we started the Monsanto Quit India campaign), where Dr. Vandana Shiva and the Navdanya team undertook a seed sovereignty yatra in Rajasthan saving seeds and meeting with local groups, scientists, and government representatives to intensify the call for the cancellation of the MoUs.

The announcement of the cancellation was yet another success of Navdanya, the seed sovereignty movement, the seed keepers of Rajasthan, NGO's, and independent scientists who worked together to roll back the power of Monsanto and the seed MNC's.

A similar issue came to the fore on April 25, 2012 when the Gujarat government decided to withdraw Monsanto's proprietary seeds from various ongoing government projects including Project Sunshine.

The hijack of the seed supply by corporations like Monsanto threatens the very survival of our peasants and our biodiversity. The costly experiment of Bt cotton and hybrid corn that Monsanto has undertaken is increasing the economic and ecological vulnerability of farmers without bringing them new benefits.

The future of the seed, the future of the farmers, and the future of food lies in the conservation of biodiversity of our seeds. Seed sovereignty is the foundation of food sovereignty. The Great Seed Robbery threatens both and it must be stopped.

Biopiracy of Brinjal

The development of Bt brinjal by Monsanto and its Indian partner Mahyco is another classic example of biopiracy. The company had accessed nine Indian varieties of brinjal to develop their genetically modified vegetables without prior permission from the NBA or the relevant State and local boards. This was a violation of the Biological Diversity Act, 2002. The Environmental Support Group (ESG) lodged a formal complaint with the Karnataka Biodiversity Board on February 15, 2010. Soon, the Government put a moratorium on Bt brinjal on health and safety grounds.[3]

Biopiracy of Climate Resilient Crops

For millennia farmers have innovated and evolved varieties with unique properties. Farmers' innovation has stressed on breeding for climate resilience and for conservation of biodiversity. Giant corporations which have destroyed biodiversity by promoting monocultures and uniformity started claiming farmers' collective, cumulative innovation as their invention through the patenting of climate resilient traits. The petitioner was conserving farmers' varieties since 1987. Once again, the corporations attempted to pirate the collective innovation of farmers in breeding crops that are resilient to droughts, floods and salinity with the biotechnology industry spreading the misconception that without genetic engineering we will not be able to evolve crops with climate resilience.

Piracy of Medicinal Plants, Recipes and Soil Organisms

The patent on neem, *Phyllanthus niruri,* and Haldi represented only the tip of the biopiracy iceberg. Other Ayurvedic drugs, e.g.,

Arjuna, Chandan, Brahmi, Tulsi, Ashwagandha, Aadabahar, and other indigenous plants, such as: *Boswellia serrata, Euphorbia hirta, Impatiens balsammina, Jatropha cruces, Melia azadirachta, Phyllanthus emblica, Punicagranatum, Quisqualisindica, Ricinus communuis,* and *Sapiumsebiferum* had already been selected for patenting in the US and other industrialized countries.

The latest addition to the list of patents to be filed in India was Nestle India's process patents on vegetable pal, parboiled rice, and cooked cereals. The Swiss based transnational had already obtained a product patent in Europe for cereals with added vegetables (vegetable pale) and a process patent for rehydrating pulses. Vegetables Pala and parboiled rice are among the seventeen items for which Nestle had sought Indian patents. For centuries, Indians have been making parboiled rice by boiling paddy in water and then drying and milling it. In many southern and eastern states, parboiled rice is the staple food.

The patenting of soil organisms is yet another area whereby Indian biodiversity is being patented by the TNCs, mainly in the area of pharmaceuticals.

Biopiracy of Vechur Cow

In 1997 Edinburg-based Roslin Institute, which produced the world's first cloned sheep 'Dolly', applied for the patent rights to the genetic material of this rare cow, which draws its name from Vechur, near Vaikom in Kerala. The Institute's commercial partner, PPL Therapeutics (Scotland) Ltd., held fourteen patent applications with the European Patent Office (EPO), of which one clearly referred to an Indian cattle breed, the Vechur cow. This patent (EP 0765390) stated that the invention provided recombinant gene technology for a milk protein, A-lactalbumin, in bovine cells.

The Vechur, one of the most famous Indian cattle breeds, is the smallest variety of cattle in the world. Its average height is 87 cm and length, 124 cm. It gives more milk in relation to the meager amount of fodder it eats. Its milk has high fat content from 6.02 to 7.86 percent while Europe's high-yielding varieties have 3.5 to 4.5 percent. Local people even say its milk has medicinal value.

The company was mainly interested in the Vechur breed because it was more 'productive', i.e., ate less fodder and gave more milk. The butter production capacity of milk depends on its fat content, and an institution in a developed country can earn billions of dollars each year by transferring the Vechur genes into foreign cattle. With RFSTE and other partnering organizations' intervention the patenting attempt came into limelight and was successfully withdrawn.

IPRs: Threats to Economic Survival of Communities

Today, these production systems and their technologies are under severe threat from the new monopolistic protections being carved out of the TNCs, through IPR regimes. In fact, in the free and neoliberal trade regimes which are pegged as ending protectionism and promoting free trade, IPRs become the very instrument of a new form of protectionism.

The new protectionism for TNCs through IPRs is becoming the major means of dismantling both local and national economies, as well as national sovereignty through piracy of both material as well as the intellectual and cultural resources. IPR regimes in the context of 'free trade' and 'trade liberalization' are instruments of piracy at three levels:

Resource Piracy in which the biological and natural resources of communities and the country are freely taken without recognition or permission and are used to build up global economies. For example, the transfer of *basmati* varieties of rice from India to build the rice economy of the US; the free flow of neem seeds from the farms, fields, and commons to corporations like W.R. Grace for export.

Intellectual and cultural piracy in which the cultural and intellectual heritage of communities and the country is freely taken without recognition or permission and is used for claiming IPRs such as patents and trademarks–even though the primary innovation and creativity has not taken place through corporate investment. For instance, the use by the US corporation of the trade name 'basmati' for their aromatic rice, or Pepsi's use of the trade name '*BikaneriBhujia*'.

Economic Piracy in which the domestic and international market are usurped through the use of trade names and IPRs, thereby destroying both local and national economies where the original innovation took place and hence wiping out the livelihoods and economic survival of millions. For example, US rice traders usurping European markets; Grace usurping market from small-scale Indian producers of neem-based biopesticides.

BIOPIRACY FACT SHEETS

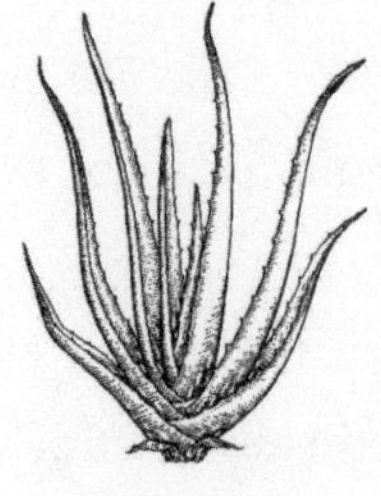

Aloe Vera

Botanical Name: Aloe barbadensis

Local Names: *Kumari* (Sanskrit), *Kunvar* (Gujarati), *Kunvar* (Hindi), *Kumari* (Kannada), *Kattalai* (Tamil), *Kalabando* (Telugu)

Use: Bleeding wounds, heavy bleeding, painful and irregular menstruation, astringent, constipation, burns, sore eyes, abscess, asthma, cough (phlegm)

Biopiracy:

US Patent	Patent Use	Patentee	Assignee
5,626,265	Production of rhein and rhein derivatives	Natale Vittori; Michael Collins	Wisconsin Alumni Research Foundation, Madison, WI, USA
5,449,517	Method and formulation for eliminating flees on animals	Edwin A. Fitzjiarrel, Sisters, OR, US	None
5,427.776	Aloe water preparation	Camille Isnard Noumea, France	None

Indian Frankincense

Botanical Name: Boswellia serrata

Local Names: *Salai* (Hindi), *Shallaki* (Sanskrit), *Parangisambrani* (Tamil), *Indian Olibanum Tree* (English)

Use: Backache, leg pain, diarrhea, dysentery, piles, skin disease, injuries, excessive bleeding, asthma, cleaning wounds, fever, fainting loss of consciousness, antiseptic, fever

Biopiracy:

US Patent	Patent Use	Patentee	Assignee
5,494,668	Method for treating musculoskeletal disease and a novel consumption thereof	Bhushan Patwardhan Pune, India	None

Golden Shower Tree

Botanical Name: Cassia fistula

Local Names: *Amaltas Sonali* (Hindi), *Bandariathi* (Bengali), *Konnel* (Tamil), *Aragvadha* (Sanskrit), *Kakkemar Konnemaran* (Kannada), *Garmala* (Gujarati); *Pudding Pipe Tree, Purging Cassia* (English)

Use: Constipation, diabetes, gout, rheumatoid arthritis, sore throat and tonsillitis, constipation (infants), ringworm, intestinal worms (infants), scabies, to kill vermin, skin disease and wounds

Biopiracy:

US Patent	Patent Use	Patentee	Assignee
5,411,733	Anti-viral agent containing crude drug	Toycharu Hozumi, Takao Matsumoto, Ooyama Tsuneo Namba, Kimiyasu Shiraki, Hattori Masao, Masahiko Kurokawa, Shigetoshi Kadota, Japan	None
5,393,898	Method of preparing diacetyl rhein	Alfons Carcsona, Wolf Grimminger, Pentti Hietala, Helga Zaeske, Klaus Witthohn	Madus AG, Cologne, Federal Republic of Germany
5,391,775	Process for production of diacetyl rhein	Alfons Carcsona, Wolf Grimminger, Pentti Hietala, Helga Zaeske, Klaus Witthohn	Madus AG, Cologne, Federal Republic of Germany

Cumin

Botanical Name: Cuminum cyminum

Local Names: *Jira Zira* (Hindi & Bengali), *Shimai Shiragam* (Tamil), *Shima Jilakan* (Telugu), *Kushna Jeerak* (Sanskrit), *Shah Jeerun* (Gujarati), *Jeerigay* (Kannada), *Black Cumin* (English)

Use: After fever, diarrhea and indigestion, syphilis and urinary infections, burning and frequent urination, difficulty during labor, stomach pain, irregular menstruation, scorpion bites, skin disorders

Biopiracy:

US Patent	Patent Use	Patentee	Assignee
5,653,981	Use of Nigella sativa to increase immune function	Rajko D. Medenica Hilton Head Island, SC, USA	None
	Use of Nigella sativa to increase immune function	Rajko D. Medenica Hilton Head Island, SC, USA	None

Asthma Plant

Botanical Name: Euphorbia hirta

Local Names: *Dudhi* (Hindi), *Chara* (Sanskrit), *Borokeruie* (Bengali), *Amampatchaiarisi* (Tamil)

Use: Blood and mucous mixed stool, worm infections, lactogenic, chronic cough and asthma, anti-emetic, skin diseases, stomach irritant and emetic, colic and dysentery, asthma and bronchial infection, warts, alleviates burning sensation, possesses anti-viral, anti-bacterial, and anti-cancer properties

Biopiracy:

US Patent	Patent Use	Patentee	Assignee
5,399,584	Use of flavone derivatives for gastro-protectin	Jeffery J. Acres, Sunil V. Kakodkar, Gary R. Kelm, Peter D. Murray, Jared L. Randall, Candice L. Slough	The Proctor and Gamble Co.

Garden Balsam

Botanical Name: Impatiens balsamina

Local Names: *Gulmendhi* (Hindi), *Dushpatrijati* (Sanskrit), *Dupati* (Bengali), *Kasihumbai* (Tamil); *Balsam, Rose Balsam, Touch-me-not, Spotted Snapweed* (English)

Use: Constipation, burns and scalds

Biopiracy:

US Patent	Patent Use	Patentee	Assignee
5,427,592	Intact seed based delayed release nutrient supplement	Peter C. Roamine, Alan Morlowe	The Penn State Research Foundation

Barbados Nut

Botanical Name: Jatrophra curcas

Local Names: *Vyaghrend* (Hindi), *Kattamanakku* (Tamil), *Mongali Erand* (Marathi), *Kodharlu* (Kannad), *Galmark* (Konkiny); *Purging Nut, Psychic Nut, Poison Nut, Bubble Bush* (English)

Use: Bleeding wounds, bleeding gums, scabies, boils, rheumatoid arthritis, increases milk secretion

Biopiracy:

US Patent	Patent Use	Patentee	Assignee
5,411,733	Anti-viral agent containing crude drug	Toycharu Hozumi, Takao Matsumoto, Ooyama Tsuneo Namba, Kimiyasu Shiraki, Hattori Masao, Masahiko Kurokawa, Shigetoshi Kadota, Japan	None
5,466,455	Polyphase fluid extract	Miles C. Huffstutler, Gary M. Steuart, USA	None

Black Mustard Seed

Botanical Name: Brassica compestris

Local Names: *Swetsarisha* (Bengali), *Avalu* (Tamil), *Sarson* (Hindi); *Brown Mustard, Chinese Mustard, Indian Mustard, Leaf Mustard, Oriental Mustard, Vegetable Mustard* (English)

Use: Influenza, gum inflammation, rheumatic pain, epilepsy, elephantiasis, ear pain

Biopiracy:

US Patent	Patent Use	Patentee	Assignee
5,638,637	Production of improved rape-seed exhibiting an enhanced oleic acid content	Raymond S. C. Wong, Wallace D. Beversdof, James R. Castagno, Ian Grant, Jayantilal D. Patel, Ontario, Canada	Pioneer Hi-Bred International Inc. Des Moines, IA, USA
5,628,145	Process for producing seeds capable of forming F. sub 1 hybrid plants utilizing self- incompatibility	Wallace D. Beversdorf, Laima S. Kott, Van L. Ripley, Jeff P. Parker, Paul R. Banks	University of Guelph, Guelph, Canada
5,463,174	Transformation and foreign gene expression in Brassica species	Maurice M. Moloney, Sharon Radke	Calgene Inc., Davis, CA, USA
5,425,885	Fire retarding extinguishing	Guansheng Zhao, Shandong, China	Fenglan Zhao, Shandong Province, Beijing, China
5,484,905	Receptor protein kinase gene encoded at the self-incompatibility locus	June B. Nasrallah, Mikhail E. Nasrallah, Joshua Stein	Cornell Research Foundation Ithaca, NY

5,625,130	Oilseed Brassica bearing an endogenous oil wherein the levels of oleic, alpha-linolenic and saturated fatty acids are simultaneously provided in an atypical highly beneficial distribution via genetic control	Ian Grant, David G. Charne, Guelph, Canada	Pioneer Hi-Bred International Inc., Des Moines, IA, USA
5,614,393	Production of gamma linolenic acid by a DELTA 6 desaturase	Terry L. Thomas, Avutu S. Reddy, Michael Nuccio, Andrew L. Nunberg, Georges L. Freyssinet, France	Rhone-Poulenc, Agrochimie, France
5,563,058	Plant lysophosphatidic acid acyltransferases	Huw M. Davies, Deborah Hawkins, Janet Nielsen	Calgene Inc., Davis, CA, USA
5,552,306	Production of gamma-linoleic acid by a DELTA 6 desaturase	Terry L. Thomas, Avutu S. Reddy, Michael Nuccio, Andrew L. Nunberg, Georges L. Freyssinet, France	Rhone-Poulenc, Agrochimie, France
5,552,139	Method for the biological control of pollen in plants	Oded Shoseyov, Levava Karmei Roiz, Givat Shmuel, Uzi Ozeri, Ben-Ami Bravdo, Raphael Goren, Rehevot, Israel	Yissum Research Development Co. of the Hebrew University of Jerusalem, Jerusalem, Israel

5,512,482	Plant thioestreases	Tori Voelker, Huw M. Davies	Calgene Inc., Davis, CA, USA
5,470,359	Regulatory element conferring tapetum specificity	Gary A. Huffman	Pioneer Hi-Bred International Inc., Des Moines, IA, USA
5,455,167	Medium chain thiosterases in plants	Huw M. Davies	Calgene Inc., Davis, CA, USA
5,420,034	Seed-specific transcriptional regulation	Jean C. Kriol, Vic C. Knauf	Calgene Inc., Davis, CA, USA

Black Pepper

Botanical Name: Piper nigrum

Local Names: *Maricha* (Sanskrit), *Kalimirich* (Hindi), *Golmarich* (Bengali), *Milagu* (Tamil), *Murem* (Marathi)

Use: Dysentery, asthmatic attack, cough and cold, colic and dyspepsia, arthritis, malaria, hemorrhoids, boils, night blindness, eye itching, headache, alopecia, toothache, distension, indigestion

Biopiracy:

US Patent	Patent Use	Patentee	Assignee
5,536,506	Use of piperine to increase bioavailability of nutritional compounds	Muhammed Majeed, VladmirBadmaev, R. Rajendran	Sabinsa Corporation, Piscataway, NJ, USA

Pomegranate

Botanical Name: Punica granatum

Local Names: *Anar* (Hindi), *Dalmia* (Bengali) *Darima* (Sanskrit), *Madulai* (Tamil)

Use: Conjunctivitis, diarrhea, vomiting, dysentery, intestinal worms, weakness, abscess, astringent

Biopiracy:

US Patent	Patent Use	Patentee	Assignee
5,411,733	Anti-viral agent containing crude drug	Toycharu Hozumi, Takao Matsumoto, Ooyama Tsuneo Namba, Kimiyasu Shiraki, Hattori Masao, Masahiko Kurokawa, Shigetoshi Kadota, Japan	None

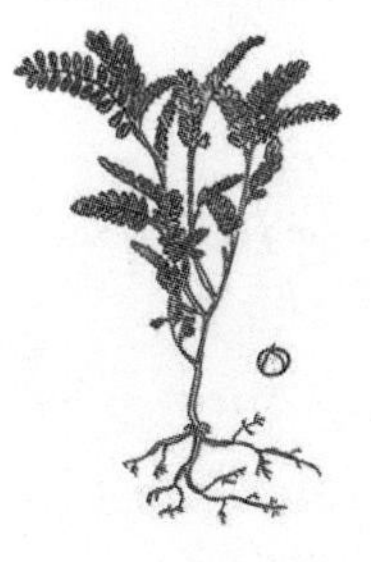

Gale of the Wind

Botanical Name: Phyllanthus niruri

Local Names: *Bhuinamla* (Bengali), *Bhuamla* (Hindi), *Bhudharti* (Sanskrit), *Kikkaynelli* (Tamil), *Nelvusai* (Telugu); *Stonebreaker, Seed-under-leaf* (English)

Use: Malaria, swelling, ulcers, dysentery, jaundice, upset stomach, sores, constipation, fever, excessive menstrual bleeding, diuretic, urinary tract issues

Biopiracy:

US Patent	Patent Use	Patentee	Assignee
4,937,074	Method for treating retrovirus infection	Pinayur S. Ventateshwaran, Irving MIlman, Baruch S Blumberg	Fox Chase Cancer Center, Pennsylvania, USA

4,859,468	Composition and method for decomposing adipose tissue	Michinori Kubo, Reiko Matsuda	Senju Pharmaceutical Co. Ltd. Japan
4,673,575	Composition, pharmaceutical preparation, and method for treating viral hepatitis	Pinayur S. Ventateshwaran, Irving Mllman, Baruch S Blumberg	Fox Chase Cancer Center, Pennsylvania, USA
5,529,778	Ayurvedic composition for the prophylaxis and treatment of AIDS, flu, TB, and other immune deficiencies	Surendra Rohatgi, India	None

Rangoon Creeper

Botanical Name: Quisqualis indica

Local Names: *Rangoon-ki-bel* (Hindi), *Ranganbel* (Bengali), *Irangumalli* (Tamil), *Chinese Honeysuckle* (English)

Use: Backache or leg pain, diarrhea, dysentery, piles, skin disease, injuries, excessive bleeding from orifices, asthma, cleaning wounds, fever, fainting or loss of consciousness, antiseptic, fever

Biopiracy:

US Patent	Patent Use	Patentee	Assignee
5,494,668	Method for treating musculoskeletal disease and a novel consumption thereof	Bhushan Patwardhan Pune, India	None

Castor Oil Plant

Botanical Name: Ricinus communis

Local Names: *Bherenda* (Bengali), *Rehri Erand* (Hindi), *Amanakkum* (Tamil), *Gandharv Hasta* (Sanskrit), *Chittamanakku* (Malyalam); *Castor, Castor seed* (English)

Use: Backache or leg pain, diarrhea, dysentery, piles, skin disease, injuries, excessive bleeding from orifices, asthma, cleaning wounds, fever, fainting or loss of consciousness, antiseptic, fever

Biopiracy:

US Patent	Patent Use	Patentee	Assignee
5,487,991	Process for production of biologically active peptide via the expression of modified storage seed protein genes in transgenic plants	Joel S, Vandekerckhove, Enno Krebbers, John Botteran, Jan Leemans	Plant Genetic Systems, Nevada, USA
5,558,834	Device and method of separating and assaying whole blood	Amy H. Chu, Lon R. Stover	Bayer Corporation, USA
5,576,428	Invertase genes and uses thereof	Yoshihira Konno, William O. Butler, Craig D. Dickinson, Leona C. Fitzmaurice, Theodore E. Mirkov, Kathryn J. Elliot	The Salk Institute, Biotechnology Industrial Association
5,475,099	Plant fatty acid synthases	Vic C. Knouf, Gregory A. Thompson	Calgene Inc., CA, USA

5,538,868	Recombinant ricin toxin fragments	Glenn T. Horn, Michael Platak Jr.	Cetus Oncology Corp, CA, USA
5,510,255	Method for making mRNA encoding a plant systhase protein	Vic. C. Knauf, Gregory A. Thompson	None
5,494,790	Alpha-3 sialytransferase	Katusitoshi Sasaki, Etsuyo Watanabe, Tatsunari Nishi, Susumu Sekine, Nobuo Hanai, Mamoru Hasegawa	Kyowa Hakko Kogya Co Ltd., Japan

Black Nightshade

Botanical Name: Solanum nigrum

Local Names: *Kakamachi* (Sanskrit), *Piludu* (Gujarati), *Gurkama*(Hindi),*Kakisopu*(Kannada),*Manathakkali* (Tamil), *Buddakasa* (Telugu), *Gudkamai* (Bengali), *Blackberry Nightshade* (English)

Use: Liver disorders, chronic skin ailments, inflammatory conditions, painful periods, diuretic, laxative. berries used for fevers, diarrhea, eye disease, hydrophobia

Biopiracy:

US Patent	Patent Use	Patentee	Assignee
5,466,662	Use of 4-chloro-3 (4-chloro -2-fluoro-phenyl)-5difluoromethoxy-1-methyl- 11 as herbal treatment	Harjinder Singhbansal, John C. Ormrod	Zeneca Limited, London, UK
5,491,285	Phytophthora resistance gene of catharanthus and its use	Robert N. Bowman	Goldsmith Seeds Inc. Gilroy, CA, USA

5,401,709	Antibiotic AB-041 derived from Streptomyces sp. NCIMB 40428, herbal compositions, and methods of use	Nunzio Andriolo, Alessandro Scacchi, Giorgio E. Borgonovi, Silvia Spera, Gianfranco Gugliemetti, Giorgio Pirali, Giovanni Confalonieri	Ministero dell Universita e della Ricerca Scientifica e Tecnologica, Rome, Italy

Arjun Tree

Botanical Name: Terminalia arjuna

Local Names: *Arjun* (Sanskrit, Bengali, and Hindi), *Vellamatta Marutae* (Tamil), *Arjun Sadda* (Marathi), *Tellamaddi* (Telugu), *Arjun* (English)

Use: Heart problems, hemorrhage, fractures, inflammations, wounds, diarrhea, irregular menstruation

Biopiracy:

US Patent	Patent Use	Patentee	Assignee
5,411,733	Antiviral agent containing crude drug	Toycharu Hozumi, Takao Matsumoto, Ooyama Tsuneo Namba, Kimiyasu Shiraki, Hattori Masao, Masahiko Kurokawa, Shigetoshi Kadota, Japan	None

Myrobalan

Botanical Name: Terminalia chebula

Local Names: *Hariraki* (Sanskrit and Bengali), *Harad* (Hindi), *Karkchettu* (Telugu), *Kadukkaya* (Tamil), *Harade* (Marathi, Gujarati)

Use: Appetizer, laxative, anti-diarrheal agent, memory, gives strength to nervous system

Biopiracy:

US Patent	Patent Use	Patentee	Assignee
5,529,778	Ayurvedic composition for the prophylaxis and treatment of AIDS, flu, TB, and other immune-deficiencies and preparation	Surendra Rohatgi, India	None

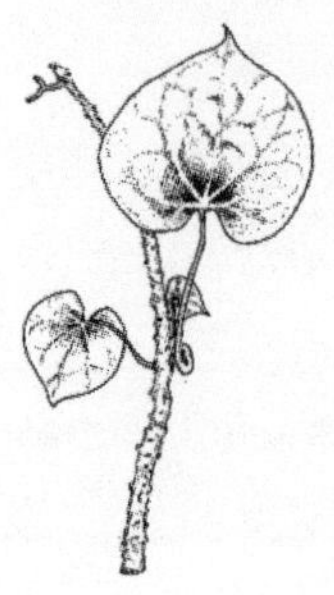

Heart-leaved Moonseed

Botanical Name: Tinosporacordifolia

Local Names: *Guduchi* (Sanskrit), *Gulancha* (Bengali), *ShidilKodi* (Tamil), *Amrita, Gulancha, Giloya* (Hindi), *Tippatigo* (Telugu), *Galo* (Gujarati), *Tinospora* (English)

Use: Immunity protection, diuretic, gout, rheumatoid arthritis, and tonic for after fever, malaria and other fevers, diabetes, urinary problems, early syphilis, skin diseases, indigestion, piles, heavy bleeding after abortion or with palpable uterine tumor

Biopiracy:

US Patent	Patent Use	Patentee	Assignee
5,529,778	Ayurvedic composition for the prophylaxis and treatment of AIDS, flu, TB, and other immune-deficiencies and the process of preparing the same	Surendra Rohatgi, India	None

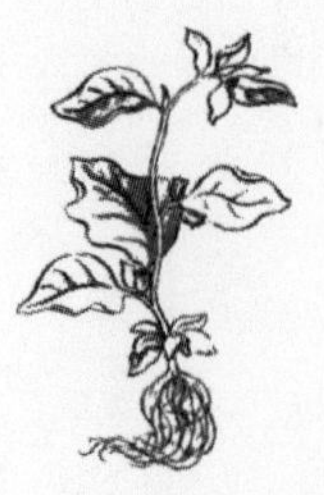

Ashwagandha

Botanical Name: Withania somnifera, Withania Ashwagandha

Local Names: *Asgand* (Hindi), *Amukkirag* (Tamil), *Amangura* (Kannada), *Asvagandha* (Bengali), *Ashvagandha* (Sanskrit), *Asundha* (Gujarati); *Indian Ginseng, Poison Gooseberry, Winter Cherry* (English)

Medicinal Properties: *Mastiksharadorbalya* (mental weakness concerning nervous system), *Hriddrbalyahar* (heart weakness), *Raktapittahar*, *Pushtikar* (gives strength to muscles), *Grahi* (anti-diarrheal) *Twachya* (improves skin condition)

Use: Backache or leg pain, diarrhea, dysentery, piles, skin disease, injuries, excessive bleeding from orifices, asthma, cleaning wounds, fever, fainting or loss of consciousness, antiseptic, fever

Biopiracy:

US Patent	Patent Use	Patentee	Assignee
5,494,668	Method for treating musculoskeletal disease and a novel composition therefore	Bhushan Patwardhan Pune, India	None

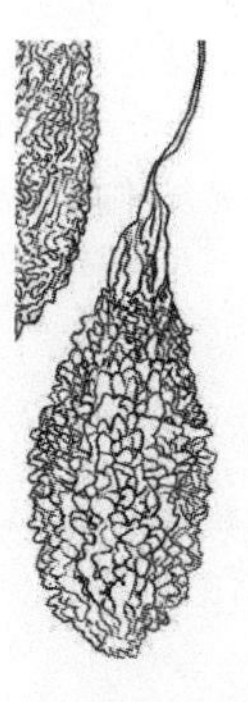

Bitter Melon

Botanical Name: Momordica charantia

Local Names: *Karela* (Hindi), *Pavakkachedi* (Tamil), *Sushavi* (Sanskrit) *Karala* (Bengali), *Bitter Gourd* (English)

Usage: Splenomegalic, chronic skin disease, abortion, migraine, burning soles, wounds, ulcers, psoriasis

Biopiracy:

US Patent	Patent Use	Patentee	Assignee
5,484,889	Plant protein useful for treating HIV infection	Sylvia Lee-Huang, Phillip L. Huang, Peter L. Nara, Hao-Chia Chen, Hsiang-Fu Kung, Peter Huang, Henry I. Huang, Paul L. Huang	New York University, New York, USA
5,466,455	Polyphase fluid extract process, resulting products and methods of use	Miles C. Huffstutler Jr., Gary M. Steuart, MN, USA	None

North Indian Rosewood

Botanical Name: Sapium sebiferum

Local Names: *Momchina* (Bengali), *Vilayeti Shisham* (Hindi), *Tayapipalli* (Sanskrit), *Chinese Tallow Tree* (English)

Use: Skin diseases, indigestion

Biopiracy:

US Patent	Patent Use	Patentee	Assignee
5,380,894	Process for the production of hydroxy fatty acids ad estolide intermediates	Bhushan Patwardhan Pune, India	None

Ginger

Botanical Name: Zingiber officinale

Local Names: *Adi* (Hindi), *Ada* (Bengali), *Adu (Gujarati), Ale* (Marathi), *Enji* (Tamil), *Alla* (Kannad), *Ginger* (English)

Medicinal Properties: Cough, cold, hoarse voice, asthma, digestion enhancer, vomiting and nausea, water retention, urticaria, ear pain, chronic arthritis, rheumatoid arthritis

Biopiracy:

US Patent	Patent Use	Patentee	Assignee
5,565,201	Pharmaceutical composition and preparation for the treatment of snoring and the use therefore	Hongzhi Li, Beijing, China	None
5,603,935	Composing for the treatment of snoring and methods of use thereof	Weng W Jain, David S. Riley	Eastern Europe, Inc. NY, USA

5,494,668	Method of treating musculoskeletal disease and a novel composition thereof	Bhusan Patwardhan, Pune, India	None
5,536,506	Use of pipernine to increase the bioavailability of nutritional compounds	Muhammed Majeed, Vladimir Badmaev, R.Rajendran	Sabinsa Corporation, Piscataway, NJ, USA

Indian Jujube

Botanical Name: Zizphus jujuba

Local Names: *Ber* (Hindi), *Kul Ber* (Bengali), *Bor* (Marathi), *Elandey* (Tamil), *Regu Chittu* (Telegu); *Jujuba fruit, Chinese Date, Chinese Apple, Indian Plum* (English)

Medicinal Properties: Fever, injuries and wounds, eye problems, digestive disorders, cough, fatigue

Biopiracy:

US Patent	Patent Use	Patentee	Assignee
5,589,182	Compositions and method of treating cardio-cerebro-vascular and Alzheimer's diseases, depression	Renki Tashiro, Tokyo, Japan. Ruth H. Pater, Yorktown, VA	None
5,411,733	Anti- viral agent containing crude drug	Toyoharu Hozumi, Takao Matsumoto, Haruo Ooyama, Tsuneo Namba, Kimiyasu Shiraki, Haltori Masao, Masahiko Kurokawa, Shigetoshi Kadota, Japan	None

Indian Soapberry

Botanical Name: Sapindus mukorossi

Local Names: *Arista* (Sanskrit), *Haithaguti* (Assam), *Ritha* (Hindi), *Rithegacha* (Bengali), *PonnarKottai* (Tamil), *Kunkunda* (Telugi); *Soap-Nut Tree of North India, Washnut* (English)

Medicinal Properties: Pain and swelling, asthama and coughing, migraine, vomiting and morphin poisoning

Biopiracy:

US Patent	Patent Use	Patentee	Assignee
5,425,885	Fire retarding and extinguishing composite	Guansheng Zhao	Fenglan Zhao, Shandong Province, Huanwen, Du, Beijing, China

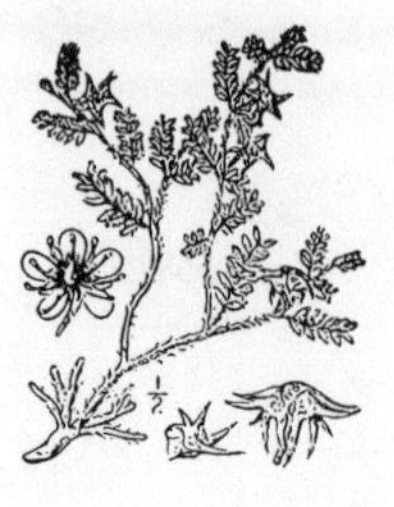

Chotagokhuru

Botanical Name: Tribulus terrestris

Local Names: *Gokshura* (Sanskrit and Bengali), *Chhotagokhru* (Hindi), *Nerinji* (Tamil), *Palleru Mullu* (Telugi), *Neggilu Mullu* (Kannad), *Puncture Vine* (English)

Medicinal Properties: Urinary infection, dysurea (difficulty in urination), highly acidic urine, highly alkaline urine (with pungent ordor), urinary calculus

Biopiracy:

US Patent	Patent Use	Patentee	Assignee
5,466,452	Pharmaceutical compositions for the treatment of skin disorders	Brain A. Whittles	Phytopharm ltd. North Humberside, UK
3,890,131	Method for controlling the growth of weed in a cotton growing area with 3.4.5 - trisubstituted isothiazoles		

Chaff Flower

Botanical Name: Achryanthes aspera

Local Names: *Apamarga* (Sanskrit), *Latjeera Chichirta* (Hindi), *Apang* (Bengali) *Adhedo* (Gujarati), *Aghada* (Marathi), *Uttarni* (Kannad)) *Apamargamu* (Telugu), *Nayurivi* (Tamil), *Atkumah* (Arabic), *Prickly Chaff Flower* (English)

Use: Skin complexion enhancer, digestion enhancer, used for gall stones, bile, and liver, hemorrhoids, acidic urine, chronic cough, scorpion and rat bites, eye inflammation, toothache/painful cavities, ear inflammation, pain, and deafness, swollen painful joints, bleeding wounds, scabies

Biopiracy:

US Patent	Patent Use	Patentee	Assignee
5,609,873	Use of an ecdysternoid for the preparation of cosmetic or dermato-logical compositions. Intended particularly for strengthening the water barrier	Alain Meyback, FredericBonte, Gerard Redziniak	LVMH Recherche, Nanterre, France

Dhaya

Botanical Name: Woodfordia floribunda

Local Names: *Dhataki* (Sanskrit), *Dhaya* (Hindi), *Dhavani* (Gujarati), *Dha* (Punjabi), *Serinjee Errapurvu* (Telegu), Fire Flame Bush (English)

Use: Diarrhea, dysentery, leucorrhea, menorrhagia, snake bites, wounds, headache

Biopiracy:

US Patent	Patent Use	Patentee	Assignee
5,411,733	Antiviral agent containing crude drug	Toycharu Hozumi, Takao Matsumoto, Ooyama Tsuneo Namba, Kimiyasu Shiraki, Hattori Masao, Masahiko Kurokawa, Shigetoshi Kadota, Japan	None

Jackfruit

Botanical Name: Artocarpus integrifolia

Local Names: *Ati Vrihatphal, Kantkiphal* (Sanskrit), *Kathal* (Hindi), *Kantal* (Bengali), *Phanas* (Gujarati), *Phanas* (Mara), *Panas* (Telugu), *Panas* (Tamil), *Chakki* (Arabic), *Jack Tree* (English)

Use: Inflammation, wounds, diarrhea, urtecaria, oligospermia, skin diseases, general weakness

Biopiracy:

US Patent	Patent Use	Patentee	Assignee
5,407,454	Larvicidal lectins and plant insect resistance based thereon	Antony Cavalieri, Thomas Czapla, John Howard, Gururaj Rao	Pioneer Hi-Bred International Inc., Des Moines, IA, USA
5,644,930	Gene and method for production of IgA binding protein	Ervin Faulmann	Medical College of Ohio Toledo, Ohio, USA
5,413,916	Gene and method for production of a 40-45-kDa IgA binding protein	Ervin Faulmann	Medical College of Ohio Toledo, Ohio, USA

*Image sources: Haridev Formulations;[4] Aim Slim;[5] USDA Natural Resources Conservation Service;[6] Aarti Draws;[7] Herb Museum;[8] Inner Path;[9] Humanity Development Library 2.0;[10] and Mother Earth Living.[11]

*Ginger, Chaff Flower, Jackfruit illustrations, and image edits by A. Müller

Bioprospecting as Sophisticated Biopiracy

Before the Biodiversity Act was implemented and laws on Access and Benefit Sharing started to regulate access, industry had floated the language of 'bioprospecting'. Like mining companies prospect minerals for mining, the biotechnology and pharmaceutical industry talked of 'bioprospecting' as prospecting for biological material and knowledge to 'mine' our genetic and intellectual wealth. However, there is a major difference between minerals and biological and intellectual wealth. The latter is living, and local communities have sovereign rights to it. Following the Biodiversity Act, regulated access has replaced the discourse of 'bioprospecting'. However, since the attempts are still being made to erode the access laws and turn biodiversity and traditional knowledge into an "Open Access" unregulated system, it is useful to revisit the bioprospecting discourse of the 1990s and remember how attempts at biopiracy were made back then, in order to recognize how they continue to be made today.

- Bioprospecting is viewed commercially as the exploration of potentially commercially valuable biodiversity and biodiversity related knowledge, assuming that prior to prospecting, the resources lie buried unknown, unused, and without value.
- Bioprospecting viewed by indigenous communities, is seen as the expropriation of their collective and cumulative innovation, which has been utilized, protected and conserved by its traditional communities since time immemorial.
- The bioprospecting model can never be a legitimate source of benefit sharing in the case of biodiversity related knowledge because it is based on two exclusions. The first takes place when one local community is treated as possessing a collective knowledge exclusively. Secondly, by signing a bioprospecting contract, a corporation makes an unjustified claim to innovation on the knowledge 'transferred' from an indigenous community, which over time excludes all communities which held and developed this knowledge their rightful share to emerging markets.

- Bioprospecting contracts, which deal with one individual or one community, fail to be equitable because prior informed consent needs to be taken from all communities and members who have contributed to the collective innovation, and who utilize the knowledge to meet their needs.
- Bioprospecting creates impoverishment within donor communities, by claiming monopolies on those resources and knowledge which previously enabled communities to meet their health and nutrition needs and charging royalties for what was originally theirs and which they had for free.
- Thus, bioprospecting leads to the enclosure of the biological and intellectual commons, through the conversion of usurped biodiversity and biodiversity related knowledge of indigenous communities into commodities protected by IPRs.

How Bioprospecting Undermines Access

Bioprospecting was promoted as the model of relationships between corporations (which commercialize indigenous knowledge) and the indigenous communities (which have collectively innovated and evolved the knowledge). It was presented as an alternative to biopiracy. However, bioprospecting was (and still is) merely a sophisticated form of biopiracy.

Bioprospecting, in effect, leads to the enclosure of the biological and intellectual commons. It takes the biodiversity and intellectual heritage of indigenous communities and converts it into commodities protected by IPRs.

Collective innovation, evolving over time, and involving many persons, is different from individual innovation which is localized in time and space. Collective innovation involves many persons who contribute to it over time. It is modified and enhanced as it is used over time and passed on from generation to generation. In some examples such collective innovation is no longer local, e.g., in the case of seeds and that of major non-western knowledge traditions–such as Ayurvedic and

Chinese medicine. In some cases, it even crosses national boundaries. This is particularly so with Ayahuasca; wherein a combination of lianas, or vines, are used to make an intoxicating ceremonial drink manufactured for ritual healing and 'enlightenment'. Traditional stories about the origins of this powerful tonic weave together the ancestral guidance, communication with spirits of the plants, and the protection of visible and invisible guardians. It is known by a variety of names including *caapi, yaje, saintodaime,* and is produced using the bark of the jaguba vine (*Banisteriopsiscaapi*).

The biological diversity of India has always been a common resource for millions of our traditional communities, who have utilized, protected, and conserved their biodiversity heritage over centuries. Their collective and cumulative innovation has been the basis of local culture and local economies which constitute the dominant economies in terms of the livelihoods provided and the needs met. In fact, their traditional knowledge in medicine, agriculture, and fisheries is the primary base for meeting their food and health needs. For them, conserving biodiversity means to conserve the integrity of the ecosystem. The right to resources and knowledge and the right to the production systems based on biodiversity are deeply connected and extremely important for their sustenance. Therefore, biodiversity is intimately linked to traditional indigenous knowledge systems as well as the people's right to protect their knowledge and resources.

However, nature's diversity and the diversity of knowledge systems are undergoing a major process of destabilization with the expansion of patents and IPRs into the domain of biodiversity, via the TRIPS Agreement of the WTO. The whole notion of TRIPS has been shaped by the objectives and interests of trade and TNCs. Through the instrument of TRIPS, TNCs have posed multiple threats to the biological and intellectual heritage of our diverse communities by appropriating and privatizing their knowledge. For TNC's commercial interests, biodiversity itself has no value and is merely a 'raw material' to be used for the production of commodities and the maximization of profits.

In the context of privatization, the mutual exchange among communities has been replaced by contracts for bioprospecting for corporations who seek to expropriate invaluable and inalienable heritage of communities often through scientific collection missions and ethnobotanical research.

The World Resources Institute defined 'biodiversity prospecting' as exploration of commercially valuable genetic and biochemical resources. The metaphor for prospecting is borrowed from the prospecting for 'gold' or 'oil'. While biodiversity has become the 'green gold' and 'green oil' for the pharmaceutical and biotechnology industry, the metaphor for prospecting suggests that prior to prospecting the resources lie buried, unknown, unused, and without value. However, unlike gold or oil deposits, the uses and value of biodiversity are long well-known to the local communities.

Taking knowledge from indigenous communities through bioprospecting is only the first step in the IPR protected industrial system which eventually markets the commodities that have used local knowledge as an input without acknowledging the ethical, epistemological, or ecological structures of the knowledge system. Biodiversity fragments are used as 'raw material' to produce biological products protected by patents. These, in turn, displace the biodiversity and indigenous knowledge which they have exploited. Bioprospecting is the first step towards occupying the dominant system of monoculture and monopolies, and thus accepting the destruction of diversity.

Indigenous knowledge is centered on the co-creation by nature and people. IPR regimes are premised on the denial of the creativity of nature. The ethical and epistemological assumption and consequences of adopting an IPR regime through bioprospecting contracts needs deeper analysis and reflection.

This consideration is particularly important as biodiversity knowledge in indigenous communities is not individual innovation but collective innovation, not privatized but a shared heritage. Therefore, all members of the community, including past generations have contributed to the innovation with many communities utilizing the knowledge and sharing the biological resources.

Bioprospecting usually involves a corporation sending an ethno-scientist to talk to a member of an indigenous community and settling for compensation with the individual or the community. However, the impact of this transaction is felt in the future by other communities who also share the innovation. Suppose the other communities do not support the privatization of this common heritage; bioprospecting has no room for respecting the rights of the people and the communities who do not want the common genetic resources enclosed. It is for those who do not accept the inevitability of the enclosure of our biodiversity that the alternatives to bioprospecting become an imperative.

The utilization of biodiversity in the people's economy is guided by a plurality of knowledge systems. The implementation of the properties, characteristics, and uses of this biodiversity is held by local communities in different languages with diverse epistemological frameworks.

In the case of reserves like land which cannot be multiplied, land-based commons have clear territorial boundaries for communities who have access to common forests or pastures and communities have very strict limits of resource use. The use of these commons goes only as far as the subsistence level and they cannot limitlessly increase its exploitation for private gain. Principles and rules of management of the commons set strict upper limits, so that no one can exploit too much, and lower limits so that no individual in the community is excluded from utilizing the commons.

In the case of agricultural resources and knowledge, which multiply by sharing and do not intrinsically reduce the givers' share, the community of users is always expanding. Thus, seeds travel across communities with increasing uses and innovations, becoming available to all communities who have shared in its biological and intellectual contribution.

The bioprospecting paradigm needs to be examined in the context of equity, specifically its effect on the following:

- The impact on donor community
- The impact on potential recipient communities
- The impact on bioprospecting corporations

Even though bioprospecting contracts are based on prior informed consent and compensation, unlike in the case of biopiracy where no consent is taken and no compensation is given, not all owners/carriers of an indigenous knowledge tradition are consulted or compensated. This leads to inequity and injustice. It also pits individual against individual within a community, and consequently pits communities against one another on a larger scale. For example, an innovation might have evolved by a group of communities, yet a bioprospecting contract enables corporations to take this collective knowledge by writing a contract with only one of those communities. This contract violates the biodiversity and knowledge rights of all other communities who also hold the knowledge and resources in common that community.

This is the reason bioprospecting models which deal with one individual or one community or one interest group can never be equitable. A commercial interest needs to take the prior informed consent of all communities and all members of each community who have used and contributed to collective innovation in biodiversity related knowledge. The partnership of the state is one mechanism for the interests of all contributing groups. In the case of biodiversity related collective innovation there are many interests involved. Farmers, the seed industry, traditional healers, pharmaceutical corporations, western and non-western scientific traditions, masculinist ways of knowing and feminist ways of knowing. All the diverse communities of interest must be included in a transaction.

Collective rights cannot be abjured or relinquished by any one community of users, or any individual of any communities, or the state on behalf of any community. The bioprospecting model, therefore, is not a legitimate source of benefit sharing in the case of biodiversity related knowledge. It is based on a double exclusion.

The first exclusion takes place when communities of users/innovators are excluded, and one local group is treated as holding the knowledge exclusively. The second exclusion takes place when the commercial enterprise signing a bioprospecting contract takes on the IPR on the knowledge transferred from an indigenous community as an unjustified claim to innovation. Over time this excludes the donor community itself as marketing systems and IPR regimes combine to make the community providing biological resources and knowledge dependent on the purchase of proprietary commodities from the corporations who monopolize the biodiversity and knowledge, e.g., farmers who contribute seeds end up buying proprietary seeds from the seed industry.

How Bioprospecting Creates Poverty

Bioprospecting was presented as a means for making the poor rich. It was often stated that the biodiversity regions are financially poor and since bioprospecting is associated with monetary compensation, it can make the biodiversity rich regions financially rich also. However, the bioprospecting model was (and still is) a model for taking away the last resources, both natural and intellectual, from the poor. It is, therefore, in reality a model for creating poverty for the community as a whole even when it might bring money to a few individuals in the community.

The poverty creating impact of biopiracy and bioprospecting can only be perceived if one recognizes the difference between the material economy and the financial economy. If people have reached biodiversity and intellectual wealth, they can meet their needs for healthcare and nutrition through their own resources and their knowledge. If on the other hand, when the rights to both resources and knowledge have been transferred from the community to IPR holders, the members of community end up paying high prices or royalties for what was originally theirs and which they had for free. They, therefore, become materially poorer.

Some communities are local users, others are non-local users. Suppose a community and a corporation engage in a bioprospecting contract, and that corporation takes on IPR on products of the medical plant; this drastically affects communities, with two major impacts being:

- All other communities no longer have access to the seed or medicine which they have used and are poorer in nutrition and health terms.
- Communities become poorer financially since they now have

to buy the seeds, agro-chemicals, or medicines which they had previously derived freely from local plant biodiversity.

Further, when biodiversity knowledge of a community is taken by a corporation, which commercializes it and transforms it into proprietary knowledge protected by IPRs, a number of impacts are felt by the donor community as the biodiversity gains commercial value globally, e.g., a medicinal plant, if it is exploited. This leads to:

- Diversion of the biological resource from meeting local needs to feeding non-local greed. This generates scarcity thus, leading to price increases.
- In the case of over-exploitation, it can lead to extinction.
- The local scarcity combined with IPRs on derived commodities eventually takes the resource and its products beyond the access of the donor communities (e.g., neem).
- The providing communities lose their rightful share to emerging markets.
- Other poor communities (whose traditions permit them to rely on free exchange or low-cost seed) which could have received the knowledge freely or at a low cost are also made dependent on the commercial interest.

The above perspective reflects the 'bioprospecting' or 'commodity paradigm', which only protects the rights of those who appropriate people's common resources and turn them into commodities. As discussed above, the benefits provided and shared by indigenous and local communities are rendered invisible and the focus is placed solely on the benefits shared by those who privatize and enclose the commons.

Reclaiming the intellectual commons of communities through asserting collective intellectual property rights combined with national and international laws on access and benefit sharing–such as the Indian Biodiversity Act–represent the real model of equitable benefit sharing.

"Give me the strength never to disown the poor or bend my knees before insolent might."

— Rabindranath Tagore

Cases of Bioprospecting

CSIR-San Hoodia Case: Who Owns What?

In 2003, a benefit sharing agreement was made between South African Council for Scientific and Industrial Research (CSIR) and the San, indigenous tribe of Kalahari in southern Africa. The San held traditional knowledge about Hoodia plant known for its hunger staving properties. CSIR, using the knowledge of the San, worked on a bioactive element from the plant and developed a pill and planned to share the benefits with San after the pill was commercialized.[12]

The San are the oldest human inhabitants of southern Africa, but after centuries of genocide and marginalization by colonialists, there are now only around 100,000 people in Botswana, Namibia, South Africa, and Angola. They used the Hoodia plant as a substitute for food and water during their hunting expeditions and so the knowledge and use of this plant dates back centuries.

In 1995, CSIR filed patent application for using biotic component of plant for its hunger suppressant properties. In 1998 it filed licensing agreement with a British company called Phytopharm which developed phyto-medicines. In the same year it was granted the patent over that component in a few countries around the world. The agreement with Phytopharm gave it license to deal with all Hoodia products. Phytopharm soon advanced the drug with its P57 program and concluded an agreement with Pfizer to develop the drug further.

The San didn't know about the CSIR's patent on P57, and until 2001 all these transactions and agreements went ahead without acknowledging San's contribution. Thus, prior informed consent was not even in the picture. CSIR cited the reason to be 'indeterminacy of authorship' and the 'difficulty' in locating the real owners of the knowledge. With the pressure from the civil society and NGOs like Biowatch, CSIR was subsequently forced to enter into some form of benefit sharing agreement which gave the San a share in the royalties from all P57 patent products.

The three organizations which negotiated this agreement with CSIR as representatives of the San were:

- The Working Group of Indigenous Minorities in Southern Africa (created on request of various San groups)
- South African San Council (created by Khomani, Xun, and Khwe communities)
- San Institute of South Africa (NGO coordinating San based organizations)

When the benefit sharing agreement was concluded in 2003, the San were recognized as the legal custodian of the Hoodia-related knowledge. The central debate soon became "who has authorship and exclusive claims of ownership."[13] These claims were extremely difficult to ascertain as the San people were spread across countries, other non-San tribes also contained Hoodia consumption and not all San groups had historically been using Hoodia. And identifying which groups had and which hadn't consumed Hoodia was close to impossible given that the San were constantly resettling throughout history.

It is interesting to note what a Khomani San leader said, "All the knowledge that Unilever and CSIR have comes from the Bushmen but they have nothing. The knowledge stays ours."

Therefore, the site of contesting claims of "who benefits" is also the site of conflicts of ownership. And solving this essentially involves erasing heterogeneity and limiting spatiality. Benefit sharing proposals thus end up reconstituting collectives and communities and permanently inscribing who is *inside* and who is *outside* the regimes of IP and benefit sharing.[14]

Similarly, in the ICBG-Aguarana case, the International Cooperative Biodiversity Groups (ICBG) along with the corporation Searle, constantly faced difficulties in identifying and locating the representatives for Aguarana, an indigenous Amazonian community in Peru with there being at least 187 different Aguarana communities.[15] A series of negotiations went on with a multitude of representative organizations coming into the picture and going out.[16] This case became one of the first cases where an indigenous group represented its interest whilst being mediated by other non-indigenous people or institutions. This agreement is considered successful with the community receiving royalty payments and a know-how license agreement. However, this success is also based on reductive site of authentic representatives. The basic presumption in benefit sharing, as reflected in this case, is that a community can be found in a homogenous quantifiable package with one voice to which law can conveniently assign authorship and subsequently assigns representation.[17] Thus, the 'rhetorical bullets' of law end up forcing the indigenous people to articulate their rights to protect their land, soil, trees, plants, and ultimately their very identity in the western colonialist discourse of exclusive ownership.[18]

In a similar fashion, we find deterritorialization at play in the Kani-TBGRI benefit sharing which was a pre-Biological Diversity Act case. The aim of benefit sharing mechanisms is to ensure that the indigenous people retain their rights to use and control their biotic realm. Deterritorialization, as articulated by Stuart Elden, happens when we are forced to "think anew on the notion of territory and to recognize how its logic is both played out and challenged in a period of globalization."[19] It leads to a production of new spatial and social relations, with new boundaries and enclaves. There is a disconnect that happens between an indigenous community and its territory, leading to the communities' displacement. This was reflected in what the Kani tribe from South India went through after the Kani-Tropical Botanical Garden Research Institute (TBGRI) benefit sharing agreement was concluded.[20] Over 70 percent of land which was the original habitat of this tribe has become "protected forests" which has restricted the tribe's access and use of the forest's resources. The forest department decides which forest produce can be accessed through a list and those produce not on the list are prohibited from being accessed. Arogyapacha, the herb which TBGRI claimed to have discovered with the Kanitribals under the benefit sharing agreement, is not on that list. Furthermore, due to fears of rapid depletion of the forest resources in the area, thousands of original inhabitants have been evicted, with many locals also carrying criminal charges for their attempt to use Arogyapacha.[21]

This shows that without secure tenure rights, these 'benefits' are empty and redundant. The IP assemblage and the ensuing rights and benefits are deterritorialized claims forming a subset of a larger global move of disconnecting territory and citizens' claims over their territory and putting in place a global order which manages these commons. Thus, to truly empower local and indigenous communities and give effect to their claims territorial rights need to be re-articulated, keeping their close relationship to indigeneity, local heritage, and resulting fairness in exchange of resources in mind.[22] These territorial rights take the form of secure land titles for the indigenous community through which determinacy can be lent to the intangible terrain of biocultural property as these land titles would ensure legal occupation of land by the community, along with establishing legal persons who own the property rights.[23] These rights would anchor the more fluid biocultural entitlements of the collectives. As suggested by Green as well, in the long run, we need more extensive recognition of people's territorial rights which may serve the interests of traditional communities more than the regime of ABS–with its empty benefits and lack of territorial entitlements.[24]

Upon closer investigation of the above mechanisms of production and representation of knowledge, one realizes that these mechanisms and frameworks are not just epistemic but political projects where the assumption of undifferentiated and homogenous communities is a deliberate strategy to shape these collectives into certain, discrete entities conducive to negotiation and lower 'transaction costs'. This necessity to assign authorship and lend central representation is rooted in the notion of an *autonomous subject* which dominates most of legal thought today. This is used by law to render the conversation between indigeneity and IP regimes smoother. The biopolitical nature of these mechanisms is further reflected in the colonialist hierarchy between an authoritative western 'science' with claims to represent 'traditional' and 'folk' knowledge through ABS. All of this put together ensures that innovators (corporations, scientists, etc.,) *receive* protection in the form of property ownership through patents and step into the roles of 'authors' and 'owners' while indigenous communities and their claims are *granted* only 'benefits'.

This is why we have evolved the concept of common, cumulative rights of indigenous communities to their knowledge and biodiversity. While laws make the colonization and biopiracy of our resources and intellectual heritage illegal, the bio-imperialists continue to make every effort to claim biopiracy as their right. On the other hand WTO, which was the preferred institution of bio-imperialism, has become the site of renewed debate on the links between CBD and TRIPS, and the need to make biopiracy illegal in Trade Law.

FIVE

The Western Corporate Bias in Knowledge and Property Rights which Facilitates Biopiracy as 'Creation' and 'Invention'

DIVERSITY AND PLURALISM are the characteristics of both the Indian environment as well as Indian society. We have a rich biodiversity of plants for food and medicine. Thus, agricultural diversity and diversity of medicinal plants have in turn given rise to a rich plurality of knowledge systems in agriculture and medicine.

Philosophy and History of Science are revealing that preference of one system of knowledge over others is part of the constructed superiority of the colonizing West.[1] Under colonial influence India's biological and intellectual heritage was devalued. The priorities of scientific development, and R&D efforts guided by a western bias, transformed the plurality of knowledge systems into a hierarchy of knowledge systems.

Western industrial systems of knowledge in agriculture and medicine were defined as the only scientific system. Indigenous systems of knowledge were defined as inferior, and, in fact, as unscientific. Thus, instead of strengthening research on safe and sustainable plant-based pesticides such as neem and pongamia, we focused exclusively on the development and promotion of hazardous and non-sustainable chemical pesticides such as DDT and Sevin. The use of DDT causes millions of deaths each year and has increased the occurrence of pests 12,000-fold. The manufacturing of Sevin at the Union Carbide Plant in Bhopal led to a disaster which killed thousands and disabled more than 400,000 people.

As recognition of the ecological failure of the chemical route to pest control increases, the use of plant-based pesticides is becoming increasingly popular in the industrialized world. Corporations that have promoted the use of chemicals are now looking for biological options. That is why, in the search for new markets and control over the biodiversity base for the production of biopesticides and chemicals, TNCs like W.R. Grace claimed IPRs on neem-based biopesticides.

The experience with agrichemicals was replicated in the field of drugs and medicines. Indigenous systems of medicine and the biodiversity of medicinal plants were totally neglected in our scientific research and health policy which focused exclusively on the western allopathic system as well as on technology transfer from the western pharmaceutical industry. Thus, the health and pharmaceutical budget was heavily weighted in favor of the development and dissemination of the western allopathic system. In spite of a lack of official support, indigenous medical systems are based on over 7,000 species of medicinal plants and on 15,000 medicines of herbal formulations in different systems. The Ayurvedic texts refer to 1,400 plants, Unani texts to 342, Siddha system to 328. Homeopathy uses 570 plants of which approximately 100 are of Indian origin. Needless to say, the economic value of medicinal plants to 100 million rural households is simply immeasurable.

The failures and non-sustainability of the chemical route to agriculture and health care provides an opportunity to re-evaluate knowledge systems and move from the false hierarchy of these systems to a plurality. Such a pluralistic view of knowledge systems would imply respect for the different systems in their own logic and in their own epistemological foundations. It would also mean that one system (viz., the western) does not have to serve as the measure of scientific adequacy for all systems, and further, diverse systems would no longer be reduced to the language and logic of the western knowledge system. The integrity of our biological intellectual heritage has to be respected and preserved. The assumption of hierarchy is also the underlying basis for legitimizing piracy as invention.

Western bias enters the IPR regimes and superimposes the diversity of knowledge systems which leads to appropriation of traditional knowledge, i.e., biopiracy, and is presented as 'innovation' and 'invention'.

This phenomenon of biopiracy and intellectual piracy is one in which western commercial interests unethically and falsely claim products and innovations directly derived from indigenous knowledge traditions as their own 'intellectual property', a claim protected through 'intellectual property rights'. This is a direct consequence of the devaluation and the resulting invisibility of indigenous systems of knowledge which in turn leads to lack of protection for these systems. This devaluation is linked to the imposition of the reductionist methods of western science to the non-reductionist approaches of indigenous knowledge systems. Therefore, as the western style IPR systems are biased towards western knowledge systems which reduce biodiversity to its chemical or genetic structures, the indigenous systems receive no protection while the piracy of these systems remains protected.

In the absence of a protection system for biodiversity and indigenous knowledge systems, and with the universalization of western style IPR regimes, such intellectual and biological piracy will only grow. Protecting our biological and intellectual heritage in the age of biopiracy requires the recognition and rejuvenation of our heritage, and the evolution of legal systems for the protection of this heritage in the context of emerging IPR regimes.

Pluralism of Knowledge Systems - Diverse but equally valid methodologies and scientific systems

Ayurveda, Siddha, Unani, Folk, Homeopathy, Allopathy
Hierarchy of Knowledge Systems - only reductionist methods of western science treated as valid

With knowledge plurality mutating into knowledge hierarchy, a horizontal ordering of diverse but equally valid systems are converted into a vertical ordering of 'unequal' systems, with the epistemological foundations of one system being imposed on others to invalidate them. Such is the case with the Western treatment of Ayurveda. In colonial times, there was an attempt to ban it; even in our times, it is being treated as a second-rate science.

Across the world there is an intense contest emerging between two paradigms of health and two paradigms of science: the first paradigm is holistic and sees connections between the health of the planet and our health. It is based on the ecological science of interconnectedness. The second paradigm is reductionist, mechanistic, and commercial. The mechanistic world views us as separate from nature and each part of our body as separate from all others, just as parts of a machine are. Thus, in this system, health is defined as a commodity we buy from the pharmaceutical industry.

Recently, in the US and UK, intense debates have taken place on Obamacare and NHS, on whether health is a public good or a privatized commodity for sale.

In India a multidimensional debate emerged when a new National Medical Commission Bill (2017) was introduced in the Indian Parliament. The Indian Medical Association (IMA) called a strike to protest this bill, which has since been sent to a select committee of Parliament.

There have been many more objections to this bill.

One element of this controversy is the 'contest' detailed above between the two paradigms of health care: the holistic ancient systems like Ayurveda and the "modern" allopathic system based on drugs and pharmaceuticals. The bill seeks to allow practitioners of Ayurveda, Yoga, Naturopathy, Unani, Siddha, and Homoeopathy to practice modern medicine once they complete a short term "bridge" course.

While the objection of allopathic doctors is to Ayurveda and other traditional medicine practitioners being able to practice 'modern medicine', my objection is to the degradation and devaluation of one of the oldest and most sophisticated health systems and how it is being swallowed by a mechanistic commercial system.

Ayurveda–the Science (Veda) of Life (Ayur)–is the most sophisticated science of health, nutrition, and diet. It is guided by 5,000 years of time-tested knowledge. I see it as one of India's greatest gifts to the world, along with agroecology and organic farming, brought to the West by Sir Albert Howard through his book, *An Agricultural Testament*.

The holistic sciences, like Ayurveda, are based on interconnectedness and living processes. On the other hand, what is called 'modern medicine' is based on a mechanistic paradigm of separation, reductionism, fragmentation, and on pharmaceuticals derived from the chemicals and dye industry a hundred years ago.

Thus the mechanistic paradigm has transformed the diversity of knowledge systems, privileging the mechanistic and reductionist paradigm as the only science, and pushing all other knowledge systems to oblivion or treating them as inferior.

"Science" is derived from the Latin *scire*, meaning 'to know'.
To live is to know.

We are all knowers of different kinds. Diverse knowledge systems are scientific within their own paradigms. Mechanistic, reductionist thinking does not just reduce the world to fragmented, separated parts; it also reduces our capacity to know. By creating hierarchies of knowledge, one creates a hierarchy of knowers. Thus creating the assumption that there are 'experts' who possess 'objective' knowledge, who are separate from, and superior to, ordinary men, women, peasants, and workers. It falsely makes the practitioner of reductionist 'science' not just superior to experts of other knowledge traditions, such as Ayurveda and agroecology, but further, tries to reduce these rich systems knowledge to a mechanistic basis, thus robbing the Systems Paradigm of its very strength. This is a 'knowledge apartheid' which prevents us from obtaining any real answers about how to live healthy lives. With the repeated failures and limitations of the reductionist approach to life in agriculture and in health, the relevance of agroecology and Ayurveda grows.

From Pluralism and Diversity of Knowledge Systems to a Hierarchy of Knowledge

The shift from the chemical era to the age of biology creates new problems of patentability. Firstly, patents on biodiversity or products and uses thereof, falsely claim properties of plant derived drugs as 'products of the mind' when they are actually products of plant biodiversity. Unlike mechanical and electrical artifacts, plant-based medicines are not merely a result of inventive human genius. They are based on existing properties and characteristics of diverse plants. The boundary between the 'product of nature' and the 'product of the mind' is, therefore, fuzzy and blurred in the case of medicines of plants.

Secondly, the use of medicinal plants in indigenous systems of knowledge is the basis of most patent claims by western enterprise. Indigenous systems are used and exploited, but not recognized or protected. Instead of recognition and protection being given to the innovation of traditional systems, recognition and protection under western style patent regimes is given to minor modifications and tiny tinkering of indigenous knowledge systems by practitioners of western science. Patents cannot offer protection to the intellectual heritage of practitioners or indigenous medical traditions, as the knowledge of utilization of biodiversity for particular health problems which is available in traditional systems becomes non-patentable by indigenous practitioners since the criteria of patentability are (a) novelty, (b) non-obviousness, and (c) industrial application.

Within the indigenous traditions, undertaken by traditional practitioners, the knowledge is an ancient heritage, continues overtime, and hence is not 'novel' even though it is based on innovation. Being traditional is by definition not new. It, therefore, cannot satisfy criterion (a). Further, since indigenous medical systems are non-industrial but part of folk traditions or small-scale production processing and use, they also do not meet criterion (c).

However, when knowledge from these ancient systems is transferred to the west, translated into western systems for commercialization on a large scale, it gets treated as 'novel', non-obvious, and having industrial application. Thus, there is a de-recognition of the innovation embodied in these indigenous systems and the possibility of claiming its appropriation is named as an 'innovative step'.

In the absence of a protection system for biodiversity and indigenous knowledge systems, and with the encroaching universalization of western corporate style IPR regimes, intellectual and biological piracy is growing. This has been illustrated by the cases of patents filed on neem, turmeric, *Phyllanthus niruri* and others (For more, see the next chapter on Biopiracy). TNCs are claiming innovations based on ancient Indian knowledge.

Translation from one system to another is not invention. Biopiracy of existing plants and knowledge is not innovation. The principle that an indigenous plant is known in indigenous knowledge to be useful for medical use is existing knowledge. Its translation into English, or reductionist science, or commercial exploitation by a corporation cannot be treated as novel. Further, given this principle, small variation in processing the indigenous plant for medicinal use is an obvious step. How then does such knowledge get patented and qualify as 'novel' and 'non-obvious'?

Again, the false claim to novelty is based on epistemic bias of western knowledge systems as well as the ignorance and denial of the existence of diverse and pluralistic knowledge systems. It is based on reducing, and thus treating, all knowledge systems based on interconnectedness as inferior. The horizontal relationship between diverse systems of knowledge is converted into a hierarchy of knowledge systems with the western reductionist system at the top. Lastly, this false claim is based on the fact that while such knowledge exists in an indigenous knowledge system, it does not exist in the western knowledge system.

Translation of the knowledge that an indigenous plant is useful for the purpose of medicinal use from an indigenous knowledge system to a western one is taken as an innovation. Translation of indigenous knowledge to western knowledge in a hierarchical perspective suggests a 'higher' level of knowledge content. This translation is misconstrued as the 'creation' of knowledge. Thus, biopiracy becomes 'invention'.

A sociological shift is thus fallaciously treated as an epistemological shift. This fallacy of sociological and cultural displacement as an epistemological shift generating new knowledge is made possible because knowledge pluralities have been transformed into knowledge hierarchies. This is a result of the colonial biases which have treated western knowledge as exclusively scientific, while treating non-western knowledge systems as unscientific. However, the difference in epistemological foundation does not make indigenous knowledge system inferior, it just makes them different.

This diversity of knowledge needs to be recognized and respected, and a pluralistic IPR regime needs to be evolved which makes it possible to recognize and respect indigenous knowledge and protect the indigenous knowledge systems and practices and livelihoods based on it.

Schematically, what is proposed is the recognition that there are diverse indigenous knowledge systems. And each has its own epistemological foundations and its own scientific community of practitioners. We, therefore, need diverse legal regimes and not just universalized TRIPS and WTO related laws which are restricted to western laws. We need IPR systems which don't just reflect the interests of the dominant economic systems of the west, nor of TNCs.

The criterion on which western laws are based fails to recognize where indigenous knowledge systems are non-western. It is only when an element of indigenous knowledge is transferred to a western knowledge system that it is recognized, and it is then treated as a western innovation. As a corollary, the interests and rights of indigenous communities find no place in western laws and are transferred to the scientific practitioners of the western knowledge system, in particular those backed by corporate capital.

It is the inappropriateness of existing corporate IPR regimes, like patents for the protection of traditional knowledge systems and biodiversity, combined with the absence of legal frameworks that protect the integrity of indigenous knowledge systems that leads to IPRs in their present state becoming restricted forms and mechanisms of piracy.

Most biodiversity related IPRs are either the enclosure of the intellectual commons of non-western traditions of science (e.g., neem, turmeric, and *Phyllanthus niruri*) or the enclosure of the intellectual commons of contemporary western traditions of science. Examples of the latter are patents on scientific processes related to genetic engineering which have been evolved through research in the public domain in universities and have been privatized through IPRs. Such examples include the particle gun used for inserting foreign genes into an organism, a basic technique in genetic engineering.

In the present world market economy, where knowledge represents money, capital represents power. Profit earning is the sole aim. Those who own capital seek IPRs to protect their 'discoveries', which are often based on the cumulative and collective innovation of traditional societies. Therefore, biodiversity based traditional knowledge systems of the forest dwellers, farmers, and healers are fast becoming the private property of the TNCs. The TNCs are usurping these systems from the domain of common knowledge through IPRs, which in essence promotes resource piracy and intellectual piracy.

The system of IPRs has expanded the domain of intellectual property to biodiversity. However, these IPR regimes, as provided under TRIPS, only recognize and provide protection to the formal innovators, not to the informal indigenous innovators. The traditional knowledge of informal innovators–farmers, indigenous medical practitioners, forest dwellers–is being pirated by the formal innovators–scientists, plant breeders, and technologists–who make minor modifications or advances, and then seek patents, thereby claiming the knowledge as their private property.

Botanists seek information free of cost from indigenous peoples which the latter have accumulated through several generations of folk experimentation and adoption. The information often pertains to the manifold uses of plant species, geographic locations and habitat preferences of individual species, time and mode of harvest of plant species, preparations, processing, formation and recipes, using one or more species for specific medicinal uses and other subject matters, particularly on folk selection procedures and ecosystem preservation.

The plant breeders and germplasm collectors often visit the farmers' fields and collect diverse genetic resources of several species of cultivated plants for use in formal plant breeding. They develop improved varieties using these local landraces adapted to diverse agroclimatic conditions.

When they release these varieties, they claim IPRs on them called 'breeders rights', from which they receive royalties, while the farmers receive nothing. IPR systems which do not recognize farmers as breeders, and which only protect the rights of the seed industry, not the rights of the farmers providing farmers' varieties are systems based on the piracy of our agricultural biodiversity.

Similarly, pharmaceutical industries investigate the efficacy of many medicines and toxic substances used by indigenous or tribal people. In fact, more than 7,000 natural chemical compounds used in modern medicines and chemical industries have been employed by indigenous healers and other people for centuries. Pharmaceutical companies have often investigated useful attributes of substances known to tribal communities and isolated the active principles. From there, they modify the products or sometimes use them as a lead for the design of a new synthetic compound; thereby potentially rendering this compound more stable or less toxic than the original substance. The pharmaceutical companies would then claim their product as 'novel' and on that basis, claim patent rights on it. Local knowledge helps increase the efficiency and decrease the costs of such isolation by almost 400 times.

Once more, patents are supposed to satisfy three criteria:

1. Novelty
2. Non-obviousness
3. Utility

Novelty implies that the innovation must be new. It cannot be part of 'prior art' or existing knowledge. Non-obviousness implies that someone familiar in the art should not be able to achieve the same step. Most patents based on indigenous knowledge appropriation violate the criteria of novelty combined with non-obviousness because they range from direct piracy to minor tinkering, which involves obvious steps to anyone trained in the techniques and disciplines involved.

In the US, many distortions in law exist which have facilitated the patenting process for companies such as those in the pharmaceutical industry. One such distortion is the interpretation of 'prior art'. It permits patents to be filed on discoveries in the US despite the fact that identical ones may already exist in other parts of the world. Patent attorney Peter J. Thoma of the Dallas firm of Thompson and Knight explains:

> *"If for example, someone in Europe were developing an invention and you independently and without knowledge of its existence in good faith developed your own device that was essentially the same invention, that fact would not prevent you from obtaining a patent in the US. The European invention would not be considered prior art in the statute. Furthermore, if the invention had been written up in a publication, or had been patented anywhere in the world more than one year before your filing date, that would be considered prior art. So, the incentive is to file promptly."*[2]

Essentially the statute of prior art states that patents cannot be filed on discoveries or inventions already existing in the US, but they can be filed on discoveries or inventions existing outside the US (because 'prior art' of these inventions is not recognized by the US).

The Economic Espionage Act, which was signed into law by the US Congress in 1996, criminalized the natural development and exchange of knowledge, and empowered its intelligence agencies to investigate the activities of ordinary people worldwide to protect intellectual property rights of US corporations. The US viewed, and continues to view, IPRs as vital to national security. The absurdity of this legislation is further increased upon the realization that what is seen as 'intellectual property' is often information 'pirated' from non-western societies and indigenous communities.

This Espionage Act implanted espionage from military domains into economic domains by redefining intellectual property infringement as a crime. It justified the use of intelligence agencies to deal with issues of science and technology exchange. While every country has the right to protect its national security, there were, however, problems with this act.

Firstly, it defined the 'nation's economic interest' as a 'nation's security interest' in a period of globalization and trade liberalization and hence used the arguments of national security asymmetrically. This is particularly problematic when globalization is being used to force other countries to give up their national interest, national security, and national sovereignty. The US is the driving force for the dismantling of national sovereignty and national security of other countries.

The Special 301 Report of the US Trade Regulations also represented an instrument of unilateralism, whereby countries identified as indulging in 'unreasonable', 'unjustifiable', or 'discriminatory' tactics that result in reduced profit for US based companies were forced to change their national laws. Unilateralism comes in the form of conditionalities attached to aid and structural adjustment programs of the IMF and World Bank, and has resulted in the lowering of health, environmental, educational and living standards of people all over the third world.

While Third World governments have sought protection from such unilateralism through multilateralism of GATT, the US held that it will continue to use unilateral instruments like Special 301 to force countries to toe its line.

While the US has been the leading voice against the piracy of intellectual property, the US is also the country leading in biopiracy *through* intellectual property in biodiversity related knowledge. India is one of the several Third World biodiversity rich countries which are losing its precious natural heritage to TNCs of the west. TNCs are making billions of dollars by pirating our genetic resources, as well as the knowledge of the local communities relating to its diverse uses by claiming patents on it.

Western patent systems were never designed for the domain of biodiversity or living resources and remain inappropriate to those subject matters. As stated by John Hoxie in *A Patent Attorney's View*:

> *"The patent system as we have it today was really very little changed by the Patent Act of 1952; it goes back to a period when invention was largely mechanical, followed by an electrical era. In both, invention was*

chiefly of physical objects. The language and much of the judicial treatment of the statutes is geared to that sort of invention. When chemical invention became more frequent... a problem arose of fitting chemical invention into a mold of words and a habit of thinking that were not developed with it in mind." [3]

The Western bias in Defining "Enclosures of the Commons" as Creation of Private Property Rights

Today we have to look beyond the state and the marketplace to protect the rights of the two-thirds majority of India–that is, the rural communities. And empower the community with the rights which enables the recovery of the commons. Commons are resources shaped, managed, and utilized through Community Control. In the commons, no one can be excluded. The commons cannot be monopolized by the economically powerful citizens or corporations, nor by the politically powerful state.

Commons and communities are beyond both the market and state. They are governed by self-determined norms and are self-managed. In the Colonial era, community power was getting undermined by the takeover of the colonial state, subsequently beginning the enclosure of the commons. Thus, water and forest were made state property, leading to the alienation of local communities, and the destruction of the resource base. Poverty, ecological destruction, social disintegration, and political disempowerment were the results of such corporate state driven 'enclosures'.

In the globalization era, the commons were (and still are) being enclosed while the power of communities was (and still is) being undermined by a corporate enclosure through life itself being transformed into the private property of corporations. The corporate enclosure functions in two ways; firstly, IPR shaped by corporations allow the "enclosure" of biodiversity and knowledge, thus eroding the commons and the community. Secondly, the corporation is treated as the only form of association with legal personality.

IPRs are the equivalent of letters patent that the colonizers have used since 1492 when Columbus set precedence in treating the license to conquer non-European people as the natural right of European men. The land title to non-European territories issued by the Pope through European Kings and Queens were the first patent. Charters and patents issued to merchant adventurers were authorization to "discover, find, search out and view such a remote heathen and barbarous land, countries and territories not actually possessed by any Christian prince or people." The colonizers' freedom was built on the slavery and subjugation of the people with original rights to the land. This violent takeover was rendered 'natural' by defining the colonized people into nature, thus defying them their humanity and freedom.

Locke's treatise on property effectively legitimized this same process of theft and robbery during the enclosure movement in Europe.[4] Locke clearly articulated capitalism's freedom to build on freedom to steal. He clearly stated that property is created in its 'spiritual' form as manifested in the control of capital by removing resources from nature and mixing them with labor. According to Locke, only capital could add value to appropriated nature, and hence only those who own the capital have the natural right to own natural resources; a right that supersedes the common rights of others with prior claims. Though capital is defined as a source of freedom, this freedom is founded upon the denial of freedom to the land, forests, rivers, and biodiversity that capital claims as its own. Because property obtained through privatization of commons is equated with freedom, those commoners laying claim to it are perceived to be depriving the freedom of the owners of that capital. Thus, peasants and tribals who demand the return of their rights and access to resources are regarded as thieves and saboteurs.

The takeover of territories and land in the past, and the takeover of biodiversity and indigenous knowledge now have been based on "emptying" land and biodiversity of all relationships to indigenous people.

All sustainable cultures, in their diversity, have viewed the earth as *terra mater* (Mother Earth). The colonial construct of the passivity of the earth and consequent creation of the colonial category of land as *terra nullius* (nobody's land), served two purposes: it denied the existence and prior rights of origin and negated the regenerative capacity and life processes of the earth.[5]

In Australia, the concept of *terra nullius* (literally meaning 'empty land') was used to justify the appropriation of land and its natural resources and declaring the entire continent of Australia uninhabited. This declaration enabled the colonizer to privatize the commons relatively easily, because as far as they were concerned, there were no commons existing in the first place!

Whether it was the gradual privatization and divisibility of community held rights or the declaration of *terra nullius*, the transformation of common property rights into private property rights implied the exclusion of the right to survival for a large section of society.

The Eurocentric concept of property views only capital investment as investment, and hence treats returns on capital investment as the only right that needs protection. Non-Western indigenous communities and cultures recognize that investment can also be of labor or of care and nurturance. Rights in such cultural systems protects investments beyond capital. They protect the culture of conservation and culture of caring and sharing. This is the culture that is dying and needs to be rejuvenated if humanity has to have a future along with other species.

There are major differences between ownership of resources shaped in Europe during the enclosure movement and during colonial takeover, and 'ownership' as it has been practiced by tribals and farmers throughout history across diverse societies. The former is based on ownership as private property, based on the concept of return on investment for profit. The latter is based on entitlements through usufruct rights based on concepts of return on labor to provide for ourselves, our children, our families, and our communities. Usufruct rights can be privately held or held in common. When held in common, they define common property.

Equity is built into usufruct rights since ownership is based on return on labor. The poor have survived in India in spite of having no access to capital because they have had guaranteed access to the resource base needed for sustenance–common pastures, water, and biodiversity.

Sustainability and justice are built into usufructuary rights since there are physical limits on how much one can labor and hence there are limits on return investment of labor and return on investment, generally. On the other hand, inequity is built into private property based on ownership of capital since there is no limit on how much capital one can own, control and invest. Today, the economy of financial capital has become a 'virtual economy' much larger than the 'real' economy of goods and services produced in the world.

Because of the inherently inequitable nature of ownership, 'ceilings' were put on ownership through capital, to ensure equity. Land reform laws such as "Land ceilings" were an instrument for limiting monopoly control over resources. Land to the Tiller policies, such as operation Barga in West Bengal, were also examples of re-introducing juridical concepts of ownership based on return on labor, rather than a return on capital. Not only is a juridical system based on usufruct more equitable, it is also more sustainable since usufruct ownership means resources are held in trust for future generations, so that the rights of future generations are not undermined for short term profits.

Corporate IPRs as Extension of the Eurocentric Concept of Property to Biodiversity and Biodiversity Related Knowledge

The enclosure of biodiversity and knowledge is the final step in a series of enclosures that began with the rise of colonialism. Land and forests were the first resources to be enclosed and converted from commons to commodities. Later, water resources were enclosed through dams, groundwater mining, and privatization schemes. Now it is both biodiversity and biodiversity related knowledge which are being enclosed through IPRs.

The destruction of commons was essential for the industrial revolution to provide a supply of natural resources as raw materials to industry. A life-support system can be shared but it cannot be owned as private property or exploited for private profit. The commons, therefore, had to be privatized and people's sustenance base in these commons had to be appropriated to feed the engine of industrial progress and capital accumulation.

The enclosure of the commons was called the "revolution of the rich against the poor."[6] However, enclosures are not just historical episodes having occurred in sixteenth century England. The enclosure of the commons is a guiding metaphor for understanding conflicts being generated by the expansion of industrial IPRs system to biodiversity, even now.

In the colonial period peasants were forced to grow indigo instead of food, salt was taxed to provide revenues for the British military, and meanwhile, forests were being enclosed to transform them into state monopolies for commercial exploitation. In the rural areas, the effects on the peasants were the gradual erosion of usufruct rights (nistar rights) of access to food, fuel and livestock grazing from the community's common lands. The marginalization of peasant communities' rights over their forests, sacred groves and 'wastelands' are the primary cause of their impoverishment.

Biodiversity has always been a local, commonly owned, and commonly utilized resource for indigenous communities. A resource is common property when a social system exists to use it based on the principles of justice and sustainability. This involves a combination of rights and responsibilities among users, a combination of utilization and conservation, a sense of co-production with nature, and sharing them among members of diverse communities. Heritage is not viewed in terms of property at all, i.e., a good which has an owner and is used for the purpose of extracting economic benefits. Instead they view it in terms of possessing community and individual responsibility. For indigenous people, heritage is a bundle of relationship rather than a bundle of economic rights. That is the reason why no concept of 'private property' existed among the indigenous communities.

Thus, the concept of individual private property rights to either the resource or to associated knowledge remains alien to the local community. This undoubtedly exacerbates the usurpation of the knowledge of indigenous people with serious consequences for them and for biodiversity conservation.

The culturally biased and narrow notions of rights and property that have shaped the western industrial IPRs paradigm are inadequate and inappropriate for indigenous cultures and for the objective of conserving biodiversity and cultural diversity. Through IPRs and TRIPS, an attempt was made to universalize and globalize a particular Eurocentric culture. When applied to biodiversity, such narrow concepts have become a mechanism for denying the intrinsic worth of diverse species and denying the prior rights and prior innovations of indigenous communities.

A frequent comment heard in scientific and lay circles is that "we should patent all our traditional knowledge and biodiversity." However, neither traditional knowledge nor biodiversity can be patented by indigenous practitioners because for indigenous societies, it is not 'novel', it is ancient.

The reason that the collective and cumulative innovation of millions of people of thousands of years can be pirated and claimed as an 'innovation' of Western trained scientists or corporation is the misguided colonial idea that science is unique to the West, and the false claim that indigenous knowledge systems cannot be treated as scientific–even when the same knowledge is pirated and later patented. Furthermore, countries like the US, where most pirated indigenous innovations are filed for patenting, do not recognize existing knowledge of other countries as prior art.

SIX

The Enclosure and Recovery of the Commons

> *"What is, then, a philosophy of relation?*
> *Something impossible, as long as it is not conceived of as poetics."*
> – Édouard Glissant

Understanding the Commons

To be is to be related, and the notion of being related is deeply intertwined with the notion of the commons. We all find ourselves in a time where there is an urgency to redefine what it means to be human, which necessitates that we redefine what it means to be in relation with one another. And if, as Glissant says, the philosophy of relation is the poetics of relation, so too, is it the poetics of the commons. A redefinition of one implies a redefinition of the other because the boundaries between humans and their environment, culture and nature, mind and body are indefinite. So, what, precisely, would carving a poetics of the commons look like?

(De)Constructing the Commons

In the current times, when the commons has become a crucial concept in carving a transformative politics, one also finds the language of the commons being co-opted by the neoliberal institutions (e.g., World Bank, The Economist, etc.,) that attack it to render a positive spin to privatization and legitimize a new wave of enclosures in the interest of 'conservation' while softening the resistance. Caffentzis and Federici put it succinctly when they say:

> *"It is almost a law of contemporary social life that the more commons are attacked, the more they are celebrated."* [1]

The literature on the commons reflects a diversity of definitions, with each discipline producing a position depending on the contours of its thought. While ecologists center their investigations on protection and conservation, economists delve deeper into 'incentives' and induced 'cooperation', political scientists explore the idea of state as an 'active agent' or 'decentralized agency' and anthropologists continue to focus more on defining the exact locus of community.[2] These debates within the community of researchers become significant to trace as these points of terminus and departures heavily shape the policies reaching the grass roots. A case in point being the famous publication of Hardin's *Tragedy of the Commons* in the 1960s and the resultant large-scale state intervention in resource management.

Most of these tangents of thought were results of the minds of men deeply entrenched in masculinist-individualist-reductionist ways of being, all the way from Aristotle who proclaimed something as ridiculous as "what is common to the greatest number has the least care bestowed upon it"[3] to Hardin who said, "ruin is the destination toward which all men rush, each pursuing his best interest in a society that believes in the freedom of the commons."[4] And at the root of most of these positions on resources and their caretaking has been the idea that all of us operate from a place of immense scarcity–rather than inner abundance–because of which the "free rider problem" becomes the biggest problem of a self-interested society. Our inner (spiritual, emotional, mental) scarcity becomes naturally reflected in the outer story of scarcity that we weave. The 'tragedy of the commons' being just one of the manifestations of that inner sense of limited space and time.

The positions, theories, and abstractions resulting from that inner scarcity then become the hegemonic paradigms governing the commons. And, as pointed out by Bonnie McCay, they become the "definitional frameworks" which decide what is considered the commons which in turn shapes how these commons are managed, protected, and recovered.[5] Therefore, the definitional frameworks are crucial to a genuine exploration of a poetics of the commons.

Commons vs. Open Access Systems

It is important to understand the difference between a system of commons per se and an 'open access' system. The latter assumes that resources are unmanaged with no ownership. This presumption of a lack of private property is instantly associated with a state of lawlessness and loss of control which in turn makes the resource ripe for a 'tragedy' as enunciated by Hardin.[6] The 'tragedy' of the commons arises as a result of this assumption about an open access system of commons; with this being further rooted in the flawed and narrow idea that resources can be managed effectively only if they are in the control of private individuals.

However, we have enough instances all over the world that show a successful system of commons in the hands of communities. A system of commons, as we perceive it, is a system not lacking in ownership but being owned at the level of a collective (instead of individuals). With these groups possessing their own rules and norms for managing the use of the common resources and ensuring that the resources don't vanish into their doom.[7]

What Hardin assumes in his 'tragedy' is that the only way a society can function in a healthy way is through competition, and if we all don't compete to control and protect property humankind will devolve into a state of complete chaos.[8] However, the works of thinkers like Marcel Mauss show that in order for societies to flourish they do *not* need to be organized around principles of the market.[9] Even now, major parts of societies in the Third World continue to work on the foundation of cooperation (instead of competition).

Thus it is crucial to understand this difference between the two systems as the idea of an open access system which is unmanaged (and hence in need of 'saving' by private individuals) is used by those who aim at enclosing the commons: whether it is the forest commons or our seeds. Corporations are trying to define our seed commons and our biodiversity as open access systems needing the management of their 'expertise' and their 'innovation' which in turn necessitates the application of intellectual property rights like patents to 'reward' this human labor.

Ostrom and the Theory of Commons

Elinor Ostrom's extensive work on the commons and theory of collective action reflects one such significant 'definitional framework'. Ostrom defined a "common pool resource" in her book as a "natural or manmade resource system that is sufficiently large as to make it costly to exclude potential beneficiaries from obtaining benefits from its use."[10]

Though subtly rooted in the same assumptions of autonomy, rational cost-benefit analysis, and utility maximization in humans, her work boldly challenged the rational-egoist model of neoclassical economics, being propounded by the likes of Hardin in his fable of the 'tragedy of the commons'. She emphasized that people are not just 'individuals' but part of a cooperative solidarity which not only leads to collective action but additionally sustains the common resource over long periods of time on the basis of 'trust' and 'reciprocity' without any external agency. Looking back, her three most crucial contributions in negating the rational-reductionist models of the 1980s and 90s were:

- Recognizing that there was interdependence amongst the commoners.
- Highlighting that human behavior was diverse and not always predictable as per the egoistic model of individual i.e., rational choice behavior was contingent on a multitude of other factors.
- Putting forth the idea that humans are *fallible* and *bounded* in their knowledge.[11]

Two of her reflections in her book on the commons still ring true:

- Neither the state nor the market is a successful system for allowing the people to sustain the use of a natural resource over a long period of time.
- The communities have relied on their own systems of governance, resembling neither the state nor the market, which have accrued tremendous success over long periods of time.

Thus, we have to look beyond the state and the market to protect the rights of the rural communities. Empowering the community with rights would enable the recovery of the commons. Commons are resources shaped, managed and utilized by an autonomous community. Neither can anyone be excluded nor can a single monopoly of corporation or state exercise its powers over that resource.

Another deeper definitional framework has been the Eurocentric and colonialist view of property itself. What this paradigm views as property has had a direct relationship with what commons were destroyed and enclosed. Throughout human history, catastrophic changes have taken place in the context in which resources are perceived. The enclosure of biodiversity and knowledge has been a part of the movement that began with colonialism. The success of the industrial revolution rode on the destruction of the commons, as natural resources in the commons had to be used as raw materials and people's sustenance base in these commons had to be appropriated if the engine of capital was to be fed. These enclosures continue to be seen all around us, with not just physical commons but also intellectual commons being subsumed through the IPR regimes shaped by the same Eurocentric perceptions of property.

From Commons to Commoning

While, on the one hand, the war on the commons is intensifying, on the other hand, we are also witnessing a stronger and ever more powerful resistance coming from the grassroots for a society that reclaims the commons and revolves around the principle of social cooperation. This is reflected clearly in various seeds of reclamation being sown all over the world: from the Zapatistas' call for a new constitution in the state of Mexico to the Bolivian Constitution recognizing communal property in 2009.[12]

The struggle for the commons is the most crucial struggle of our time and it is all around us in different forms and manifestations. Like any living organism, it is also mutating and becoming increasingly dynamic with new forms of social cooperation being created in various movements from 'free software', 'solidarity economy', 'time banks', 'urban gardens', and 'Community Supported Agriculture' to 'food co-ops', 'local currencies', and 'creative commons' licenses. There is a whole paradigm of new social relations being brought to life standing on the foundation of communal sharing.[13]

In lieu of how this struggle is mutating all over the world, another definitional framework being evolved by a set of critical theorists is the articulation of the process of '*commoning*' (practices that lead to the production and reproduction of the commons) and a different social relation involved in creating such a system.[14] This shift is reflective of the transition we are seeing all around us towards a process oriented systems approach. Whilst, initially, the commons were seen merely as resources or things that needed to be managed and protected, they are now widely being embraced as a relational politics, embedded in fluidity and our mutual vulnerability. From being viewed as a "mere technical management of resources (in space)" they are now seen as part of the "struggle to perform common livable relations (in time)."[15]

What our indigenous communities already embodied in their worldview of the commons as a way of life is now slowly being moved towards by the rest of the world. In gradually tracing our way back we are walking forward into a future embracing that liminality and inseparability between the communities and their common resources. Between us and our environment. This is the true poetics of the commons.

Reclaiming the Commons

> *"We know enough of our own history by now to be aware that people exploit what they have merely concluded to be of value, but they defend what they love. To defend what we love we need a particularizing language, for we love what we particularly know. The abstract, objective, impersonal, dispassionate language of science can, in fact, help us to know certain things, and to know some things with certainty...but it cannot replace and it cannot become the language of familiarity, reverence and affection by which things of value ultimately are protected."*
>
> -Wendell Berry, Life is a Miracle

Indigenous Knowledge and the Knowledge Commons

Indigenous knowledge by its very nature defies all attempts at its compartmentalization. Boven and Morohashi rightly caution:

> *"It is only when we try to translate these local practices into western terms that we are confronted with the need to choose a certain definition and we see how difficult it is to give voice to a worldview which is sometimes completely different from our own."*[16]

'Original participation' is a concept expressed by the worldview of indigenous cultures which means that their members are born into an integral world community where they speak on behalf of the four-legged-ones, the winged-ones, the finned-ones, the forest, the mountain, the bees, the river, and the seas. This is a reflection of a consciousness that is supremely evolved, not 'primitive' or 'backward', and it is more crucial than ever to safeguard the increasingly precarious future of our planet.

Indigenous knowledge strongly situates itself in the commons of knowledge which is intricately linked to the commons of nature. And we are increasingly seeing reclamation of the categories of commons simultaneously supported by the emergence of new rights which are universal in nature. Some examples being: 'the right to access information' emerging for the digital commons, and third or fourth generation 'fundamental rights' being created for the commons of nature.[17]

The Imperative to Recognize and Respect Knowledge Pluralism, and the Collective Cumulative Knowledge Commons of Indigenous Communities

In an ecologically diverse and technologically plural society such as ours the objective of legal systems cannot be to merely protect the interest of transnational corporations or practitioners of western science and technology systems. It has to be wide enough in scope to protect diverse economic organizations and diverse knowledge systems.

Indigenous knowledge systems aimed at self-provisioning and local self-reliance in nutrition and health care need a criterion for protection which is different from the 'novelty' and 'industrial application' criteria for patents. Instead of individual rights, such protection needs to be based on community rights and collective innovation.

Instead of novelty there needs to be a heritage criterion based on innovation over time.

Indigenous knowledge producers innovate collectively. This innovation also takes place over time–it is accretional and informal. The knowledge evolves as it modifies, adapts and builds upon the existing knowledge. A redefinition of 'innovation' is therefore needed that reflects this process of innovation cumulatively over time, and collectively across a community. The current definition is based on a false and artificial construction of individual innovation as a one-shot step in time. In the case of biodiversity patents, it is more often than not based on biopiracy. Neither in traditional indigenous system, nor in western scientific tradition is innovation an isolated activity in the temporal or the social context.

I worked with a team of scientists and lawyers of the Third World Network in the 1990s and in lieu of the same, we proposed to define 'innovation' to reflect the innovation taking place within indigenous systems in order to protect the 'collective rights' of indigenous innovators:

> *"Innovation includes any collective and cumulative knowledge or technology of the use, properties, values and processes of any biological material or part thereof, rendered of any or enhanced, use or value as a result of the said cumulative knowledge or technology whether documented, recorded, oral, written, or howsoever otherwise existing including any alteration, modification, improvement thereof; and shall also include derivatives which utilize the knowledge of indigenous peoples and local communities in the commercialization of any product as well as to a more sophisticated process for extracting, isolating, or synthesizing the active chemical in the biological extracts of compositions used by the indigenous peoples.*

Further, such a Community Rights (CR) regime needs to be the basis against which patent applications are considered. With access and benefit sharing laws in place in India and Internationally, the disclosure in patent applications needs to also disclose prior art and prior community rights as contained in community biodiversity registers. If indigenous innovations are protected by CRs, such innovations cannot be treated as novel–they have to be recognized as derived in obvious ways from prior innovation with its associated set of rights. CRs thus set the boundary conditions for IPRs in the era of TRIPS and the World Trade Organizations.

Further, since the issue of piracy and IPR claims an indigenous knowledge has become a global pandemic and western style corporate IPRs have been globalized, steps need to be taken to ensure that CRs are the basis of which IPRs in any country are issued and that piracy of CRs can be challenged anywhere."

This is why India has joined hands with Brazil, South Africa, and China to revive WTO talks to check biopiracy.[18]

Juridical Innovation for the Recognition and Protection of Indigenous Knowledge

"A village shall ordinarily consist of foot habitation or group of habitations or a hamlet or group of hamlets comprising a community and managing its affairs in accordance with traditions and customs."

"Every Gram Sabha shall be competent to safeguard and preserve the traditions and customs of the people, their cultural identity, community resources and the customary mode of dispute resolution."

The preceding sections are part of the Provisions of the Panchayats (Extension to the Scheduled Area) Act which came into effect December 1996. This Act represented groundbreaking legislation based on the fact that, for the first time in India juridical history, a community–in this case a community of tribals in scheduled areas–had been granted legally recognizable collective rights over its own community resources, and the power to manage its own affairs.

The Act accepted two important premises: firstly, that the community is the basic building block of the system and secondly, a formal system can be built on the firm foundation of the tradition and custom of the tribal people. The new provisions for the schedule areas made a break from the impasse in which the formal system refused to recognize the vibrant tribal community which has been managing its own affairs in accordance with its traditions through the ages, meeting effectively the challenges which have been coming its way. This Act not only formally recognized the community, which is designated as Gram Sabha, but treated the same as pivot of the system of self-government in the scheduling areas.[19]

However, further juridical innovation is therefore needed, which would achieve three tasks simultaneously:

- Protect the biodiversity and cultural integrity of indigenous communities, allowing them continued use of their resources and knowledge freely as they have done through times immemorial.
- Prevent the privacy and privatization of indigenous biodiversity and indigenous knowledge through IPRs, both nationally and internationally.
- Carve out a public domain of commons in the areas of biodiversity and knowledge.

To reflect the collective and community nature of the innovation and the rights related to indigenous biodiversity utilization, we have called these rights 'Community Intellectual Rights' (CIRs).

TRIPS provide countries the option of formulating its own *sui generis* regime for plants as an alternative to patent protection. Collective rights are a strong candidate for such *sui generis* systems for agricultural biodiversity and medicinal plants biodiversity. Therefore, it is crucial that community lead and utilized biodiversity knowledge systems are accorded legal recognition as the 'common property' owned by the communities concerned.

Building such an alternative is essential to prevent biodiversity and knowledge monopolization by an unbalanced mechanistic non-innovation implementation of TRIPS.

Examination of existing national and international legal community rights' legislation reveals that there are no binding legal instruments or standards that adequately grant rights to indigenous peoples' collective knowledge and innovations, thereby protecting their knowledge from biopiracy. That is not to say there is no scope for such developments. To the contrary, trends and precedents set in the area of international indigenous rights legislation and case law signify a strong movement in this direction.

The CBD instrument passed in 1992 represented the boldest move in the direction of recognizing indigenous knowledge traditions and innovation. The convention deals specifically with biodiversity and makes biodiversity conservation the obligation of members states. It also recognizes the role of local communities and tribals and conservation of knowledge for biological wealth.

> In the preamble, the convention states:
> *"That contracting parties recognize the close and traditional dependence of many indigenous and local communities embodying traditional lifestyles on biological resources and the desirability of sharing equitable benefits arising from the use of traditional knowledge, innovations and practices, relevant to the conservation of biological diversity and sustainability use off its components."*

The Convention not only recognized the sovereign rights of the nation state to the biodiversity and the method of its utilization through Article 3 and 4 but also gave them the right to enact their own laws for protecting their biodiversity, in a manner best suited to their particular needs and priorities. Hence, under the obligation of the CBD, it is the duty of the Government of India to enact laws to protect community rights to biodiversity and its utilization.

The United Nations declaration on the rights of indigenous peoples, which was drafted in 1993 and later adopted in 2007, promised to strengthen the position of indigenous collective rights considerably. For instance, Article 26 stated:

> *"Indigenous peoples have the right to the lands, territories and resources which they have traditionally owned, occupied or otherwise used or acquired."*

The articles indicate a strong international consensus on the positive assertion of indigenous community rights. It constitutes a powerful tool in changing attitudes as well as a focus for dialogue and debate at the national and international levels.

The Fourth Technical Conference on Plant Genetic Resources held in 1996 by FAO produced the Leipzig declaration on Farmers' Rights'. This declaration gave legal recognition to farmers' innovation and contribution to the rich diversity of agricultural crops to the world.

In light of the preceding legal instruments talked about above, and others talked about in the preceding chapters, there are obligations placed upon India to develop its own intellectual property rights regime to provide protection to community knowledge and resources.

The research foundation, together with a group of scientists and lawyers of the Third World Network, has, since 1993, developed a model biodiversity related Community Intellectual Property Rights Act.

This model can be used as a framework for developing *sui generis* systems of IPRs for protecting biodiversity by keeping resources and knowledge about its utilization in the Commons i.e. freely accessible to the community of users and conservers, but accessible by commercial interests, including TNCs–in terms of the community.

In concrete terms, the following steps need to be taken to protect our sovereignty, our biodiversity and our knowledge system:

- All IPR regimes, be they copyright, design, patent, trademarks, or breeders' right, should have a section on CIRs which allows collective claims to be registered by communities as areas of exclusions from the logic of privatization and monopolization, and which allows communities to challenge IPRs on the grounds of 'prior art' of commonly held and practiced knowledge.
- When TRIPS is finally reviewed in the context of CBD India and other countries should insist that the effective *sui generis* systems have to be effective in reflecting the human rights of indigenous communities to their indigenous knowledge and their environmental rights to their biodiversity. This implies that any IPR regime in any country that relates to biodiversity has to have a mechanism of institutionalizing CIRs for respecting the indigenous people, protecting biodiversity and preventing biopiracy.

It is quite evident that there is a lack of fit between the structure of commons and communities, and the structure of Western, especially US concept of right and property based on privatization.

If commons and communities do not fit into the narrow, non-sustainable, and parochial framework of Eurocentric jurisprudence then it is that framework that needs changing rather than collective nature of right of communities.

This is the context in which we propose a rights and responsibility framework which reflects the values of India's composite culture and protects all such biological and cultural heritage.

The collective rights framework is not aimed at changing the common, traditional practices of indigenous communities, or overburdening people with new state interference in their daily use of biodiversity for their survival needs. The legal framework is aimed at the protection of indigenous communities and societies *externally* by regulating the access and rights of powerful commercial interests. The communities themselves would then be left free, internally, to organize their biodiversity utilization and knowledge exchange on the basis of their own customs, values, beliefs, and epistemologies which would be explicitly recognized and respected, though not regulated by state structures and commercial interests.

The society of self-regulation and organization would dispense with the needs of communities having to remold themselves into western judicial frameworks based on individualism, private property, and value based on expropriation alone. On the other hand, a western usurped regulatory system would form an interface with external access to their knowledge and resources and externally imposed right. This would protect their rights from external abuse.

The Colonial Legacy: Erosion of Community Rights

Historically, in the villages, private and unequal land holding existed side-by-side with common and equally shared resources. It was not necessary that the legal rights of ownership of common resources had to be with the Village Community. Even though legally, common resources were recognized as state property, they were commonly held resources if the local community had enjoyed traditional access to them.

However, under the British, the colonial methods of common resource management symbolized the erosion of traditional norms and community control of the commons. The British began the process of commercialization of the CPRs (common property resources). Management of these resources became entirely commercial, despite the fact that the village people were dependent on these resources for their food and nutrition, and that their traditional right over these resources were recognized. The process of commercialization, and the subsequent usurpation of common natural resources, occurred through the complex network of laws concerning forest, minor forest produce, common water resources, common land, industrial and agrarian laws, and policies.

The privatization of common resources in inequitable manner by the

British led to the non-recognition of rights of communities over these resources and increasing restrictions over their use. The consequence of legalized and *de facto* privatization of CPRs was to turn the non-cash economy into the market economy by affixing a price for most primary resources, which were earlier free. The introduction of the concept of private or individual ownership over resources by the British continued to be 'promoted' even after the independence.

Community control of common resources was well depicted by none other than Englishman Dr. Francis Buchanan in 1801. While studying the condition of forests Buchanan noted that:

> *"The forest are the property of the Gods of villages in which they are situated, and the trees ought not be cut without having obtained leave from Gauda, or the headman of the village, whose office is hereditary, and is also the priest (Pujaris) to the temple of the village God. The idol receives nothing for granted this permission, but the neglect of the ceremony of asking his leave brings his vengeance on the guilty person."*

The observation highlighted the concept of community ownership over natural resources through worship and as something which was regarded as sacred. However, in the legal paradigm of the North, the rest dwellers and tribal communities never truly 'owned' the forests in the sense of private property. What they possessed were occupancy rights (or *nistar* rights defined as usufruct rights of local communities on forests and its produce).

The Artha Veda, Brihat Parasara, and other related texts, clearly revealed that in the Vedic Period the Aryan Kings, after conquering an area, realized taxes for land granted but did not take over the inhabitants' occupancy rights. This practice was even more pronounced during the Mauryan and Buddhist period. Even the Hindu and Muslim rulers continued with the same practice and did not interfere with the forest dwellers, tribal communities, nor their use of forest produce, though they did proclaim sovereignty over all land under their jurisdiction.

Therefore, in contrast to the western formal legal system where property rights belong to the individual only, there are multiple examples in which societies retained the community control over their resources. In fact, throughout history, societies have been protecting the commons which have remained the domain of the community only. All members of the community have equal access to and responsibility for the commons, like pastures, forests, water resources, seeds, and biodiversity which provide the conditions of life and have been managed as the CPRs of communities.

The commons have successfully existed beyond state and market control. Commons are not property, nor are they public in the sense of state control. They are a public resource under the control of a community.

Reclaiming the Sovereignty of the Community

Community control is still a living tradition in some of the tribal societies of India. Due to the imposition of incongruous laws such as Land Acquisition Act(s) and Forest Act(s), and the complex administrative system which disregarded their rights over the commons, the local people and members of traditional villages have been struggling since the British Raj against the criminalization of the whole community.

The tribal people of Santhal Parganas protected their community rights over village tanks even at the risk of their lives. The Kevats of Ganga rejected the rights of Zamindars over water and fought to establish their own rights over water resources. The people of Kolhan stuck to their traditional system of self-management and did not surrender their rights in favor of formal institutions established by the state. The Rai Sabha of Adilabad managed all affairs of the village community on their own. The people of Bastar and Gardchiroli claimed primacy of community in the management of social matters, forests, and other resources. They took the resolve of "our government in our village" (*'mawa mate mawa sarkar'*).

The deep-rooted aspirations of the people for self-government were finally given formal recognition by the parliament of India through a legislation accepting the communities as the real sovereign and at last honoring the verdict, *"We, the People of India,"* of our Democratic Constitution. This legislation not only treated the communities as the pivot of the system of self-governance in the scheduled areas, but also recognized them as a competent authority in all matters concerning community.

The work to reclaim the sovereignty of our communities still continues, given that the US has kept pressuring India to adopt US style patent regimes (implying an erosion of communities' sovereign rights). However, as I wrote in an open letter to Prime Minister Modi and President Obama when Obama came to India for Republic Day, while US laws might be 'strong' for establishing corporate monopolies based on false claims to inventing that which they cannot invent–and promoting biopiracy of our biodiversity and traditional knowledge–Indian laws are strong when assessed in terms of true inventions and equity. Our laws protect the integrity of life and avoid the hubris of defying living organisms and seeds as "manufactured" and "machines" "invented" by corporations.[20] In 2016, I wrote an article in Indian Express called "Rogue Companies Must Be Stopped from Taking over India's Rich Biodiversity" highlighting the same issue.[21]

When we first wrote this book in 1997 before our laws on Biodiversity and Patent Amendment had been implemented, the dominant assumption was that western industrialized countries and their corporations are 'innovators' and 'knowledge generators'. Our work and the work of indigenous communities worldwide created a global discussion on traditional knowledge and IPRs. WIPO was the original international platform for Intellectual Property before the global corporations hijacked IPRs and dragged them to GATT/WTO to fashion IPR regimes to facilitate their unjust, unscientific and immoral monopolies.

WIPO recognized that:

"The current international system for protecting intellectual property was fashioned during the age of industrialization in the West and

developed subsequently in line with the perceived needs of technologically advanced societies. However, in recent years, indigenous peoples, local communities, and governments, mainly in developing countries, have demanded equivalent protection for traditional knowledge systems."[22]

In 2000, WIPO members established an Intergovernmental Committee on Intellectual Property and Genetic Resources, Traditional Knowledge and Folklore (IGC), and in 2009 they agreed to develop an international legal instrument (or instruments) that would give traditional knowledge, genetic resources and traditional cultural expressions (folklore) effective protection. Such an instrument could range from a recommendation to WIPO members to a formal treaty that would bind countries choosing to ratify it.

Traditional knowledge is not so-called because of its antiquity. It is a living body of knowledge that is developed, sustained and passed on from generation to generation within a community, often forming part of its cultural or spiritual identity. As such, it is not easily protected by the current intellectual property system, which typically grants protection for a limited period to inventions and original works by named individuals or companies. Its living nature also means that traditional knowledge is not easy to define.

Recognizing traditional forms of creativity and innovation as protectable intellectual property would be an historic shift in international law, enabling indigenous and local communities as well as governments to have a say over the use of their traditional knowledge by others. This would make it possible, for example, to protect traditional remedies and indigenous art and music against misappropriation and enable communities to control and benefit collectively from their commercial exploitation.

The WIPO refers to a new moment in the historical evolutionary leap, which transcends the North South Divide of WTO/TRIPS. It refers to 'defensive protection' which aims to stop people outside the community from acquiring intellectual property rights over traditional knowledge. This includes access and benefit sharing in national and international law and includes the cases against biopiracy that we have mentioned in this book.

WIPO also refers to 'positive protection' which involves granting of rights that empower communities to promote their traditional knowledge, control its uses and benefit from its commercial exploitation. Some uses of traditional knowledge can be protected through the existing intellectual property system, and a number of countries have also developed specific legislations for the same.

This is the deepening of common intellectual rights that RFSTE and Navdanya have evolved. However, any specific protection granted by recognizing indigenous knowledge under national law may not hold for other countries. And this is the one reason why many indigenous and local communities, as well as governments, are pressing for an international legal instrument on the positive protection of their biological resources, territories, and knowledge.

Community control over common resources represents the only real mechanism for ensuring sovereign control over natural resources. This framework does not determine how community norms function. It merely recognizes the rights of communities and hence opens the legal option of limiting the rights of corporations. National legislation needs to recognize community rights through alternatives to intellectual property regimes. A framework for such an alternative at the national level is model Community Intellectual Rights and Biodiversity Rights Act put forth by the Research Foundation for Science and Technology and Ecology.

There is also a national and international demand for disclosure requirements. Many countries like India have already implemented this in the Biodiversity Act.

These issues are also being discussed in WIPO and the World Trade Organization's Council on Trade Related Aspects of Intellectual Property (TRIPS).

We are also seeing various openings of proposals of governments during the Mandatory TRIPS Review of Article 27.3(b) which should have been completed in 1999 to exclude lifeforms from patentability, since living organisms are not invented by man, and not being inventions, are not patentable.

The inadequacy of existing IPR arrangements for the protection of indigenous knowledge and Indian medical systems makes it an imperative that Biopiracy is made illegal in international IPR law. Communities shall be able to use their biodiversity and get a fair share in the context of others commercializing their resources and knowledge.

The evolution of a *sui generis* system of community rights, on an international level, for traditional practitioners is an urgent imperative. While India's amended Patent Act has ensured that Biopiracy patents are not granted at the domestic level, international laws are needed to prevent Biopiracy of India's biological and intellectual heritage at the international level. IPR policy globally needs to be based on the recognition that the largest numbers of 'knowledge providers' in the area of biodiversity are the practitioners of systems based on indigenous knowledge. Knowledge is not 'created' when it is merely transferred to a lab practicing western science in India, or to practitioners in the west. Protection of such transfer by IPRs is based on a false definition of translation from one knowledge system to another as 'innovation' and 'creation' – and it perpetuates piracy, both within the country and internationally.

Piracy will eventually destroy our intellectual heritage by displacing our knowledge systems, our practices, as well as our decentralized, self-reliant biodiversity-based economies. To stop this destruction, the granting of patents must be made conditional to a screening of prior innovation and prior rights of indigenous systems. This is why we started the movement for Community Biodiversity Registers in Pattuvam in Kerala in 1994.

TRIPS has universalized the framework of IPR regimes on the assumption that the only knowledge that exists is in the western scientific journals. However, in the area of medicinal plants, patent claims are increasingly being based on indigenous knowledge that exists outside the information and communication systems of western scientific research in the language, epistemology, and communication systems of diverse cultures and knowledge systems. The lack of recognition of these systems and the lack of legal regimes to ensure their protection leads to the phenomena of piracy.

Such an establishment of a community rights regime would ensure that the sovereign rights to biodiversity are made real and the benefits from the biological resources and our knowledge tradition first flow to us. This would not prevent either innovation or our sharing of benefits with other countries; however, it would in fact ensure that what is rewarded is real innovation, and not mere piracy. Lastly, it would ensure that over time TNCs' monopolies, strengthened through patents, do not block the flow of knowledge of how plants can heal and cure us.

The conflicts and debates unleashed by the introduction of IPRs in biodiversity have forced us to reassess the value of our biological and intellectual heritage. To stop the piracy of this and hence its destruction, the IPR and biodiversity legislation being evolved have to define and defend our sovereign rights to our social creativity and our natural wealth, in the past, in the present, and the future.

We need to remember that what is being pirated is not one invention of one individual or corporation, rather it is the collective creativity and inventiveness of millions of people over millennia, a creativity that has shaped one civilization's distinctiveness and steadfastness. A creativity which is necessary for meeting the needs of our people in the future. We need to recognize that knowledge of medicinal plants has been evolved and perfected in our civilization over thousands of years of innovation. The issue of protection of knowledge of medicinal plants is not a narrow legal issue or technical issue. It is an issue of the continuity and survival of the knowledge values of an ancient civilization as reflected in the ancient hymn from the Rig Veda, The Healing Plants, which have been called mothers:

Mothers, you have a hundred forms
and a thousand growths.
You who have a hundred ways of working,
make this man whole for me.
Be joyful, you plants that bear flowers
and those that bear fruit.
Like mares that win the race together,
the growing plants will carry us across.
You mothers who are goddesses:
let me win a horse, a cow, a robe-and
your very life, O man.
When I take these plants in my hand,
yearning for the victory prize,
the life of the disease vanishes as if before
a hunter grasping at his life.
He through whom you plants creep
limb by limb, joint by joint,
you banish disease from him like a huge man
coming between fighters.
Fly away, disease from him like a huge man
coming between fighters.
Fly away, disease, along with the
blue jay and the jay;
disappear with the howl of the wind,
with the rainstorm.
Let one of you help the other;
let one stand by the other.
All of you working together, help
this speech of mine to succeed.

Recovery of the Commons

> *"The spread of the commons discourse in recent years has had a double effect; it has helped identify new commons and, in providing a new public discourse, it has helped develop these commons by enabling people to see them as commons."*
>
> -David Bollier (2007)

Very similar to the endeavor of studying nuanced social processes is the task of a biologist to investigate complex processes. A biologist's approach involves observing the simplest possible organism in which the process to be investigated is seen in a clarified and exaggerated form. The reason for choosing this organism is not that it is the most representative but that it allows the process under investigation a more effective study.[23]

The organism we consider in this section is the commons.

The aim of this section is to look at processes and systems that are increasingly recovering our commons, protecting our commons, and reclaiming the sovereignty of our communities. Through this, it aims to achieve the double effect of Bollier's where it recognizes efforts at creating and recovering commons as well strives to reinforce and inspire new ways of creating more commons.

Community Seed Banks

> *"Bija Swaraj (Seed Sovereignty) is our Birthright and we shall defend it with our life. For Seed is life and without the seed there can be no life. It is a gift of Mother Nature that has sustained the Indian civilization for over 8,000 years. In our culture the seed is sacred and revered as the progenitor of life and not a commodity."*

Diversity is life and the very basis of ecological stability. Diverse ecosystems birth diverse life forms and diverse cultures. And seed is integral to this diversity.

Seed is life. Reclaiming the seed commons is reclaiming the commons of life.

This seed commons has been guarded and stewarded by our farmers through their collective and shared knowledge and knowledge systems which have evolved over generations. Communities all over the globe have cultivated knowledge and found ways to derive their livelihood from nature's bounty of diversity in both wild and domesticated forms. The corporate hijack of our diversity that we face today threatens the intergenerational weaving of knowledge and ways of being. The indigenous knowledge of seed saving and conservation has almost been wiped off from our collective fabric and memories because of the agro-tech companies forcing their hybrid seeds and chemicals on our farmers. Thus, community seed banks have become the physical and metaphorical site of resistance against this new seed imperialism to defend our *Bija swaraj* (seed sovereignty), our *Anna swaraj* (food sovereignty), and reclaim our commons.

Community Seed Banks (CSBs) are essentially local, informal institutions which collectively maintain, protect, and conserve seeds for local use. While there are multitudes of seed saving initiatives going by different names, e.g., Community Gene Bank, Farmer Seed House, Seed Hut, Seed Wealth Center, Seed Savers Group, Community Seed Reserve, Seed Library, Seed Cooperative Networks, etc., they are all geared toward the reclaiming of the seed commons.

In a 1997 paper by Lewis and Mulvany, one finds the first scientifically studied typology of community seed banks globally.[24] They classify the community seed banks into five types: de facto seed banks, community seed exchanges, organized seed banks, seed saver networks, and ceremonial seed banks. More recently, Vernooy et al., expanded the classifications and identified different seed banks based on their functions.[25]

Function	Services
Conservation	— Short term conservation of mostly local varieties — Longer term conservation of heirloom and rare varieties — Restoration of 'lost' varieties — Development of protocols for conservation of healthy seed and training of local communities
Access and Availability	— Platform of offering multiple channels of access and availability of seeds at the community level — Maintenance of locally adapted seed at low cost — Fostering of seed exchanges at local and supra local levels — Access to novel diversity not conserved locally — Capacity to respond to local crises/disaster/shortage of seeds — Seed multiplication including varieties bred through participatory activities
Seed and Food Sovereignty	— Maintenance of local control over seed conservation, exchange and production activities (community-based biodiversity management) — Income generation through the sale of seeds — Sharing knowledge and expertise — Links between *ex situ* and *in situ* conservation — Support of traditional and ethnic food culture — Contribution to ecological and food sovereignty movements
Source: Table 1 from Vernooy, R., Sthapit, B., Galluzzi, G., & Shrestha, P. (2014). The Multiple Functions and Services of Community Seedbanks.	

Despite these classifications, it is important to understand that most community seed banks not only serve interconnected and holistic functions but also broadly facilitate four kinds of interlinked rejuvenations:[26]

- Rejuvenation of agricultural biodiversity as a common property resource;
- Rejuvenation of farmers' self-reliance in seed locally and nationally;
- Rejuvenation of sustainable agriculture as the foundation for food security, both locally and nationally;
- Rejuvenation of Farmers' Rights as common intellectual rights of agricultural communities.

Navdanya Seed Bank

"Bija Swaraj is our birthright and we shall defend this right by all means necessary."

To conserve agrobiodiversity in different agroecological zones of India, Navdanya began establishing community seed banks and identifying seed keepers/seed producers. These community seed banks are a step towards the identification and conservation of important traditional seed varieties. These also help in orienting the agricultural community towards conservation and cultivation of important, highly nutritious traditional crops and varieties.

In the recent past community seed banks within Navdanya working areas have helped conserve the traditional agrobiodiversity. These seed banks are being managed by the farming community itself.

To date, Navdanya has set up 124 community seed banks in twenty-two states of India. Many seed banks are now running independent of Navdanya's support. Navdanya has also trained and created awareness amongst nearly 750,000 farmers in seed sovereignty, food sovereignty, and sustainable agriculture over the past two decades, and helped set up the largest direct marketing, fair trade organic network in the country. It has also established a conservation and training center at village Ramgarh in Doon Valley, in Secunderabad in Uttar Pradesh, and Balasore in Orissa.

In Navdanya's living seed banks the contributions of farmers to identifying, studying, modifying, and cultivating varieties to suit their ecological, economic and other needs are recognized. Farmers are the experts, situated at the center of conservation activity. Conservation starts and ends in the fields–it is carried on within the environment where the diversity grows. While corporate agriculture does not acknowledge farmers' agricultural skill and contributions to breeding, therefore awarding breeders' rights only to the seed industry and researchers, Navdanya' partnership model of conservation recognizes that farmers and scientists are equals. This partnership model is committed to creative solutions that fall far from the mainstream and question the dominant model of food production and distribution.

More than 4,000 rice varieties have been collected, saved, and conserved by Navdanya in the last twenty-six years. Forgotten food crops such as millets, pseudo-cereals, and pulses have been conserved and promoted by Navdanya, which were previously pushed out by the green revolution and expanding monocultures.

How the Community Seed Bank functions:

- Groups of farmers (mostly women) are organized to collect, multiply, and exchange traditional seeds and indigenously derived knowledge. Members are responsible for conservation of indigenous crop varieties. Each farmer conserving Seeds is known as a Seed Keeper.
- The farmer members collect the seeds available in their village. The seed bank is provided with the initial supply of seeds by Navdanya, either from the farmers who are already cultivating them in surrounding villages or from the existing seed banks or farmers of similar agroclimatic regions.

- Farmers who are interested in growing indigenous varieties are also given technical know-how on cultivation of these crops, raising seeds and pest management organically.
- At season's end, farmers return the seed with some additional amount (25%) that they borrowed from the seed bank.
- These seeds are then given to other farmers in the next season to multiply and also to increase the number of member farmers.

Initially, Navdanya provides each community assistance in running the seed bank, but with time, the community takes over the management.

Community Biodiversity Registers

To give more strength to CBD and defend the attacks from GATT and IPR regimes which aim at the enclosure of our biodiversity commons, documenting and archiving knowledge and resources on biodiversity becomes essential. India's National Biodiversity Action Plan prepared by the central government took a step in that direction and called for preparing People's Biodiversity Register or Community Biodiversity Registrar (CBR).

Simply put, CBR is a document of local, collective, and folk knowledge of bioresources which have constantly sustained and nourished the people of that region. Archiving this crucial knowledge helps in rejuvenating the ecological basis of agriculture and the economic status of the community. This helps them claim the knowledge which is rightfully theirs in the face of threats of biopiracy through IPR. CBR helps recognize and allow a greater role of local people in managing their biodiversity and claiming their sovereignty over their resources.

The purposes of Community Biodiversity Register are ensuring an acknowledgement of alternative knowledge systems which recognize the informal, collective, and cumulative systems of innovations of indigenous peoples and local communities; further, revitalizing and reviving traditional knowledge and ways of being and sharing the local knowledge with other communities in India.

Consonant with this, these community registers help define innovation broadly to include not only the technologically improved end product, but knowledge relating to the use (or enhanced use) of properties, values, and processes of any biological resource. This definition can be wide enough to include any alteration, modification, improvement or derivative which utilizes the knowledge of indigenous groups or communities in the commercialization of any product, as well as more sophisticated processes for extracting, isolating or synthesizing the active chemical in the biological extracts or compositions used by the indigenous peoples and communities;

Consequently, preventing exploitation by commercial users which includes protection against imposition of IPR by corporations and other outsiders by providing proof of prior use and facilitating a mechanism to take prior informed consent of the concerned community. Additionally, CBRs accomplish the following:

- Making local communities/indigenous peoples the stewards of such innovations, defining such rights as 'non-exclusive' and 'non-monopolistic' and encouraging its non-commercial and free use and exchange
- Permitting rights to be held in common with other communities
- Preventing the erosion of knowledge in communities. As knowledge about biodiversity becomes eroded, and only a few remember it, corporations find it easy to steal the knowledge and pirate it, as it has already vanished from the commons.

On a deeper level, the act of locally building up such a register affects the social fabric of people through:

- Building self-rule in the management of biodiversity
- Making people aware of their rights to seed, food, medicines, and more empowered to challenge biopiracy and resist monopolization of knowledge through IPRs.
- Providing the community with a means to assert rightful sovereign control over what is their own and better equipping them with bargaining power.

Provisions of the Panchayats (Extension to the Scheduled Area) Act

At a time when we need to learn from tribals in order to defend the future of our civilization, the future of the tribals is itself under threat. The most intense expression of a violent appropriation of resources, which Gandhi condemned in Hind Swaraj, continues to be played out in tribal areas. We have no right to uproot tribal societies from their homelands for mining bauxite, iron ore, or coal. We have no right to define their deployment.

In this context, PESA recognizes the right to resources and the right to define development as the sovereign right of tribal communities of Adivasi Swaraj.

Article 243(1) of the Indian Constitution prohibits the extension of 73rd Amendment to Scheduled Areas. However, tribal leaders and communities protested and the need for enacting this Act by the Parliament was felt. This was entrusted with the high level Bhuria Committee Report. Eventually a bill based on the committee's recommendation was enacted and made into an act which extended the 73rd Amendment Act to the Scheduled Areas mentioned under Article 244(2) making it mandatory for the states to amend their existing Panchayat Acts in conformity with PESA.

The Act provides that the Gram Sabha is empowered to safeguard the traditions and customs of the people, their cultural identity, community resources, and customary mode of dispute resolution. It has the power to approve plans, programs and projects for social and economic development, and is responsible for identification of beneficiaries under different programs. It is endowed with ownership over minor forest produce. It is also empowered to prevent alienation of land in the scheduled areas. Consultation of the Gram Sabha is mandatory before making acquisition of land in scheduled areas. It also made it a prerequisite for states to formulate their own acts, rules and regulations to give effect to that.

Section 4 of the Act states:

"Notwithstanding anything contained under Part IX of the Constitution, the Legislature of a State shall not make any law under that Part,

which is inconsistent with any of the following features, namely:

(a) a State legislation on the Panchayats that may be made shall be in consonance with the customary law, social and religious practices and traditional management practices of community resources;

(b) a village shall ordinarily consist of a habitation or a group of habitations or a hamlet or a group of hamlets comprising a community and managing its affairs in accordance with traditions and customs;

(c) every village shall have a Gram Sabha consisting of persons whose names are included in the electoral rolls for the Panchayat at the village level;

(d) every Gram Sabha shall be competent to safeguard and preserve the traditions and customs of the people, their cultural identity, community resources and the customary mode of dispute resolution;

> *(i) the Gram Sabha or the Panchayats at the appropriate level shall be consulted before making the acquisition of land in the Scheduled Areas for development projects and before re-settling or rehabilitating persons affected by such projects in the Scheduled Areas; the actual planning and implementation of the projects in the Scheduled Areas shall be coordinated at the State level;*

(k) the recommendations of the Gram Sabha or the Panchayats at the appropriate level shall be made mandatory prior to grant of prospecting licence or mining lease for minor minerals in the Scheduled Areas;

(l) the prior recommendation of the Gram Sabha or the Panchayats at the appropriate level shall be made mandatory for grant of concession for the exploitation of minor minerals by auction;

(m) while endowing Panchayats in the Scheduled Areas with such powers and authority as may be necessary to enable them to function as institutions of self-government, a State Legislature shall ensure that the Panchayats at the appropriate level and the Gram Sabha are endowed specifically with-

> *(i) the power to enforce prohibition or to regulate or restrict the sale and consumption of any intoxicant;*
>
> *(ii) the ownership of minor forest produce;*

(iii) the power to prevent alienation of land in the Scheduled Areas and to take appropriate action to restore any unlawfully alienated land of a Scheduled Tribe;

(iv) the power to manage village markets by whatever name called;

(v) the power to exercise control over money lending to the Scheduled Tribes;

(vi) the power to exercise control over institutions and functionaries in all social sectors;

(vii) The power to control over local plans and resources for such plans including tribal sub-plans;

(n) the State Legislations that may endow Panchayats with powers and authority as may be necessary to enable them to function as institutions of self-government shall contain safeguards to ensure that Panchayats at the higher level do not assume the powers and authority of any Panchayat at the lower level or of the Gram Sabha."

The Provisions of the Panchayats (Extension to the Scheduled Area) Act marked the beginning of a new chapter in the history of democracy in India, and perhaps even in the world. It demonstrated the existence of legal innovation for the recognition and protection of indigenous knowledge and indigenous commons of tribals in the country. It is therefore necessary that what follows is an expansion of such rights to cover all communities within India.

SEVEN

Vasudhaiva Kutumbukam: From Corporate Anthropocentrism to Earth as Family

Since 1992, when the Earth Summit was organized in Rio and the Convention on Biodiversity was signed and since 1995, with the coming into force of the WTO, the ecological crisis and the crisis of marginalization and exclusion has only increased and accelerated.

The reason the Biodiversity Convention and Climate Convention were agreed to by the International Community at the Earth Summit in Rio in 1992 was so that we could see the imminent danger of failing to protect biodiversity and stabilize the climate system. We had scientific evidence of the consequences of violating the earth's planetary boundaries and ecological limits. The danger now is no longer a subject of scientific discussion. It is facing us starkly. All evidence indicates that with business as usual, based on greed and corporate anthropocentrism, the human species could be extinct within a century.

There are multiple imperatives to create a shift from the anthropocentric, corporate dominated paradigm of reductionism, greed, and the privatization of life on Earth to a paradigm of Earth Community. This paradigm of an Earth Community is one of ecological knowledge as a commons, based on an understanding of the relationships between species. It is also the paradigm of the recovery of our biodiversity and intellectual commons which are cared for by the local communities who have deep ecological knowledge of this biodiversity.

The first imperative is one of survival for humans and other species. If humans are to protect other species from extinction, and consequently avoid human extinction, we need to make a shift from corporate anthropocentrism which puts humans as masters and owners of other species, and corporations as masters and owners of the intellectual and biological commons. Scientists estimate that we're now losing species at 1,000 to 10,000 times the background rate, with literally dozens going extinct every day.[1] Researchers have also started talking of the sixth mass extinction and of a widespread 'biological annihilation'.[2] To avoid this path, it is crucial to recognize that we are members of an Earth Family, Vasudhaiva Kutumbukam, characterized by diversity and relationships.

The second imperative is the scientific and epistemic imperative of a necessary transition from a mechanistic, reductionist paradigm of knowledge which treats nature as dead, uncreative, and is at the root of the crisis of species extinction, of biopiracy, and Patents on Life. New research is confirming what indigenous communities always knew: that nature and all beings–including the tiniest microbes–are alive, self-organized, and intelligent.

The third is a shift in the paradigm of ownership and private property to the commons and the common good. A shift from IPR systems based on false claims of corporate 'invention' of life and biodiversity leading to privatization and enclosures of the biological and intellectual commons of local communities to the recovery of the commons through regulation of access and limits on patentability–as enshrined in Section 3(j) of Indian Patent Act.

This book, based on thirty years of work dedicated to articulating a biodiversity paradigm, and practicing biodiversity based organic farming, is also inspired by an awareness that we are part of the earth, and are deeply interrelated with all beings. We are not separate from the earth and biodiversity. We are not the masters, owners, nor the creators of life.

Navdanya, as a movement, operates with the recognition that man does not 'invent' life. Therefore, patents on life are scientifically and ontologically flawed. We feel happy and proud that this scientific recognition is central to our laws–our Biodiversity Laws and our Patent Laws, which through section 3(j), clearly state that living organisms are not inventions, and hence not patentable.

The fourth is the imperative of creating sustainable, fair, and just economies. The Biodiversity Act of India and the Nagoya Protocol already make fair and just benefit sharing an obligation in all commercial activities. The Sustainable Development Goals (SDGs) are dedicated to sustainability and to removing hunger and poverty by 2030. The recovery of the biodiversity commons is not only a justice and equity imperative; it is a civilizational imperative to ensure that on a fragile planet with limits no one is deprived of their basic needs.

We have talked about the second and third imperative in various other sections of the book. The fourth imperative of creating sustainable, fair, and just economies is elaborated below.

The Sustainability and Justice Imperative

Biodiversity is the alternative to a fossil fuel economy which is leading to both climate change and species extinction. From the growth and processing of food to systems of health, biodiversity provides safe and sustainable alternatives and livelihoods to more people compared to the fossil fuel economy, which is based on displacing people.[3]

Biodiversity and biodiversity-based economies are a sustainability imperative in times of climate change and high unemployment. The realization that under conditions of limited availability, uncontrolled exploitation of natural resources involves robbing resources from those who need them for survival, has been an underlying element of Indian philosophy–which views prudent and restrained use of resources as an essential element of social justice.

> According to an ancient Indian text, the Ishopanishad:
> *"A selfish man over utilizing the resources of nature to satisfy his own ever-increasing needs is nothing but a thief, because using resources beyond one's needs would result in the utilization of resources over which others have a right."*

This relationship between restraint regarding use of resources in social justice was also a core element of Mahatma Gandhi's political philosophy. In his view: "the Earth provides enough for everyone's need, but not for everyone's greed."

To create the possibility and potential of a future we need a massive paradigm and worldview shift.

This shift is gradually being seen through the emergence of 'Rights of Nature'. After civil, political, economic, and social rights have been recognized we are now moving towards more expansive rights: the rights of nature. The emergence of these rights lends a fresh momentum to the idea of the commons and pushes us towards a deeper reflection on the relationship between nature, indigenous knowledge and the commons.

Rights to Nature

The movement for Rights of Nature is rooted in recognizing that ecosystems and natural communities are not merely property that can be owned but are living beings that have an independent right to exist and flourish.

Protecting biodiversity is protecting our future. This requires a shift away from anthropocentrism that privileges the human species and has resulted in what some scientists refer to as the 'Anthropocene' age. However, while the industrial and corporate man can be a determining factor in destruction, only earth citizens can be stewards, and co-creators with other species. Man cannot replace the ecological web of life of which he is a part. Man cannot be the master and owner of biodiversity, nor of creation.

Thomas Berry's *The Great Work,* which called for co-creating humanity's transition into the Ecozoic Era, laid one of the major foundations for the creation of a legal paradigm for speaking on behalf of and defending the community of life. [4]

Laws recognizing the rights of nature now only shift the status of natural communities and ecosystems, so too they create a new context where nature and her components become rights-bearing entities. These rights can then be enforced by people, governments, and communities.

While a majority of our current legal paradigm is still based on the narrative of separation that enables corporations and governments to criminalize opposition to crimes against nature, Berry's vision of an Earth Jurisprudence has inspired many leaps of thought and, already, we have started to see glimpses of "the more beautiful world our hearts know is possible" where humankind and nature are one. [5] We are gradually moving towards such a world through the work of organizations like the Gaia Foundation, The Pachamama Alliance, Navdanya, and EnAct which have deepened and resiliently navigated this conversation about Earth Law.

That is why Ecuador put the Rights of Mother Earth in its constitution.

Declaration of the Rights of Mother Earth

In April 2010, Bolivia hosted the Peoples Conference on Climate Change and the Rights of Mother Earth. At the conference, the Universal Declaration of the Rights of Mother Earth was drafted and approved after the failure of the Copenhagen Climate Summit. Modeled on the Universal Declaration of Human Rights, The Global Alliance for the Rights of Nature is now working to take this Declaration forward to the United Nations where it can either be adopted or become an inspiration for the drafting of an official Declaration. This Declaration embodies the wisdom and knowledge of people from both the ancient and modern societies all over the world and reflects a beautiful way of aligning our laws with those of Nature.

The Global Alliance on the Rights of Mother Earth, of which I am a founding member, was created on the basis of this Declaration of the Rights of Mother Earth.

Proposed Universal Declaration of the Rights of Mother Earth

Preamble

"We, the Peoples and Nations of Earth:

Considering that we are all part of Mother Earth, an indivisible, living community of interrelated and interdependent beings with a common destiny; gratefully acknowledging that Mother Earth is the source of life, nourishment and learning and provides everything we need to live well;

Recognizing that the capitalist system and all forms of depredation, exploitation, abuse, and contamination have caused great destruction, degradation, and disruption of Mother Earth–putting life as we know it today at risk through phenomena such as climate change;

Convinced that in an interdependent living community it is not possible to recognize the rights of only human beings without causing an imbalance within Mother Earth;

Affirming that to guarantee human rights it is necessary to recognize and defend the rights of Mother Earth and all beings in her and that there are existing cultures, practices and laws that do so; conscious of the urgency of taking decisive, collective action to transform structures and systems that cause climate change and other threats to Mother Earth;

Proclaim this Universal Declaration of the Rights of Mother Earth, and call on the General Assembly of the United Nation to adopt it, as a common standard of achievement for all peoples and all nations of the world, and to the end that every individual and institution takes responsibility for promoting through teaching, education, and consciousness raising, respect for the rights recognized in this Declaration and ensure through prompt and progressive measures and mechanisms, national and international, their universal and effective recognition and observance among all peoples and States in the world."

Article 1. Mother Earth

1. *Mother Earth is a living being.*
2. *Mother Earth is a unique, indivisible, self-regulating community of interrelated beings that sustains, contains and reproduces all beings.*
3. *Each being is defined by its relationships as an integral part of Mother Earth.*
4. *The inherent rights of Mother Earth are inalienable in that they arise from the same source as existence.*
5. *Mother Earth and all beings are entitled to all the inherent rights recognized in this Declaration without distinction of any kind, such as may be made between organic and inorganic beings, species, origin, use to human beings, or any other status.*
6. *Just as human beings have human rights, all other beings also have rights which are specific to their species or kind and appropriate for their role and function within the communities within which they exist.*
7. *The rights of each being are limited by the rights of other beings and any conflict between their rights must be resolved in a way that maintains the integrity, balance, and health of Mother Earth.*

Article 2. Inherent Rights of Mother Earth

1. *Mother Earth and all beings of which she is composed have the following inherent rights:*
   a. *the right to life and to exist;*
   b. *the right to be respected;*
   c. *the right to regenerate its bio-capacity and to continue its vital cycles and processes free from human disruptions;*
   d. *the right to maintain its identity and integrity as a distinct, self-regulating and interrelated being;*
   e. *the right to water as a source of life;*
   f. *the right to clean air;*

g. the right to integral health;
h. the right to be free from contamination, pollution and toxic or radioactive waste;
i. the right to not have its genetic structure modified or disrupted in a manner that threatens it integrity or vital and healthy functioning;
j. the right to full and prompt restoration the violation of the rights recognized in this Declaration caused by human activities;

2. *Each being has the right to a place and to play its role in Mother Earth for her harmonious functioning.*
3. *Every being has the right to wellbeing and to live free from torture or cruel treatment by human beings.*

Article 3. Obligations of human beings to Mother Earth

1. *Every human being is responsible for respecting and living in harmony with Mother Earth.*
2. *Human beings, all States, and all public and private institutions must:*

a. act in accordance with the rights and obligations recognized in this Declaration;
b. recognize and promote the full implementation and enforcement of the rights and obligations recognized in this Declaration;
c. promote and participate in learning, analysis, interpretation and communication about how to live in harmony with Mother Earth in accordance with this Declaration;
d. ensure that the pursuit of human wellbeing contributes to the wellbeing of Mother Earth, now and in the future;
e. establish and apply effective norms and laws for the defense, protection, and conservation of the rights of Mother Earth;
f. respect, protect, conserve, and where necessary, restore the integrity, of the vital ecological cycles, processes and balances of Mother Earth;
g. guarantee that the damages caused by human violations of the inherent rights recognized in this Declaration are rectified and that those

responsible are held accountable for restoring the integrity and health of Mother Earth;

h. *empower human beings and institutions to defend the rights of Mother Earth and of all beings;*

i. *establish precautionary and restrictive measures to prevent human activities from causing species extinction, the destruction of ecosystems or the disruption of ecological cycles;*

j. *guarantee peace and eliminate nuclear, chemical and biological weapons;*

k. *promote and support practices of respect for Mother Earth and all beings, in accordance with their own cultures, traditions and customs;*

l. *promote economic systems that are in harmony with Mother Earth and in accordance with the rights recognized in this Declaration.*

Article 4. Definitions

- *The term "being" includes ecosystems, natural communities, species, and all other natural entities which exist as part of Mother Earth.*
- *Nothing in this Declaration restricts the recognition of other inherent rights of all beings or specified beings.*

The notion of granting rights to entities other than human beings is not something new and has been a widely accepted legal fiction through which a variety of entities, especially corporations, have enjoyed legal personhood.[6] However, its possibilities are being explored, in giving rights to nature, only recently. Stone, in the year 1972, proposed a methodology for recognizing the rights of nature in his pioneering paper *Should Trees Have Standing?* Where the idea that was being explored was protection of nature for the sake of nature itself instead of the utility it held for humans. The history of law suggests that with every development in the moral landscape of human beings there was a parallel legal development in the discourse of rights. And each successive extension of rights to some entity was "unthinkable" before it got those rights. Women, Slaves, or African Americans were once rightless, but as Stone highlights that "until the rightless thing receives its rights" we can't see it as "anything but a thing for the use of us–those holding the rights at the time."[7]

The three criteria he identified that would make something count jurally were:

- Whether the thing can initiate legal actions at its behest
- Whether the court must take the injury caused to that entity into account while deciding the relief
- Whether that relief directly benefits that entity

Ecuador

In 2008, in a revolutionary way, the Ecuadorian government rewrote the country's Constitution, rejected all debt which had accrued due to its past corrupt government, became a part of the Bolivarian Alliance for the Americas, and started developing a vision for life in Ecuador to revolve around the principles of *Buen Vivir* or Sumak Kawsay (Good Living). Articles 71–74 in chapter seven of its constitution recognizes the rights of nature and reflect a shift in the constitutional framework of the country:

> *Article 71. Nature, or Pachamama, where life is reproduced and occurs, has the right to integral respect for its existence and for the maintenance and regeneration of its life cycles, structure, functions and evolutionary processes.*
>
> *All persons, communities, peoples, and nations can call upon public authorities to enforce the rights of nature. To enforce and interpret these rights, the principles set forth in the Constitution shall be observed, as appropriate.*
>
> *The State shall give incentives to natural persons and legal entities and to communities to protect nature and to promote respect for all the elements comprising an ecosystem.*
>
> *Article 72. Nature has the right to be restored. This restoration shall be apart from the obligation of the State and natural persons or legal entities to compensate individuals and communities that depend on affected natural systems.*

In those cases of severe or permanent environmental impact, including those caused by the exploitation of nonrenewable natural resources, the State shall establish the most effective mechanisms to achieve the restoration and shall adopt adequate measures to eliminate or mitigate harmful environmental consequences.

Article 73. The State shall apply preventive and restrictive measures on activities that might lead to the extinction of species, the destruction of ecosystems and the permanent alteration of natural cycles.

The introduction of organisms and organic and inorganic material that might definitively alter the nation's genetic assets is forbidden.

Article 74. Persons, communities, peoples, and nations shall have the right to benefit from the environment and the natural wealth enabling them to enjoy the good way of living.

Environmental services shall not be subject to appropriation; their production, delivery, use and development shall be regulated by the State.

Bolivia

On October 15, 2010, the government of Evo Morales in Bolivia launched the *Ley de Derechos de la Madre Tierra* or Law of Mother Earth. In September 2012 the law was upgraded by the National Legislative Assembly as the Framework Law of Mother Earth and Integral Development to Live Well (Ley Marco de la Madre Tierra y Desarrollo Integral para Vivir Bien). As part of a complete restructuring of the Bolivian legal framework, after a change of constitution in 2009, this law draws strongly from the indigenous Andean spiritual worldview which places the environment and the earth deity (known as the Pachamama) at the center of all life, and where all other living entities are equal to humans. The Pachamama has been described as: "sacred, fertile, and the source of life that feeds and cares for all living beings in her womb. She is in permanent balance, harmony, and communication with the cosmos. She is comprised of all ecosystems and living beings, and their self-organization."

CHAPTER III of the Constitution: RIGHTS OF MOTHER EARTH

Article 7:

I. Mother Earth has the following rights:

1. *To life: The right to maintain the integrity of living systems and natural processes that sustain them, and capacities and conditions for regeneration.*
2. *To the diversity of life: It is the right to preservation of differentiation and variety of beings that make up Mother Earth, without being genetically altered or structurally modified in an artificial way, so that their existence, functioning or future potential would be threatened.*
3. *To water: The right to preserve the functionality of the water cycle, its existence in the quantity and quality needed to sustain living systems, and its protection from pollution for the reproduction of the life of Mother Earth and all its components.*
4. *To clean air: The right to preserve the quality and composition of air for sustaining living systems and its protection from pollution, for the reproduction of the life of Mother Earth and all its components.*
5. *To equilibrium: The right to maintenance or restoration of the interrelationship, interdependence, complementarity and functionality of the components of Mother Earth in a balanced way for the continuation of their cycles and reproduction of their vital processes.*
6. *To restoration: The right to timely and effective restoration of living systems affected by human activities directly or indirectly.*
7. *To pollution-free living: The right to the preservation of any of Mother Earth's components from contamination, as well as toxic and radioactive waste generated by human activities.*

Rivers Have Rights

The world found its first examples of rights being carved for specific and bounded natural features (i.e., rivers) holding a powerful precedent to establish a whole new tangent in environmental law. In 2011, a hybrid mix of rights of nature was applied to the rivers of Victoria in Australia. And even more recently, in 2017, four rivers were given the legal status of persons: Whanganui River in New Zealand, Ganga and Yamuna in India, and Atrato in Columbia. In these cases, rights have been granted with a guardian appointed to act on the behalf of the rivers. These cases have the following commonalities:[8]

1. Legal rights have been created not in any abstract realm of nature as a whole but for a specific natural entity
2. Each context pertains to responses to environmental degradation (over-extraction of water in Victoria, Pollution in India, illegal mining in Columbia)
3. There is not only a creation of these rights but also laying down of provisions that deal with the enforcement of these rights.

Rivers in Victoria, Australia

Victoria is located in the southeast of Australia and historically has had its own state laws for water resources management. The Victorian Water Act 1989 was the main regime of law, and Victorian Environmental Water Reserve (EWR) was the main body handling access to water to ensure a healthy flow of the rivers throughout Victoria's wetlands and estuaries to maintain a balanced ecosystem.

After the millennium draft it became apparent that the water entitlements had to be moved away from the control of the ministry of environment. Finally, in 2010, a new body was established to handle all the decisions regarding its water management. This entity is known as the Victorian Environmental Water Holder (VEWH). Drawing from Stone's work, this entity was created as a body corporate (legal person), consisting of three commissioners and employees of state public service, which would hold water rights as a guardian to keep aquatic health intact.[9] The VEWH would decide how the water would be used, and who would be able to buy and sell the water in the water market, all while keeping the interest of the aquatic ecosystem in mind. The VEWH had the power to sue, enter into a contractual relationship and acquire and dispose of property on behalf of the environment. To ensure sustainable resource management, it is funded through a water levy imposed on all the users in Victoria.

Whanganui River, New Zealand

It is since 1873 that the indigenous Whanganui Maori tribe have contested the legal arrangement under the Treaty of Waitangi (because of which the Crown always owned the riverbed). The dispute finally settled with the Te Awa Tupua (Whanganui River Claims Settlement) Act, 2017 after eight years of negotiation between the tribe and the Crown. This legislation granted legal personhood to the Whanganui River while creating a fully-fledged framework for its governance. It recognizes and respects the Whanganui Iwi's worldview of perceiving the river as a sacred living whole. It creates rights, powers, duties, and liabilities for the river just like those of any legal person. While the ownership is vested in Te Awa Tupua, who can sue and be sued in the court of law, when the time arises, it can be represented by a steward or guardian known as Te Pou Tupua who would act and speak for the wellbeing of the river's ecosystem. The Te Pou Tupua would be composed of two people, one appointed by the tribe and other by the Crown and act as one entity. This guardian would receive the advice and guidance from an advisory group called Te Karewao, and a strategy group called Te Kopuka na Te Awa Tupua which would monitor and regulate the interest of the river through seventeen stakeholder representatives coming from across the spectrum from the government to the tribe to conservationists and hydropower plant operators. This is supported by the NZ$30 million fund made by the Crown.

Ganga and Yamuna Rivers, Uttarakhand, India

On March 20, 2017 the High Court of Uttarakhand declared that "The rivers Ganga and Yamuna, all their tributaries' streams, every natural water flowing with continuously and intermittently of these rivers are declared as legal persons/living entities having the status of a legal person with all corresponding rights, duties, and liabilities of a living person."[10]

The basis of this grant of status as a legal person was rooted more in the Indian philosophy where rivers were considered sacred, divine, and "central to the existence of half the Indian population." The court went on to carve a guardianship regime where the rivers would be considered minors under the law. By following the model laid down by Stone, the court called for the government to act as *loco parentis* for the rivers. This consisted of the Director of NAMAMI Gange project, the chief secretary of Uttarakhand, and the Advocate General of Uttarakhand.

Later, on July 7, the Supreme Court, on hearing an appeal by the state government stayed the High Court judgement. The state government filed an appeal on the ground that these rivers flowed much beyond the borders of the state of Uttarakhand and so it was unclear as to how it could act as a guardian of the whole river with the existing legal and administrative difficulties. The current status (as of August 2018) of the rivers stands in limbo.

Atrato River in Colombia

Illegal mining activities near this river and its tributaries were polluting the health of its whole ecosystem along with the livelihoods connected to this river. Local testimony and recent analysis of satellite imagery indicates that more than 100km of the Quito's (tributary of Atrato) river channel and floodplain had been almost completely destroyed in less than twenty years.

Center of Studies for Social Justice (Tierra Digna) demanded that the government take action and stop this mining. Upon the government's denial of this request, the center then initiated a case in which they argued that the activities of illegal miners in Chocó violated the fundamental human rights of the communities living alongside the river, causing extreme degradation of the river; destroying the natural course of the river, flooding the rainforest, and contaminating the river with chemicals. In May 2017, the court ruled that the Atrato River, its basin and its tributaries have the right to be protected and restored by the State and the Communities. The judgement said that "only an attitude of profound respect and humility with nature and its beings makes it possible for us to relate with them in just and equitable terms, leaving aside every utilitarian, economic, or efficient concept." The river was given legal personhood and to give effect to the same, the court appointed two representatives of the river: one from the community and one from the government. The claiming communities represented by the

Tierra Digna organization will have to create a commission of guardians with two delegates to follow up on the protection and restoration that the State must provide for the river. The Humboldt Institute and the World Wildlife Fund (WWF) will advise this commission. This posed a watershed moment for indigenous and environmental rights in Latin America. However, while the court explicitly acknowledged an ecocentric approach–referring to the interconnectedness of nature and humans with nature, and the superior interest of the environment and obligations to protect nature's rights–it also remained rooted in anthropocentricity where the river's rights flowed only as a consequence of recognizing the communities' human rights which included 'biocultural' rights.[11]

How these rights for the river would translate on the ground depends largely on how the government proceeds, and how the court monitors this development as the court has created a mechanism for regular reports to be submitted to it giving updates on the implementation from the government.

The following table gives a brief analysis of the nature of these rights.[12]

Legal and institutional attributes	Rivers of Victoria (Australia)	Whanganui River (New Zealand)	Ganges and Yamuna (India)	Atrato River, Columbia
Legal standing	Yes	Yes	Yes	yes
Aim	Political and economic : to create one voice for decision making about water in Victoria's legislation	Treaty settlement	Environmental and religious	An 'accion de tutela' (action for protection of constitutional rights)

Right to enter contracts	Yes	Yes	Yes	Uncertain
Right to own property	Yes	Yes	Yes	Uncertain
Legal form	Statutory body corporate (corporation and public entity hybrid)	Legal entity with a status of legal person	Legal entity with a status of legal minor with all corresponding rights, duties and liabilities of living persons	Legal entity with status of legal person
Explicit creation of legal rights for nature	No	Partial	Yes	Partial
Natural elements protected	Water rights used to provide environmental flows for rivers, wetlands in	Whanganui river from mountains to the sea and the corresponding catchment	Ganga and Yamuna rivers (extent unclear)	Atrato River, tributaries and river basin

Jaiv Panchayat–Living Democracy

Ecological agriculture is not possible unless biodiversity is in the commons and is free from the threat of extinction posed by technologies like genetic engineering. Hence, on June 5, 1999, World Environment Day, Navdanya launched Jaiv Panchayat–the Living Democracy Movement–to fight against biopiracy and IPR monopolies on life forms.

Panchayats are local institutions of self-governance which have been in existence in India since pre-independence. Sabha and Samiti were the popular institutions through which the masses had a direct say in village affairs and had direct control over Gramini. The village was a self-dependent unit. It generated its own resources, had its own functionaries and its own functional domain. The State performed only those functions which the village could not perform itself.

Post-Independence, the Panchayat system was formally introduced in the Constitution through Article 40 which was a directive to all states to take steps to organize village Panchayats and endow them with such powers and authority as may be necessary to enable them to function as units of self-government. The Balwantrai Mehta Committee suggested three tier Panchayati Raj Institutions to fulfill the goals of democratization of the society. The 64th Amendment Bill, which became the 73rd Constitutional Amendment Act of Indian Constitution, provided Constitutional status to the Panchayati Raj Institutions. This devolved administrative powers to the local village level and institutionalized the three-tier governance system (Center, State, and Panchayat).

The "Jaiv Panchayat" is the Biodiversity Panchayat. It is living democracy–both in being the democracy of all life, and democracy in everyday life. It consists of the entire Gram Sabha (gram ke sab log): women, children, and minority communities, and not merely those who are on the electoral rolls of the village. This form of the Panchayat renders the community the decision-maker on all matters pertaining to biodiversity and its conservation. In doing so, the Jaiv Panchayat lays down the parameters within which the elected Panchayat body can take action vis-à-vis biodiversity. The community ownership it asserts is not aimed at putting different communities in conflict with each other over the use and control over biodiversity. It is actually rejuvenating the traditional systems of common property resource management, which was based on equitable sharing of scarce resources for the common good of all the communities, as an alternative to the privatization and monopolization propagated by corporations.

Such alternatives are also envisioned in the Convention on Biological Diversity (CBD) and Agenda 21. The Jaiv Panchayat movement is in the spirit of the CBD and is our local Agenda 21. The obligations to implement the commitments under CBD are part of the government's mandate and are broader and deeper than that of the trade commitments.

Local grassroots initiatives like the Jaiv Panchayat are crucial in this context and they do not have to be limited to structures of the formal elected Panchayat. Such local decentralized democratic bodies are in fact in the spirit of the Panchayati Raj Amendment 1992 and the Panchayat Act 1996. Genuine commitment to the process of democracy implies that even the processes of globalization and free trade have to be based on recognition of primary ownership of village communities to their natural resources and their decision-making power to determine the utilization of these resources.

The first Jaiv Panchayat was brought to life by a gathering of about 1,000 villagers of Agastyamuni village in district Rudraprayag, Garhwal, Uttaranchal on June 5, 1999. The Jaiv Panchayat campaign launched by Navdanya is a part of the much broader movement called Bija Satyagraha. As a part of the movement over 6,000 village communities have affirmed their rights to their biodiversity and have taken a pledge to conserve, rejuvenate, and protect their biodiversity. There are more than 200 Jaiv Panchayats in Garhwal alone, where people have asserted their inalienable and common rights to their natural resources. In many of the Jaiv Panchayats, the elected leaders are also the leaders of the movement. Many of them have declared their villages GM-free zones as well.

Jaiv Panchayat records the biodiversity of the village in their own Community Biodiversity Register (CBR) to protect and reclaim the biological and intellectual commons. It has rejuvenated indigenous knowledge and promoted its propagation from grandmother to grandchildren. Another important function of the Jaiv Panchayat is to strengthen the concept of Community Intellectual Rights to resources and traditional knowledge and innovation through documentation of local diversity and knowledge in CBRs.

The Mandakini Milan Declaration of June 5, 1999 was created at Agastyamuni, Dist. Rudraprayag, Garhwal, Uttaranchal.

June 5, 1999 was the auspicious occasion of World Environment Day. It was that day that the people of Agastyamuni took a solemn pledge to continue to protect their plants, trees, animals, cattle, and their entire diverse biological wealth, as a revered gift and ancestral heritage.

This pledge assumed more significance as it was taken in Agastyamuni, the sacred land of Rishi Agastya, who through his dedication and research stabilized the mighty Himalayan Mountain (hence the name Agastya–the stabilizing force). Both humanity and nature have greatly benefited from the diligent research of Maharishi Agastya, Maharishi Jagdamni, Rishi Atri, Mata Anusuiya, and other saints. Their work has contributed to the conservation and sustainable use of all kinds of medicinal plants and floral wealth and other precious biodiversity of these mountains. The research has been further enriched by Maharishi Charak and other saints and health practitioners who compiled the volumes of Samhita and Nighantu detailing the uses and properties of our biological resources. These volumes were bestowed to the community for well-being and continue to live through Ayurveda.

From our forefathers we have inherited the right to protect the biodiversity of our Himalayan region and also the corresponding duty to utilize these biological resources for the good of all people.

Therefore, that pledge, by way of the Declaration, was to ensure that no destructive elements would unjustly exploit and monopolize the precious resources through illegal means. It was to truly establish a living people's democracy wherein each and every individual could associate themselves with the conservation and sustainable, just use of these biological resources in their everyday practical living.

This tradition of sharing is kept alive through the Jaiv Panchayat–the Living Democracy. The Jaiv Panchayat decides on all matters pertaining to biodiversity. Through such decentralized democratic decision-making we make real democracy for life.

This democracy of life acknowledges that the cows, buffaloes, goats, sheep, lions, tigers, and in fact all animals, birds, plants, trees, precious medicinal plants, manure, water, soil, and seeds are our shared biological resources, and we shall not let any outsider exercise any control over them through patents, or destroy it through genetic engineering.

As a community, we need together to be the guardians of our biological heritage.

The basic purposes of the Jaiv Panchayat are to:

- Strengthen people's rights over biodiversity to defend local economies
- Heal the diseased and decaying system of political democracy
- Counter and resist the WTO rules for free trade in agriculture, patents on seeds, and medicines which are threatening the environment, livelihood and domestic rights of the common citizens.

The launch of the Jaiv Panchayat marked the commencement of a movement towards relocating control and decision making over knowledge and biodiversity from global to local, from the MNCs to the people.

The Jaiv Panchayat is Living Democracy because through it, people live economic and political democracy in their daily lives, the democratically structured society is vibrant and alive, and the family of species, our earth family of diverse life forms, is included in the Democracy of Life.

The democratic functions of a Jaiv Panchayat are to:

- Protect cultural diversity and cultural activities
- Rejuvenate indigenous knowledge of biodiversity
- Create mechanisms to conserve it
- Create mechanisms to regulate it and use it sustainably
- Document the biological wealth past and present
- Conserve medicinal plants and encourage traditional health practices
- Defend the livelihoods based on biodiversity
- Promote sustainable agriculture
- Facilitate setting up of community seed banks

- Regulate the trade of biodiversity, and shape laws for ownership and control over biodiversity and its knowledge
- Make decisions on IPRs and knowledge conflicts

Natural Rights Flow from Rights of Nature

We are part of Vasudhaiva Kutumbukam–the Earth family. As members of the earth family we have natural rights that flow from being part of nature. The fact that Nature has rights and the fact that the discourse on "rights of nature" has taken flight is a positive development. The future demands that our concepts of 'political', 'economic', 'social', and 'human rights' reflect our being part of this Vasudeva Kutumbukam–which on the one hand creates responsibilities and duty to care and share, and on the other hand creates our natural rights to life; to food, water, air, and the space which we share with all other beings.

Western Bias 'Naturalizes' Anthropocentrism and Enclosures of the Commons to Define Rights to Private Property as a Natural Right

The concept of 'rights' which is familiar to all of us today takes its origin in the 18th century, in the European Enlightenment and its tradition of individualism, materialism, and rationalism. It was Locke who wrote:

> *"Though Earth and all inferior creatures be common to all Men, yet every Man has a property in his own person…whatsoever then he removes out of the State that Nature hath provided and left it in, he hath mixed his Labor with, and joined it to something that is his own, and thereby makes it his Property."*[13]

This created the artificially constructed anthropocentric divide between 'man' and 'inferior creatures' while simultaneously enclosing the commons of indigenous communities and dividing humans on the basis of a construct of capital. Locke clearly states that it is not the labor of the horse or the serf that creates "property" but the "spiritual" labor of the one who owns the horse and the serf. Interestingly, it was also Locke who said that there must be "enough and as good left in common for others" and that no person shall take from the commons more than he can use. But the dominant culture took the former, disposed of the latter, and this completely changed how we view ourselves, how we view nature, how we view labor, property, and how we view our natural, 'inalienable' rights.

To see private property, not the commons that weave our common life support, as the fundamental attribute of our being, and inseparable expression of being a human was what completely twisted how we view rights, as well as our relationship with the earth and her diverse beings.

This dominant narrative of the inalienable rights of economically powerful men, defined as the right to private property created through enclosures, is the foundation of colonialism and capitalist patriarchy. While natural rights that flow from being part of nature are *sui generis* and arise from our being alive and being a part of the Earth Family, the notion that for a right to be framed there first has to be a demand by an individual which the state will then grant, or refuse, is a deeply embedded Western construct which has ridden on the universalization of 'their' ideas and concepts. Timothy Mitchell says:

> *"How is the general character of law produced? How do the rules of property achieve the quality of being universal? In the positive accounts of law...the genealogy of what is taken to be a universal system of rules is not open to investigation."*[14]

The language of inalienable rights and the most *natural* rights being the right to property in the anthropocentric capitalist patriarchy became this 'universal' system which was not open to investigation, even though it was a particular system created by men in power and imposed on the commons, which were and are the truly universal system.

And at the root of this paradigm of rights was the perception that we are all separate and autonomous individuals, independent from our environment and our society rather than part of it.

Natural Rights are not given, they arise naturally from being living beings. Natural rights are not political rights

The assumption that the source of all rights are institutions that privilege human beings, and among humans, privilege the economically powerful men organized in corporate form, is marred by the fallacy of dubious assumption. It is anthropocentric and involves a premise based on multiple other premises which are not kept open to question. Thus, it is important to ask whether all types of rights are the same and emanate from the same sources.

Natural Rights are indigenous, common rights shared by every being, including human beings. They have come before man. They will remain after man. It is our anthropocentric arrogance that makes us think that our sophistry, our civility, and our culture have endowed us with the concept of 'rights' and 'responsibilities'. Nature has always had its own Hohfeldian matrix of rights, duties, power, etc. Everything in nature has always had a 'correlative' as everything is always interconnected. It is us and our individualist-reductionist mindsets that have seen things as separate.

By saying that something exists, it is implied that one didn't know it existed before. We never say: "air exists" or "I am breathing in air right now." It is a basic quality of life that air is something with which we are interconnected: we are a part of it, and it is a part of us. It doesn't have to be said, affirmed or highlighted.

That is why it is interesting how so many languages and cultures don't have a word or language for rights: like the cultures of Algonquin, Aymara, Bangla, Basque, Khmer, Korean, Japanese, que-chua, Turkish, Shuswap, etc.[15]

There is no language for rights because rights simply are.

Similarly, we see in other realms of nature that rights are already embodied in the behaviors of living beings. For example, hyenas abruptly terminate the chase of a potential prey as soon as they reach the border of neighboring hyena territory, even though no other predators are in sight.[16] Mammals, birds and fish mark off their territories and their rights are always respected in intra-species as well as inter-species interactions.

These natural rights exist because of the universality of cause and effect relations. And they take form through the checks and balances built into the way the universe unfolds. Thus, the rights exist by the very fact of being born into the community of the earth family.

Denial of these natural rights doesn't mean they have been extinguished

The landmark Mabo Case (Mabo v Queensland, no. 2) was a decision in the Australian Courts in 1992 which gave 'native title' in Australia for the first time.[17] Native title was described as the interests and rights of indigenous inhabitants in land, whether communal, group or individual, possessed under the traditional laws acknowledged by and the traditional customs observed by the indigenous inhabitants. This case pertained to the rights and interests of the Meriam people to their traditional land.

The main question that was framed in the case was: whether the rights of the indigenous people survived after the colonization by the Crown. Justice Brennan, in Paragraph 61 of the Judgement, answered: "Mere change in sovereignty does not extinguish native title to land."

He quoted another case called Calder v Attorney-General of British Columbia where Justice Hall had rejected as "wholly wrong" the "proposition that after conquest or discovery the native people have no rights at all except those subsequently granted or recognized by the conqueror or discoverer."[18]

Similarly, in India we have the Fifth Schedule of India's Constitution, along with many state laws, which affirms the non-alienability of tribal land as an elementary right.

All of these instances reflect the idea that natural rights are ontological, ecological, and biological. These ontological rights have always existed and will continue to exist. No human law or court can "create" these rights. It can only affirm them. They exist de facto.

A statement from 2003, from a meeting of indigenous people in the autonomous communities in Mexico states:

> *"The government resolved not to recognize our fundamental rights in the constitution, but to intensify its plundering, destruction and robbery policies towards our lands, territories and natural resources...confronted with the aforementioned, we have decided to stop demanding further recognition for the exercise of our own rights, so now we demand respect for our lands, territories and autonomy. We have resolved that this state has lost its legitimacy, by its legal practices, we must exercise our autonomy de facto, thus addressing our grave situation and looking forward to a better future for our children"*[19]

The Western Paradigm of natural rights as involving the inalienable right to property, is therefore, completely flawed. This is why it is the "tyranny" of rights which is at the root of all the violence, terror, rape, exploitation, and deprivation today. As long as we stay in this western paradigm of rights, violence and destruction will only grow.

By telling us that rights don't just flow from the fact of being an ecological and biological being, what this western paradigm has ingrained in us is the idea that by being who we are, by our very existence, is not enough. This thinking has inflicted a massive, pervasive, and deep mental, emotional, and spiritual damage upon us all.

If this rights regime is not corrected, we are led on a path as devastating and destructive as our colonial pasts have been. And this time colonization will end in the extinction of biodiversity, including the human species. This colonizing past has decimated our agricultural system, our economic system, our educational system, our political system, and even more importantly, our interpersonal ways of being. The right to possess and hold property has deeply damaged and altered something within us.

This healing is the potential that the future holds. The future that you, and I, and all of us have the power to carve together.

Potential for the Future

In the following diagram, Quadrant A and B represent the Western Paradigm of Rights which is rooted in viewing all of us as individuals and a set of individuals with no permeability. Its spectrum remains anthropocentric and restricted to human beings. And if we remain in that paradigm, the seeming 'expansion' of rights will still be restricted as it will still see everything as separate with distinct boundaries.[20]

On the other hand, Quadrants C and D represent the Paradigm of the Rights of the Earth family, or Vasudeva Kutumbukam. It perceives every living being in a related-ness with every other living being. There is a permeability which is recognized. Each being is also seen as carrying the past and future time and space with it and within it.

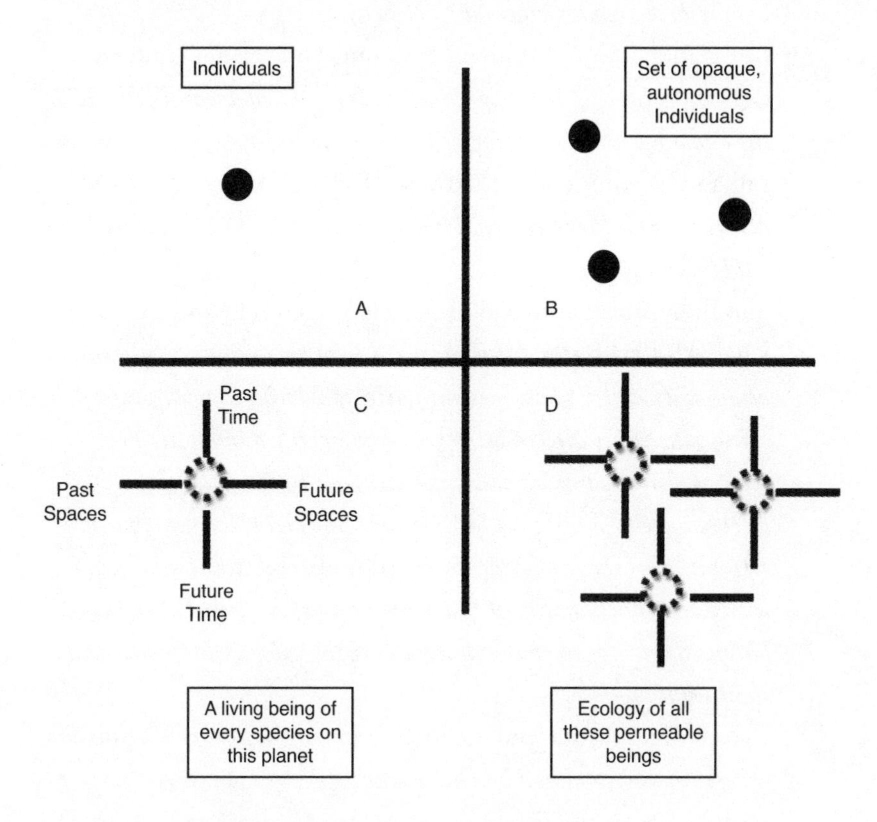

This is the potential for the future: recognizing and celebrating the natural rights which arise from being a part of the earth family. Where these rights are born from the ecology of our being. Where the very membership of every species and living creature of this Vasudeva Kutumbukam implies the existence of these natural rights.

Interconnected Space of Rights

- Universal Declaration of Human rights: Human Rights have to be seen as a subset of rights of the Earth Family. Article 1 of the UDHR states that "*All human beings are born free and equal in dignity and rights.*" Even Article 3 states, "*Everyone has the right to life, liberty and security of person.*" This 'everyone' includes all members of the Earth Family.
- International Covenant on Civil and Political Rights says, "*every human being has an inherent right to life.*"
- International Convention on Economic, Social and Cultural rights, 1966 says, "*these rights derive from the inherent dignity of the human person.*"
- Indian Constitution in its Article 21 states *"No person shall be deprived of his life or personal liberty except according to a procedure established by law."*
- The Bolivian constitution in Article 7. (RIGHTS OF MOTHER EARTH) states: "*It is the right to preservation of differentiation and variety of beings that make up Mother Earth, without being genetically altered or structurally modified in an artificial way, so that their existence, functioning or future potential would be threatened.*" And goes onto state: "*The right to maintenance or restoration of the interrelationship, interdependence, complementarity and functionality of the components of Mother Earth in a balanced way for the continuation of their cycles and reproduction of their vital processes.*"
- Ecuadorian constitution in *Article 71 states: "Nature, or Pachamama, where life is reproduced and occurs, has the right to integral respect for its existence and for the maintenance and regeneration of its life cycles, structure, functions and evolutionary processes."*

All of these diverse rights (Constitutional Rights, Rights in International Covenants, and Rights for Nature) are interconnected rights and can become the starting point to begin embodying the Paradigm of the Rights of the Earth Family. This paradigm of rights has three main characteristics which we already see at play in the commons, viz., Interconnectedness, Anna Swaraj as a natural right, and rights as they exist with responsibility.

Interconnectedness

The interconnected space of rights, responsibilities and duties is the commons. This sense of separate-ness and lack of sight as to how all these rights are interconnected is the reason why countries end up intervening militarily in other countries like Afghanistan, Kosovo, etc., in the name of human rights. Once we see everything in relationship with another, like how it is in the commons, only then will we be able to move into a future of peace and sustainability.

Anna Swaraj is a Natural Right

Food is the most basic right of all living beings. As soon as one is born, the right to food is naturally exercised. The cause and effect of nature takes care of it. No one should be fighting and struggling for this right. B. Kneen puts it well: "as for food, human beings are no different than any other organism in requiring reliable nutrition to maintain life. Yet, humans, I dare say, are the only organisms to come up with the idea of a right to food, which transforms a human necessity into legal claims to be granted by some authority or other. There are no legal or government bodies for all the other organisms to appeal to for rights, including the right to food."[21]

Therefore, Anna Swaraj is the most natural right there is. The right to food is a right borne out of us being ecological creatures. And the commons have always ensured that.

Rights Always Exist with Responsibilities

Responsibility has to do with the fact that we exist in a related-ness. Our reality is to be in relationship with every life form around us. Marcelo

Saavedra-Vargas, an indigenous Aymara from Bolivia, says that they don't have a concept of rights but "have notions that talk about our existence as integral parts of a dynamic set of relationships and responsibilities." For example, we have the idea of Suma Qamana, which, more or less, translates into 'living and coexisting well'.[22] These natural rights of the earth family are the rights for *Suma Qamana*. And inherent to these rights are the responsibilities that each one of us takes to live and co-exist well together.

This is also what the Commons have always embodied. People have lived well together, in peace and harmony, and continue to live that way in some parts of the world.

The struggle for the future is this interconnected struggle for the Commons.

For the Rights of the Earth Family.

For Vasudeva Kutumbukam.

'The poison of the snake is lodged in its fangs,
The poison of a fly is in its head;
The poison of a scorpion is in its tail,
The poison of a wicked is all-over spread.'

Notes

ONE

1. Preamble of Convention on Biological Diversity; available at https://www.cbd.int/doc/legal/cbd-en.pdf.
2. Cartagena Protocol available at https://www.cbd.int/doc/legal/cartagena-protocol-en.pdf.
3. Nagoya Protocol (1993 available at https://www.cbd.int/abs/doc/protocol/nagoya-protocol-en.pdf.
4. Biological Diversity Act, 2002 available at http://nbaindia.org/uploaded/Biodiversityindia/Legal/31.%20Biological%20Diversity%20%20Act,%202002.pdf

TWO

1. Trade Related Intellectual Property Rights available at https://www.wto.org/english/docs_e/legal_e/27-trips.pdf.
2. Speech by Edmund T Pratt to US Council for International Business , Intellectual PropertyRights and International Trade , available at www.pfzer.com/pfizerinc/plocy /forum , cited in Peter Drahos and John Braithwaithe , Information Feudalism , The New Press , New York , 2003.
3. IN THE HIGH COURT OF DELHI AT NEW DELHI Reserved on: 09.03.2018 Pronounced on: 11.04.2018 FAO (OS) (COMM) 86/2017, C.M. APPL.14331, 14335, 15669, 17064/2017.
4. Seed Price Control Order available at http://pib.nic.in/newsite/PrintRelease.aspx?relid=137599.
5. The Patents Act 1970 available at http://www.wipo.int/edocs/lexdocs/laws/en/in/in065en.pdf.
6. WIPO, "Intellectual Property and Traditional Knowledge"; available at http://www.wipo.int/edocs/pubdocs/en/tk/920/wipo_pub_920.pdf.
7. Economic Times, "India pitches for WTO talks on checking theft of traditional knowledge"; available at https://health.economictimes.indiatimes.com/news/industry/india-pitches-for-wto-talks-on-checking-theft-of-traditional-knowledge/64399276.
8. Nuziveedu Seeds ltd. and ors. vs. Monsanto Technology LLC and ors. Delhi High Court. Available at http://lobis.nic.in/ddir/dhc/SRB/judgement/12-04-2018/SRB11042018FAOOSCOMM862017.pdf.
9. Para 67, Nuziveedu Seeds ltd. and ors. vs. Monsanto Technology LLC and ors. Delhi High Court. Available at http://lobis.nic.in/ddir/dhc/SRB/judgement/12-04-2018/SRB11042018FAOOSCOMM862017.pdf.
10. Times of India, "Bt cotton: Govt admits Monsanto never had patent in India" available at http://timesofindia.indiatimes.com/city/nagpur/Bt-cotton-Govt-admits-Monsanto-never-had-patent-in-India/articleshow/48674689.cms.
11. Shiva, V. (2018) "A victory for 'seed freedom'" available at http://www.asianage.com/opinion/oped/020518/a-victory-for-seed-freedom.html.
12. Bangalore Mirror, "Bt Brinjal: HC says Monsanto will have to face bio-piracy

case" available at https://bangaloremirror.indiatimes.com/bangalore/cover-story/esg-bt-brinjalhigh-court-kbb-uas-justice-as-pachhapure-biological-diversity-act/articleshow/24303637.cms; Economic Times, "NBA to file bio-piracy case against developers of BT Brinjal: Official", available at https://economictimes.indiatimes.com/news/politics-and-nation/nba-to-file-bio-piracy-case-against-developers-of-bt-brinjal-official/articleshow/16658168.cms.

13. See https://en.wikipedia.org/wiki/Arabidopsis_thaliana; https://en.wikipedia.org/wiki/Cauliflower_mosaic_virus.
14. Reference Case No. 2 of 2015 & Case No. 107 of 2015, Competition Commission of India. Available at https://www.cci.gov.in/sites/default/files/Ref%2002-2015%20and%20107-2015%20-26%281%29%20order_10.02.2015.pdf.
15. See Hagedorn, C (1997), The Bollworm Controversy -Monsanto's Bt Cotton in 1996; Available at https://www.sites.ext.vt.edu/newsletter-archive/cses/1997-01/1997-01-01.html.
16. See Wan, P., Huang, Y., Wu, H., Huang, M., Cong, S., Tabashnik, B. E., & Wu, K. (2012). Increased frequency of pink bollworm resistance to Bt toxin Cry1Ac in China. PLoS One, 7(1), e29975; Zhang, H., Yin, W., Zhao, J., Jin, L., Yang, Y., Wu, S., ... & Wu, Y. (2011). Early warning of cotton bollworm resistance associated with intensive planting of Bt cotton in China. PLoS one, 6(8), e22874; Dhurua, S., & Gujar, G. T. (2011). Field-evolved resistance to Bt toxin Cry1Ac in the pink bollworm, Pectinophora gossypiella (Saunders) (Lepidoptera: Gelechiidae), from India. Pest management science, 67(8), 898-903; Tabashnik, B. E., Van Rensburg, J. B. J., & Carrière, Y. (2009). Field-evolved insect resistance to Bt crops: definition, theory, and data. Journal of economic entomology, 102(6), 2011-2025.
17. Amar Singh, (3rd April 2018), "Doubling the Cotton Farmers' Income: Economic Perspective", cotton association of India, available at www.caionline.in/download_publication/547
18. International Conference on the TRIPS CBD Linkage 7-8 June 2018 in Geneva, available at http://pib.nic.in/newsite/PrintRelease.aspx?relid=179635

THREE

1. Navdanya , The Manifesto on the Future of Seed available at https://www.navdanya.org/attachments/Know_Your_Food1.pdf ; Navdanya, Law of the Seed, available at https://www.navdanya.org/attachments/lawofseed.pdf.
2. See Shiva, V., & Singh, V. (2011). Health Per Acre.
3. Refer to US Supreme Court Case No. 92-2038, Asgrow Seed Company v Winterboer [1995].
4. Refer to *Bija*, issue 17 and 18.
5. Tracy Clunis Ross, "Growing problems: the issue of sovereignty over seeds."
6. "*Sui Generis*" can be defined as a form of intellectual property rights which is derived from itself or in other words is not part of the patent system. This does not suggest however that each country is free to have its own IPR system.
7. Prof. (Dr.) N.S. Gopalakrishnan, (6 July 2018) "Problems with the Indian Plant Variety Regime: Old Vine in Newly "Enclosed" Bottle?" available at https://spicyip.com/2018/07/problems-with-the-indian-plant-variety-regime-old-vine-in-newly-enclosed-bottle.html; Prof. (Dr.) N.S. Gopalakrishnan, (11 July 2018) "Problems with the Indian Plant Varieties Regime (II): Helping Seed Companies at the Cost

of the Farmer?" available at https://spicyip.com/2018/07/problems-with-the-indian-plant-varieties-regime-ii-helping-seed-companies-at-the-cost-of-the-farmer.html.

8. Shalini Bhutani, (9 June 2018) "Plant Breeder Rights on the Table, Farmers' Rights for the Chair", available at https://thewire.in/agriculture/plant-breeder-rights-on-the-table-farmers-rights-for-the-chair.
9. See Hagedorn, C (1997), The Bollworm Controversy -Monsanto's Bt Cotton in 1996; Available at https://www.sites.ext.vt.edu/newsletter-archive/cses/1997-01/1997-01-01.html.
10. See Wan, P., Huang, Y., Wu, H., Huang, M., Cong, S., Tabashnik, B. E., & Wu, K. (2012). Increased frequency of pink bollworm resistance to Bt toxin Cry1Ac in China. *PLoS One*, *7*(1), e29975; Zhang, H., Yin, W., Zhao, J., Jin, L., Yang, Y., Wu, S., ... & Wu, Y. (2011). Early warning of cotton bollworm resistance associated with intensive planting of Bt cotton in China. *PLoS one*, *6*(8), e22874; Dhurua, S., & Gujar, G. T. (2011). Field-evolved resistance to Bt toxin Cry1Ac in the pink bollworm, Pectinophora gossypiella (Saunders) (Lepidoptera: Gelechiidae), from India. *Pest management science*, *67*(8), 898-903; Tabashnik, B. E., Van Rensburg, J. B. J., & Carrière, Y. (2009). Field-evolved insect resistance to Bt crops: definition, theory, and data. *Journal of economic entomology*, *102* (6), 2011-2025.
11. As reported in Livemint. Available at: https://www.livemint.com/Politics/oZHYGceXXVZB3lit9PytEN/Centre-tells-Delhi-high-court-Bt-cottons-resistance-to-pest.html.
12. Latham, J. R., Love, M., & Hilbeck, A. (2017). The distinct properties of natural and GM cry insecticidal proteins. *Biotechnology and Genetic Engineering Reviews*, *33*(1), 62-96.
13. Halewood, M., (2013). What kind of goods are plant genetic resources for food and agriculture? Towards the identification and development of a new global commons. International Journal of the Commons. 7(2), pp.278–312.
14. Safrin, S (2004). Hyperownership in a Time of Biotechnological Promise: The International Conflict to Control the Building Blocks of Life. *American Journal of International Law* 98: 641.
15. See Halewood, M., (2013). What kind of goods are plant genetic resources for food and agriculture? Towards the identification and development of a new global commons. International Journal of the Commons. 7(2), pp.278–312.
16. Sutherland, Peter, Seeds of Doubt: Assurance on "Farmers' Privilege," India Times, Mar. 15, 1994.
17. International Conference on the TRIPS-CBD Linkage 7-8 June 2018 in Geneva, available at http://pib.nic.in/newsite/PrintRelease.aspx?relid=179635.

FOUR

1. The claim states: "*The medicament or therapeutic composition of the present innovation may be administered using any amount and method effective for inhibiting growth of hepatitis virus.*"
2. Hindu Business Line, 11 May 2001, Hyderabad.
3. PriscilaJebaraj, 'Development of Bt brinjal a case of bio-piracy', The Hindu, August 10, 2011.
4. http://haridevformulations.com/catalog/herbal-extracts/shallaki.

5. http://www.aimslim.com/allaboutaimslim.html.
6. https://plants.usda.gov/java/largeImage?imageID=trte_001_avd.tif.
7. http://aartidraws.blogspot.com/.
8. http://www.herbmuseum.ca/content/ashwagandha.
9. https://www.innerpath.com.au/matmed/herbs/Sapium~sebiferum.htm.
10. http://www.nzdl.org/gsdlmod?e=d-00000-00---off-0hdl--00-0----0-10-0---0---0direct-10---4-------0-0l--11-en-50---20-home---00-0-1-00-0-0-11-1-0utfZz-8-00-0-0-11-10-0utfZz-8-00&cl=CL1.10&d=HASHdef7cdefa-42f3a2a3a9a85.3.6>=1.
11. https://www.motherearthliving.com/health-and-wellness/the-heart-of-the-hematter.
12. Wynberg, R., & Chennells, R. (2009). Green diamonds of the South: An overview of the San-Hoodia case. In *Indigenous Peoples, Consent and Benefit Sharing* (pp. 89-124). Springer, Dordrecht.
13. Chandra, R. (2016). The Cunning of Rights: law, life, biocultures. Oxford University Press. p.107.
14. Chandra, R. (2016). The Cunning of Rights: law, life, biocultures. Oxford University Press. p.107; Coombe, R. (2005). Protecting cultural industries to promote cultural diversity: Dilemmas for international policy-making posed by the recognition of traditional knowledge.
15. Greene, S. (2004). Indigenous People Incorporated?. *Current Anthropology*, *45*(2).
16. For more details see Greene, S. (2002). Intellectual property, resources or territory? Reframing the debate over indigenous rights, traditional knowledge, and pharmaceutical bioprospection. *Truth claims: Representation and human rights*, 229-49.
17. Hayden, C. (2003). From market to market: Bioprospecting's idioms of inclusion. *American Ethnologist*, *30*(3), 359-371.
18. Vermeylen, S. (2010). Law as a narrative: legal pluralism and resisting euro-american (intellectual) property law through stories. *The Journal of Legal Pluralism and Unofficial Law*, *42* (61), 53-78.
19. Elden, S. (2005). Missing the point: globalization, deterritorialization and the space of the world. *Transactions of the Institute of British Geographers*, *30*(1), 8-19.
20. For details of the agreement see Chaturvedi, S. (2007). *Intellectual Property Regime, Indigenous Knowledge System and Access and Benefit Sharing: Drawing Lessons from Kani Case* (No. 22089).
21. Chandra, R. (2016). The Cunning of Rights: law, life, biocultures. Oxford University Press. p.114.
22. *Ibid.*
23. *Ibid.*
24. Greene, S. (2002). Intellectual property, resources or territory? Reframing the debate over indigenous rights, traditional knowledge, and pharmaceutical bioprospection. *Truth claims: Representation and human rights*, 229-49.

FIVE

1. Navdanya, Manifesto on the future of knowledge systems, available at https://www.navdanyainternational.it/images/manifesti/conoscenze/conoscenze_ing.pdf; Shiva, V. (1988). *Staying alive: Women, ecology and survival in India*. Kali for Women.
2. Warshofsky, F. (1994). *The Patent Wars: The Battle to Own the World's Technology* (p.

122). New York: Wiley.Pg. 51-52.
3. *A Patent Attorney's View* by J. Hoxic, (1965) quoted in S. Kadil, "Plants, Poverty and Pharmaceutical Patents", The Yale Law Journal, Vol. 103, No. 1, October, (1993).
4. Locke, J. (1988). Two treatises of government, ed. *Peter Laslett (Cambridge, 1988), 301.*
5. Von Werlhof, C. (1989). 'Women and Nature in Capitalism' in Mies, M (ed), "Women: the Last Colony", Zed Books, London.
6. Polanyi, K. (1944). The great transformation: Economic and political origins of our time. *Rinehart, New York.*

SIX

1. Caffentzis, G., & Federici, S. (2014). Commons against and beyond capitalism. *Community Development Journal, 49* (suppl_1), i92-i105.
2. See Appadurai , A and Rao, Vyjayanthi, 2008, "Scale and Mobility in defining the commons" in Bardhan, P., & Ray, I, *The Contested Commons Conversations between Economists and Anthropologists.* Oxford University Press. P.163.
3. Aristotle, *Politics*, Book II, ch.3.
4. Hardin, G. (1968). The Tragedy of the Commons' (1968) 162. *Science, 1243*, 63.
5. McCay, B. J., & Acheson, J. M. (Eds.). (1990). *The question of the commons: The culture and ecology of communal resources.* University of Arizona Press.
6. Shiva, V. (2002). *Water wars: Privatization, pollution, and profit.* Indian Research Press. p. 26.
7. *Ibid.*
8. *Ibid.*
9. See Mauss, M. (1924). *The gift: The form and reason for exchange in archaic societies.* New York: Routledge.
10. Ostrom, E. (1990). *Governing the commons.* Cambridge university press.
11. See Velicu, I., & García-López, G. (2018). Thinking the Commons through Ostrom and Butler: Boundedness and Vulnerability. *Theory, Culture & Society*, 0263276418757315.
12. Caffentzis, G., & Federici, S. (2014). Commons against and beyond capitalism. *Community Development Journal, 49* (suppl_1), i92-i105.
13. See Bollier, D., & Helfrich, S. (Eds.). (2015). *Patterns of commoning.* Commons Strategy Group and Off the Common Press.
14. See Caffentzis, G., & Federici, S. (2014). Commons against and beyond capitalism. *Community Development Journal, 49*(suppl_1), i92-i105.
15. Velicu, I., & García-López, G. (2018). Thinking the Commons through Ostrom and Butler: Boundedness and Vulnerability. *Theory, Culture & Society*, 0263276418757315.
16. Boven, K., & Morohashi, J. (2002). *Best practices using indigenous knowledge.* The Hague: Nuffic.
17. Aguiton, C. The Commons. *Systemic Alternatives*, 77.
18. Business line, "India seeks to generate more support at WTO on linking TRIPS to bio-piracy, available at https://www.thehindubusinessline.com/news/world/india-seeks-to-generate-more-support-at-wto-on-linking-trips-to-bio-piracy/article24039104.ece; S.S. Rana & Co. Advocates, "Bio-Piracy Initiative By India", available at http://www.mondaq.com/india/x/720484/Patent/BioPiracy+Initia-

tive+By+India.

19. Sharma, B. D. (1997). *Tide Turned: The Makings of Tribal Self-Rule in the First Central law in the wake of Bhuria Committee Report*. National Front for Tribal Self-Rule.
20. Vandana Shiva, (19 December 2014) "An Open Letter to Prime Minister Modi and President Obama from Democratic, Concerned Citizens of India and the US", available at https://www.organicconsumers.org/news/open-letter-prime-minister-modi-and-president-obama-democratic-concerned-citizens-india-and-us.
21. Vandana Shiva, (4 June 2016), "Rogue companies must be stopped from taking over India's rich biodiversity", available at https://indianexpress.com/article/blogs/biodiversity-national-intellectual-property-rights-policy-modi-us-visit-biopiracy-trips-wto-2834379/.
22. WIPO, "Traditional Knowledge and Intellectual Property – Background Brief", available at http://www.wipo.int/pressroom/en/briefs/tk_ip.html.
23. Drawn from Ostrom's analogy in Ostrom, E. (1990). *Governing the commons*. Cambridge university press.
24. Lewis, V., & Mulvany, P. M. (1997). A typology of community seed banks. *Natural Resource Institute, Chatham, UK, Project A, 595*, 47.
25. Vernooy, R., Sthapit, B., Galluzzi, G., & Shrestha, P. (2014). The multiple functions and services of community seedbanks.
26. Shiva, V., Shroff, R., & Lockhart, C. (2012). Seed freedom a global citizens' report. *RS (Coordinators).. India: Navdanya, October*.

SEVEN

1. See Center for Biological Diversity, "The Extinction Crisis", available at https://www.biologicaldiversity.org/programs/biodiversity/elements.../extinction_crisis/.
2. Carrington, D. (10 July 2017). Earth's sixth mass extinction event underway, scientists warn. *The Guardian*.
3. Navdanya , (2017), "Annam: Food as Health"; Vandana Shiva , Andre Leu and Navdanya, (2018), "Biodiversity , Agroecology and Regenerative Agriculture", forthcoming.
4. See Berry, T. (1999). *The great work: Our way into the future*. New York; Swimme, B., & Berry, T. (1992). The universe story: From the primordial flaring forth to the ecozoic era. *San Francisco: HarperSanFrancisco, 992*.
5. Eisenstein, C. (2013). *The more beautiful world our hearts know is possible* (Vol. 2). North Atlantic Books
6. Stone, C. D. (1972). Should Trees Have Standing--Toward Legal Rights for Natural Objects. *S. CAl. l. rev., 45*, 450.
7. *Ibid.*
8. O'Donnell, E., & Talbot-Jones, J. (2018). Creating legal rights for rivers: lessons from Australia, New Zealand, and India.*Ecology and Society, 23*(1).
9. O'Donnell, E., and J. Talbot- Jones, 2017. Legal rights for rivers: what does this actually mean? *Australian environment Review* 32 (6): 159-162; O'Donnell, E., & Talbot-Jones, J. (2018). Creating legal rights for rivers: lessons from Australia, New Zealand, and India.*Ecology and Society, 23*(1).
10. *Mohd. Salim v State of Uttarakhand & Others*, WPPIL 126/2014, Uttarakhand

High Court.
11. Macpherson, E., "Rio Atrato, Columbia" in *New developments in the legal status of rivers 11 August 2017*; Available at: https://law.unimelb.edu.au/__data/assets/pdf_file/0007/2516479/Legal-rights-for-rivers-Workshop-Report.pdf.
12. Based on the analysis from O'Donnell, E., & Talbot-Jones, J. (2018). Creating legal rights for rivers: lessons from Australia, New Zealand, and India.*Ecology and Society*, *23*(1).
13. Locke, J. *Second Treatise of Civil Government. Chapter 5, Section 27, Of Property.*
14. Timothy Mitchell, rule of Experts- Egypt, techno-politics, modernity, university of California Press, 2002. P. 55.
15. Kneen, B. (2009). The tyranny of rights. Ottawa: Ram's Horn.
16. Kruuk, Hans (1972), *The Spotted Hyena: A Study of Perdition and Social Behaviour*, p. 160 as cited in Mehran Banaei and Nadeem Haque, (12 June 2013), "Are rights prescribed to animals and nature, or are they inherent and pre-existent?"
17. Mabo v Queensland (No. 2) HCA 23, (1992) 175 CLR 1.
18. Calder v. Attorney-General of British Columbia(124) (1973) SCR.
19. Statement of the Pacific- Center Region of the *Congreso Nacional Indigena* meeting in Tlanixco state, Mexico, 25- 26/1/03.
20. Framework is built upon what Kneen has done in Kneen, B. (2009). The tyranny of rights. Ottawa: Ram's Horn.
21. Kneen, B. (2009). *The tyranny of rights*. Ottawa: Ram's Horn.
22. Personal conversation with Kneen, B., author of "the tyranny of rights".

Index